THE
PASTOR
HIS LIFE
AND WORK

Charles u. Wagner

Col. 1: 18

THE
PASTOR

HIS LIFE
AND WORK

CHARLES U. WAGNER

REGULAR BAPTIST PRESS
1300 North Meacham Road
Schaumburg, Illinois 60173-4888

Library of Congress Cataloging–in-Publication Data

Wagner, Charles U.
    The pastor.
    Bibliography: p.
    Includes index.
    1. Pastoral theology. I. Title.
BV4011.W27   1988   253   88-32248
ISBN 0-87227-001-7

THE PASTOR: HIS LIFE AND WORK
© 1976
Regular Baptist Press
Schaumburg, Illinois
Printed in the U.S.A.

Revised edition, 1988

TO THE MEMORY OF MY PARENTS. They were the first to recognize that the Lord had set me apart for Christian service, and they encouraged me in the things of the Lord by their love and godly example.

TO MY FORMER PASTOR, Dr. David Allen. He best exemplified the principles set forth in this volume, and was the greatest single influence in my life as a pastor.

TO MY WIFE. She has faithfully stood with me as a co-laborer in the Lord's work and has shared for over thirty-six years in the challenges and blessings of the ministry.

I want to express my gratitude to the many pastors and college and seminary professors who encouraged me to put the pastoral theology syllabus into print.

I also extend my thanks to the seminary students I taught at the Los Angeles Baptist Theological Seminary and the Northwest Baptist Seminary; their participation in the classroom helped in ascertaining the needs of a young pastor.

THE TASK

I would express him simple, grave, sincere;
In doctrine uncorrupt; in language plain,
And plain in manner, decent, solemn, chaste,
And natural in gesture; much impress'd
Himself, as conscious of his awful charge,
And anxious mainly that the flock he feeds
May feel it too; affectionate in look,
And tender in address, as well becomes
A messenger of grace to guilty men.

William Cowper

"To this end was I born, and for this cause came I into the world."

John 18:37

CONTENTS

Foreword

The gospel ministry is the most serious responsibility ever assigned to a man. It involves that extra dimension of spiritual experience that is known only to those who are called of God to positions of Biblical leadership. Its dimensions are so broad and varied that the most gifted and energetic of men have never exceeded them, for within the work of God are possibilities of service that are never completely exploited.

Two questions come to mind. First, what is the gospel ministry in its essential substance? Second, how is the gospel ministry effectively fulfilled? This book will answer these questions.

Many years ago I had the happy privilege of first meeting Dr. and Mrs. Charles Wagner. They were "up to their ears" in the work of the First Baptist Church of Richland, Washington. This pastorate was a combination of the joy of preaching, the love of people, the creative challenge of reaching men and respect for local church stability. Subsequent pastorates at Calvary Baptist Church, Everett, Washington, and Temple Baptist Church, Tacoma, Washington, have confirmed Dr. Wagner's pastoral leadership.

The Pastor: His Life and Work has been substantiated by extensive pastoral experience and several years of classroom evaluation. It is a standard text in several Christian colleges as well as the Northwest Baptist Seminary, Tacoma, of which Dr. Wagner was president and professor of pastoral theology. It is a privilege to commend it to pastors of all ages as they begin or review their responsibilities as stewards of the mystery of the gospel.

John R. Dunkin, Th.D.

Introduction

Most of the material in this work is the result of my own pastoral ministry, which includes five pastorates, representing over thirty-six years in the ministry. It first appeared in a syllabus written for and used in classes in pastoral theology and church administration in both the Los Angeles Baptist Seminary and the Northwest Baptist Seminary. Much material has been added and other areas have been expanded. I have tried to keep the material more practical than theoretical so that it can be used not only by the young man in seminary preparing for the ministry, but also by the pastor who feels a need of help in various areas of his ministry.

I believe the principles and practices as outlined in the book are tested and tried. It is hoped that some of them will be beneficial to the pastor in any size church.

Some of the material is very basic—such as the material on the call to the ministry and the view of the ministry. The material on the pastor and people relationship is a result not only of my own observations, but also of the many pastors I have consulted concerning such problems. While some pastors may handle some situations differently, basically I feel that the course recommended is the wisest one.

In my mind, one of the interesting areas is that which deals with the study life of the pastor. The material on evangelism is a result of many years of establishing visitation programs in churches large and small.

Some of the material here would be classified in the area of church administration as much as pastoral theology. Believing that these two areas overlap, I have included material bearing on both subjects.

Finally, some new material, such as chapters on the pastor and the computer and the pastor's appearance and health, has been added with this edition after long and careful thought to their importance and relevance.

If the material in this book will help the pastor to "finish his course with joy" and bring glory to his Savior, the labor in writing it will have been worthwhile.

CHAPTER ONE
The Call to the Ministry

It is incongruous to think that an ambassador would go to a country as a representative of his homeland without being sent. This is even more true in the ministry. One of the most vital areas of pastoral theology is that of the call to the ministry; the awareness of such a call is imperative. To go, without being sent, is to walk in failure.

The Dangers and Misconceptions of the Ministry
The danger of entering the ministry when there is no call. Why would a person enter the ministry without a call? Yet it is felt by some that a call is unnecessary. This philosophy is held by those who espouse a more liberal view of the ministry. In such cases aptitude tests may be used to determine a person's vocational ability. Then, counselors recommend certain educational pursuits to develop the *natural* acumen. While some are more suited for sciences, others are channeled to social or humanitarian pursuits, one of which might be an involvement in the religious field. Of course, the born-again believer understands that although natural intelligence and aptitudes are not to be scorned or considered unimportant, these are not the final criteria in determining one's call to the ministry. While the believer ought to be aware of the needs of people, both physically and spiritually, the awareness of those needs and a human ability to help alleviate the condition of man are not in themselves suffi-

cient grounds to enter the ministry.

It is conceivable that some may enter the ministry because of parental encouragement. Some fathers insist that the eldest son be encouraged to go into the ministry; hence, a young man may be told from his earliest years that he is the appointed one for that service. Others may enter the ministry to compensate for the wasted years of their lives.

There is also the person who is simply intrigued with the idea of going into the ministry. To him there is a glamour in standing before men and doing the work of God. While this may seem juvenile, it is a very real problem that can end in disillusionment and ultimate failure. Spurgeon wrote:

When living as a child at my grandfather's in the country, I saw a company of huntsmen in their red coats riding through his fields after a fox. I was delighted! My little heart was excited; I was ready to follow the hounds over the hedge and ditch. I have always felt a natural taste for that sort of business, and, as a child, when asked what I would be, I usually said I was going to be a huntsman. A fine profession, truly! Many young men have the same idea of being parsons as I had of being a huntsman—a mere childish notion that they would like the coat and the horn-blowing; the honor, the respect, the ease; and they are probably even fools enough to think, the riches of the ministry. (Ignorant beings they must be if they look for wealth in connection with the Baptist ministry.) The fascination of the preacher's office is very great to weak minds, and hence I earnestly caution all young men not to mistake whim for inspiration, and a childish preference for a call of the Holy Spirit.[1]

Probably one of the most subtle dangers is a genuine misunderstanding as to the difference between a specific call to the ministry and the call for every believer to be surrendered to the Lord and effective as a witness. Obviously, every saint is not called to be a pastor, although it is the responsibility of every child of God to be in "the work of the ministry" in the broad sense of that word. This is made clear in Paul's epistle to the Ephesians. "And he gave some, apostles; and some, prophets; and some, evangelists; and some, pastors and teachers; For the perfecting of the saints, for the work of the ministry..." (Eph. 4:11, 12).

This passage makes it clear that there are specific functions in the church, one of which is the function of the pastor-teacher. He, in turn, is to equip or perfect the *saints* for the work of the ministry. This passage, then, makes it clear that in a broad sense of the term "ministry," *every* believer should be involved in Christian work and should put on the equipment to be used by God in the local New Testament church. But the perfecting is done by pastors and others called to specific services. Therefore, a young person who surrenders his life to the Lord is not always called to the ministry of the pastor. The surrendered life and heart might well mean that he is to be used of God as an exemplary layman, actually engaged in a ministry of the church.

Martyn Lloyd-Jones, in his excellent book *Preaching and Preachers*, has written:

This distinction is brought out in a most interesting way in Acts 8, in verses 4 and 5. There we are told in the first verse that a great persecution of the church arose in Jerusalem, and that all the members of the Church were scattered abroad except the Apostles. Then we are told in verses 4 and 5, "Therefore they that were scattered abroad went everywhere preaching the Word. Then Philip went down to the city of Samaria, and preached Christ unto them." That is the King James Version translation, and in both cases you have the word "preached." But in the original the same word was not used in the two verses; and this is the vital distinction. What the people who went everywhere did was, as someone has suggested it might be translated, "to gossip" the Word, to talk about it in conversation. Philip on the other hand did something different; he was "heralding" the Gospel. This is, strictly speaking, what is meant by preaching in the sense that I have been using it. It is not accidental that such a distinction should be drawn into the actual text.[2]

The danger of refusing to enter the ministry when there is a definite call. Must there be a struggle when one is called to the ministry? Generally a struggle is a result of unyieldedness. If, for example, God speaks to a man regarding the ministry and that man turns from the Lord's direct leading, he is grieving the Spirit (Eph. 4:30). The Spirit cannot properly work *through* him as He is busy working *with* him, seeking to make him conscious of the sin of rebellion. More specifically, the rebel is guilty of quenching the Spirit (1 Thess. 5:19). To quench the Spirit is to say no to Him. However, if a person is walking in the Spirit (Gal. 5:16) in a spirit of yieldedness, a struggle is not necessarily a part of that process whereby God calls one to the ministry. However, this does not preclude the wrestling in prayer which often accompanies the earnest Christian's desire to know the will of God.

Must there be great intellectual endowments to be called to the ministry? While it is true that God does not put a premium on ignorance (it is never smart to be dumb), intellectual endowment is not a prerequisite to entering the ministry. Many Bible colleges and seminaries will agree that some of the finest preachers in our pulpits are average students. Recognizing this, however, we must be careful that we do not encourage all "A" students to be teachers in seminaries, suggesting that any other ministry is inferior. There is no higher calling than the call to preach the Word! But God often chooses "the foolish things of the world to confound the wise" and "the weak things of the world to confound the things which are mighty" (1 Cor. 1:27). This is true of all areas of Christian service, including the pastorate.

The Necessity of a Divine Call

It should be noted that, in Ephesians 4, apostles, prophets, evangelists, pastors and teachers were *given by God* (v. 11). He set them apart specifically in these areas to equip the saints.

There are a number of examples in the Old Testament of a divine call. However, there is something very special and unique in the New Testament with regard to the call to the ministry. The impartation of specific spiritual gifts to men to function in the local church is unique to our present dispensation.

As the pierced hand of the Lord ordained the apostle Paul to serve Him, so God lays His hand on those who are separated unto the work of the ministry. "He is a chosen vessel unto me, to bear my name before the Gentiles, and kings, and the children of Israel" (Acts 9:15). "Even so hath the Lord ordained that they which preach the gospel should live of the gospel" (1 Cor. 9:14). Every minister of the gospel must then conclude as Paul did, "For though I preach the gospel, I have nothing to glory of: for *necessity* is laid upon me; yea, woe is unto me, if I preach not the gospel" (1 Cor. 9:16—italics mine)! There must be a divine call and an acute consciousness that one must preach and teach the Word. What God did in the life of Paul He has done in thousands of men the world over. J. H. Jowett wrote:

> You cannot get away from that wonder in the life of the Apostle Paul. Next to the infinite love of his Saviour, and the amazing glory of his own salvation, his wonder is arrested and nourished by the surpassing glory of his own vocation. His "calling" is never lost in the medley of professions. The light of privilege is always shining on the way to duty. His work never loses its halo, and his road never becomes commonplace and grey. He seems to catch his breath every time he thinks of his mission, and in the midst of abounding adversity glory still more abounds. And, therefore this is the sort of music and song that we find unceasing, from the hour of his conversion and calling to the hour of his death: "Unto me, who am less than the least of all saints, is this grace given, that I should preach among the Gentiles the unsearchable riches of Christ."[3]

Dr. Adam Clarke, in a letter to a preacher, stated:

> No man should engage in the work in which you are engaged, unless he verily feels that he is inwardly moved by the Holy Ghost to take upon him this office. He must not presume that he is thus moved because he has been educated for the ministry; in cases of this kind, man may propose but God must dispose.[4]

Rev. John Brown of Haddingon said:

Suppose my connections with the great, and my address to the people, should ever so easily procure a license, a charge, yet, if I run unsent to Christ, in my whole ministration I must act the part of a thief, a robber, a traitor to Christ, and a murderer of souls, not profiting them at all.[5]

Spurgeon is often quoted in this regard:

If any student in this room could be content to be a newspaper editor, or a grocer, or a farmer, or a doctor, or a lawyer, or a senator, or a king, in the name of heaven and the earth let him go his way; he is not the man in whom dwells the Spirit of God in its fullness, for a man so filled with God would utterly weary of any pursuit but that for which his inmost soul pants.[6]

The Nature and Evidences of a Divine Call

Assuming, then, that one should not enter the ministry unless he is called, and that he should be very careful to distinguish between a general call to serve and the specific call to the ministry, how can one determine whether or not he is called to the ministry?

The personal conviction. When one believes that God has called him into the ministry, he will surely have a sense of God's will that he is God's man, in this unique sense of the word, to preach God's Word . Theodore Cuyler wrote:

When God calls a man to the ministry, He is apt to let the man know it. I believe in answers to honest prayer, and I believe in the leadings of the Holy Spirit; and if you believe in them also, and will keep your eyes open and heart humble and docile, you will be likely to get some clear indications as to your duty. During the first eighteen months after I graduated from college—

months mostly spent in teaching—I was balancing between the law and the ministry. Many of my relatives urged me to become a lawyer, as my father and grandfather had been; but my godly mother had dedicated me to the ministry from infancy and her counsels all leaned toward the pulpit. One winter afternoon I rode off five miles to a prayer meeting in a neighboring village. It was held in the parlor of a private house. I arose and spoke for ten minutes; and, when the meeting was over, a person said to me, "Your talk did me good." On my way home the thought flashed into my mind, "If ten minutes' talk today helped one soul, why not preach all the time?" That one thought decided me on the spot. Our lives turn on small pivots; and, if you will let God lead you, the path will open before your footsteps.[7]

I can give a similar testimony. A short time after I was saved I was aware that the Lord had laid His hand upon me for the ministry. It was a personal conviction that was very marked, and while there were seasons when I was not in the will of the Lord, there was never a time that I doubted the Lord would have me preach, and that the only calling for me was the ministry.

C. E. Colton has written:

Every genuine preacher must feel the hand of God laid upon him for this specific task; otherwise his ministry will be unhappy and unproductive. Only the consciousness of a divine call to do a great and awful work can give that confidence and feeling of authority necessary to make one's ministry successful.[8]

In 1 Timothy 3, the most complete passage in the Bible on the qualifications of a bishop, Paul deals with the subject of a pastor's own feelings about the ministry. In spite of recent claims that there can be no subjective "feeling" about a divine call, this passage makes it clear that personal desire and conviction are clear evidences of divine ordination. "This is true saying, If a man *desire* the office of a bishop, he *desireth* a good work" (1 Tim. 3:1— italics mine). The New International Version renders this passage, "If anyone sets his heart on being an overseer, he desires a noble task." The word *desire* means to "reach out after something." It is used in only two other places in Scripture—1 Timothy 6:10 and Hebrews 11:16. Hebrews speaks of those heroes of the faith who "*desire* a better country, that is, an heavenly" (italics mine). Thus we see an earnest "reaching out" to Heaven. A careful examination of the Hebrews passage shows that this desire is based upon the promises of God. God spoke to Abraham and he responded in faith (Heb. 11:8). Later, Abraham again obeyed, having "received the promise" (v. 17) and his desire was in direct response of obedience to God's promise. It is clear that this is not an obscure, blasé desire but a fervent, ardent longing.

Kent observes:

> Two strong verbs depict the yearning for this office which is commended by Paul. *Orego* means to reach out after, and the middle voice employed here indicates that the subject is reaching after this object for himself. Such a yearning is described by a second verb *epithumeo,* to desire, to fix the ardor or passion upon a thing. Here it is used in the good sense of strong desire. This godly desire for the responsible task of overseership, if controlled by the Spirit of God, may deepen into a sacred conviction. Such a desire is the motive for preparation in college, Bible school, and seminary. Of course, desire for this task merely for the prestige or honor involved is

not praiseworthy, but if longed for in the will of God is to be commended.[9]

Certainly an ordination council is justified in asking a candidate about his call to the ministry. After all, God has given pastors to churches, and they have the right to know if his call is genuine. The process seems to be that God speaks specifically to hearts and men respond in faith, having a strong desire to obey the specific call and do the will of God.

The imperativeness of the mission. Once again, we remember the words of the apostle Paul, who said, "Woe is unto me, if I preach not the gospel" (1 Cor. 9:16)! A man who receives a divine call from God to preach is aware that there are no options or alternatives. Certainly it is not an "either-or" proposition. Preach he must!

It was Vince Lombardi, the great football coach, who once said, "Winning is not everything—it is the only thing." This can certainly be applied to preaching—it is the *only* thing.

J. H. Jowett said:

Now I hold with profound conviction that before a man selects the Christian ministry as his vocation he must have the assurance that the selection has been imperatively constrained by the eternal God. The call of the Eternal must ring through the rooms of his soul as clearly as the sound of the morning-bell rings through the valley of Switzerland, calling the peasants to early prayer and praise. The candidate for the ministry must move like a man in secret bonds. "Necessity is laid" upon him. His choice is not a preference among alternatives. Ultimately he has no alternative; all other possibilities become dumb only one clear call sounding forth as the imperative summons of the eternal God.[10]

The conviction of others. Certainly one way to corroborate one's calling is to understand how others feel about his call to the ministry. Remember that Paul said to Timothy, "Neglect not the gift that is in thee, which was given thee by prophecy, with the laying on of the hands of the presbytery" (1 Tim. 4:14). Again, Paul said, "Wherefore I put thee in remembrance that thou stir up the gift of God, which is in thee by the putting on of my hands" (2 Tim. 1:6).

A human ordination is simply man's recognition of what God has already done. Usually, long before the ordination service, there is the awareness on the part of others that one has been called to the ministry. There are some notable exceptions to this, one of whom is G. Campbell Morgan, who was turned down for ordination in the Methodist church!

When there is a strong conviction that one should be in the ministry, nothing should deter that person from obeying God and pursuing such work in spite of what man might say. However, often godly men have felt led to express their feelings as to the hand of God upon others. This was the case with Dr. George W. Truett. "The whole church at Whitewright was impressed of God that Truett should preach, and so expressed it, before he himself felt and answered the call."[11]

Spurgeon gives a rather humorous incident in this regard:

From someone or other I heard in conversation of a plan adopted by Matthew Wilks, for examining a young man who wanted to be a missionary; the drift, if not the detail of the test, commends itself to my judgment though not to my taste. The young man desired to go to India as a missionary in connection with the London Missionary Society. Mr. Wilks was appointed to consider his fitness for such a post. He wrote to the young man, and told him to call upon him at six o'clock next morning.

The brother lived many miles off, but he was at the house at six o'clock punctually. Mr. Wilks did not, however, enter the room till hours after. The brother waited wonderingly, but patiently. At last, Mr. Wilks arrived, and addressed the candidate thus, in his usual nasal tones, "Well, young man, so you want to be a missionary?" "Yes, Sir." "Do you love the Lord Jesus Christ?" "Yes, Sir, I hope I do." "And have you had any education?" Yes, Sir, a little." "Well, now, we'll try you; can you spell 'cat'?" The young man looked confused, and hardly knew how to answer so preposterous a question, but in a moment he replied steadily, "C-a-t, cat."

"Very good," said Mr. Wilks; "now, can you spell 'dog'?" Our young martyr hesitated, but Mr. Wilks said in his coolest manner, "Oh, never mind; don't be bashful; you spelled the other word so well that I should think you would be able to spell this: high as the attainment is, it is not so elevated but what you might do it without blushing." The youthful Job replied, "D-o-g, dog." "Well, that is right: I see you will do in your spelling, and now for your arithmetic; how many are twice two?" It is a wonder that Mr. Wilks did not receive "twice two" after the fashion of muscular Christianity, but the patient youth gave the right reply and was dismissed.

Matthew Wilks at the committee meeting said, "I cordially recommend that young man; his testimonials and character I have duly examined, and besides that, I have given him a rare personal trial such as few could bear. I tried his self-denial—he was up in the morning early; I tried his temper, and I tried his humility; he can spell 'c-a-t' and 'd-o-g' and can tell that 'twice two make four,' and he will do for a missionary exceedingly well."

Now, what the old gentleman is thus said to have done with exceedingly bad taste, we may with much propriety do with ourselves. We must try whether we can endure brow-beating, weariness, slander, jeering, and hardship; and whether we can be made the offscouring of all things, and be treated as nothing for Christ's sake. If we can endure all these, we have some of those points which indicate the possession of the rare qualities which should meet in a true servant of the Lord Jesus Christ.[12]

The evidence of gifts in the fruit of one's ministry. Earlier we mentioned that God gives various gifts to men with which to function. One of these is the gift of a pastor-teacher (Eph. 4:11). It is regrettable that there are a number of people in the ministry who do not have the *evidence* of being called by God.

We take the liberty of quoting Spurgeon here again:

As a worker, he is to work on whether he succeeds or no, but as a minister he cannot be sure of his vocation till results are apparent. How my heart leaped for joy when I heard tidings of my first convert! I could never be satisfied with a full congregation, and the kind expressions of friends; I longed to hear that hearts had been broken, that tears had been seen streaming from the eyes of penitents. It is a marvel to me how men continue at ease in preaching year after year without conversions. Vain are their talents, their philosophy, their rhetoric, and even their orthodoxy, without the signs following. How are they sent of God who will bring no men to God? Prophets whose words are powerless,

sowers whose seed all withers, fishers who take
no fish, soldiers who give no wounds—are
these God's men? Surely it were better to be a
mud-raker, or a chimney sweep, than to stand
in the ministry as an utterly barren tree. The
meanest occupation confers some benefit upon
mankind, but the wretched man who occupies
a pulpit and never glorifies his God by conversions is a blank, a blot, an eyesore, a mischief.[13]

End Notes

[1] Charles H. Spurgeon, *Spurgeon's Lectures to His Students*, condensed and abridged by David Otis Fuller (Grand Rapids: Zondervan Publishing House, 1945), pp. 30–31.

[2] D. Martyn Lloyd-Jones, *Preaching and Preachers* (Grand Rapids: Zondervan Publishing House, 1971), p. 102.

[3] J. H. Jowett, *The Preacher, His Life and Work.* Reprint (Grand Rapids: Baker Book House, 1968), pp. 20–21.

[4] Wilson T. Hogue, *Homiletics and Pastoral Theology*, (Winona Lake, IN: Free Methodist Publishing House, 1946), p. 454.

[5] Ibid. p. 268.

[6] Spurgeon, *Lectures to Students*, pp. 29–30.

[7] Theodore Cuyler, *The Young Preacher*, (Old Tappan, NJ: Fleming H. Revell Co., 1893), p. 111.

[8] C. E. Colton, *The Minister's Mission* (Grand Rapids: Zondervan Publishing House, 1951), p. 14.

[9] Homer Kent, Jr., *The Pastoral Epistles* (Chicago: Moody Press, 1958), p. 123.

[10] Jowett, *The Preacher*, pp. 12–13.

[11] Colton, *The Minister's Mission*, p. 17.

[12] Spurgeon, *Lectures to Students,* pp. 38–39.

[13] Ibid. pp. 33–34.

CHAPTER TWO

A View of the Ministry

Just what is the ministry all about? Probably the reason so many start out like "atom bombs" and end up like "firecrackers" is because they do not view the ministry as it really is and as God expects it to be. Could it be that they lack an understanding of the divine concept of the ministry as opposed to a preconceived idea given to them by another source?

We will examine the different concepts of the ministry.

The Distorted Concept of the Ministry

The minister as the world sees him. It would be interesting to take a survey to determine the concept that the average man on the street has of the ministry. Doubtless there would be a variety of responses.

To some the minister is a social worker whose major interest is strictly humanitarian. Others look upon him as an impractical dreamer in an unreal world. They see him as lacking the down-to-earth pragmatism of the average man on the street. To use a vernacular, he is "out of it," and is seldom taken seriously. Still others view the minister as a meek and weak man disseminating pious platitudes on Sunday morning.

On the other hand, in some parts of the country the minister is considered the articulate, educated man of the town. This view may be more characteristic of rural areas. It was especially true half a century ago.

There is little doubt that the world's concept of the

ministry has been influenced by the minister's portray-
al in Hollywood presentations.

The minister as the evangelical church sees him. Even
here the minister is often misunderstood. He is sometimes thought of as the one who "does all the work." There
are certain expectations of him which, if fulfilled, determine his success in the ministry. These expectations include preaching sermons twice on Sunday and once on
prayer meeting night. He is to be available to help when
called upon in times of need. He is the administrator of
the church, heads up the major activities and functions
of the church and is considered the "professional" one
among them. He is expected to do all the visiting, and
while he is not seen as a priest per se, he is considered as
being on a different level from the average church member. While the priesthood of the believer is held by the people, his priesthood is usually looked upon as distinctly
different and above theirs.

The Divine Concept of the Ministry

This is not to suggest that some of the concepts of both
the world and the church are not valid. Certainly if a man
is to be a preacher he should be articulate as he declares
God's Word. He should possess the qualities of an administrator. Nor is it wrong for a pastor to be humanitarian
and be concerned about the needs of man. However, any
of these things taken individually, if not seen in the right
perspective, can be distorted and will give a wrong view of
the ministry as God sees it.

A. It is a high and holy calling.

It requires divine power. The ministry involves first
and foremost the preaching of the message of the gospel,
beseeching men to be reconciled to God. When Paul
talked about the goal set before him, he said with regard to
some of the circumstances of the day: "None of these
things move me, neither count I my life dear unto myself,

so that I might finish my course with joy, and the ministry, which I have received of the Lord Jesus, to testify the
gospel of the grace of God" (Acts 20:24). Paul saw that his
first and foremost responsibility was testifying "both to
the Jews, and also to the Greeks, repentance toward God,
and faith toward our Lord Jesus Christ" (Acts 20:21). It
can readily be seen, therefore, that the pastor is dealing
with eternal matters. He is an ambassador for Christ, a
representative of the Lord; he cannot preach a divine
message without divine power.

It requires special shepherding grace. This, of
course, involves various areas of the church and pastoral administration. As an undershepherd over the flock,
the pastor will require special shepherding grace and
strength from the Chief Shepherd. The pastor must see
that every area of church life, whether it is attending a
meeting of the trustees or working with the custodian in
general problems, is sacred. In each of them he is the
shepherd-pastor; in such work there is no division between the sacred and the secular.

Well has Hogue said:

> No seraph from glory was ever instructed with
> so important an errand to the children of men as
> that for which the Son of God calls and commis-
> sions the ministers of His gospel. The exalted
> objects of the Christian ministry give to the of-
> fice a most exalted character. "Its grand aims,"
> says Mr. Murphy, "are to exalt Jehovah, the
> Creator, Redeemer, and Judge of the world; to
> overthrow the power of Satan, the prince of all
> evil; to save mankind from sin and hell; to ban-
> ish vice and all other evil from the earth; to bring
> true happiness to the lost children of Adam; to
> build up a glorious church amidst the ruins
> which sin has wrought; to prepare citizens for
> the heavenly world who shall behold all and

share the infinite blessedness of the Son of God.
Surely it must be a calling of no ordinary impor-
tance which God has appointed for such ends.
Who can describe its solemn grandeur."[1]

B. It is the hardest of all callings.

The power of the enemy. The major reason for the
ministry being a hard calling is the constant threat of the
enemy, the Devil. Paul talked about this in Ephesians
6:10 when he said, "Finally, my brethren, be strong in the
Lord, and in the power of his might." Strength is needed,
but it is strength "in the Lord." It is apparent that *inner*
strength comes from Christ; the armor is *outward* and
comes from the Father. "Put on the whole armour of God,
that ye may be able to stand against the wiles *[methodei-
as]* of the devil" (Eph. 6:11). Power is needed, but it is the
power of His Spirit (Zech. 4:6). It is imperative that the
pastor understand that no amount of college or seminary training is sufficient in preparation to do battle
against this enemy. Remember that the Devil is also in-
telligent, well educated, and a master of deceit and craft.
Paul recognized this when he said, "We are not ignorant
of his devices" (2 Cor. 2:11).

The pull of the secular world. While the pastor is to be
insulated from the world, he is not *isolated* from it. A
pastor does not go off in cloistered seclusion like a monk in
a monestery. Rather, he mixes with people, rubs elbows
with the man on the street, and makes contacts with people, many of whom are adverse to the gospel. The pastor
deals with many classes of people. If he is not careful, in
working with the poor he will find himself pitying them;
as he works with the rich, he is in danger of envying them
and catering to their whims. The pastor must be in constant touch with the Lord because the pull of the secular
world is strong.

The demands of the congregation. Pressure is not

necessarily wrong. Sometimes the greatest power comes to those who are under the greatest pressure. When, however, the pressure comes from a congregation whose concept is different from the divine concept, the pastor will find himself in danger of being occupied as a man-pleaser and engaged in a hopeless task. The following rather facetious example will certainly make the point. It was prepared by a leading layman of a Baptist church in Michigan, and was first read at a Layman's Sunday program.

Man Wanted: Minister for Growing Church. A real challenge for the right man! Opportunity to become better acquainted with people!

Applicant must offer experience as shop worker ... office manager ... educator (all levels, including college) ... artist ... salesman ... diplomat ... writer ... theologian ... politician ... Boy Scout leader ... children's worker ... minor league athlete ... psychologist ... vocational counselor ... psychiatrist ... funeral director ... wedding consultant ... master of ceremonies ... circus clown ... missionary ... social worker.

Helpful but not essential: experience as a butcher ... baker ... cowboy ... Western Union messenger.

Must know all about problems of birth, marriage and death; also conversant with latest theories and practices in areas like pediatrics, economics, and nuclear science.

Right man must hold firm views on every topic, but be careful not to upset people who disagree. Must be forthright but flexible; return criticism and backbiting with Christian love and forgiveness.

Should have outgoing, friendly disposition at all times; should be captivating speaker and intent listener; will pretend he enjoys hearing women talk.

Education must be beyond Ph.D. requirements, but always concealed in homespun modesty and folksy talk. Able to sound learned at times, but most of the time talks and acts like good-old-Joe. Familiar with literature read by average congregation.

Must be willing to work long hours; subject to call any time day or night; adaptable to sudden interruption. Will spend at least 25 hours preparing sermon; additional 10 hours reading books and magazines. Applicant's wife must be both stunning and plain; smartly attired but conservative in appearance; gracious and able to get along with everyone. Must be willing to work in church kitchen, teach Sunday school, baby-sit, run Multilith machine, wait on tables, never listen to gossip, never become discouraged.

Applicant's children must be exemplary in conduct and character; well-behaved, yet basically no different from other children; decently dressed.

Opportunity for applicant to live close to work. Furnished home provided; open-door hospitality enforced. Must be ever mindful the house does not belong to him.

Directly responsible for views and conduct to all church members and visitors; not confined to direction or support from any other person.

Salary not commensurate with experience or need; no overtime pay. All replies kept confidential. Anyone applying will undergo full investigation to determine sanity (clipped).

Along the same line is this quote from an unknown

source, captioned "The Perfect Preacher Has Been Found."

> After hundreds of years, a model preacher has been found to suit everyone. He preaches exactly 20 minutes and then sits down. He condemns sin, but never hurts anyone's feelings.
>
> He works from 8 A.M. to 10 P.M. in every type of work, from preaching to custodial service. He makes $60 a week, wears good clothes, buys good books regularly, has a nice family, drives a good car, and gives $30 a week to the church. He also stands ready to contribute to every good work that comes along.
>
> He is 25 years old and has been in the ministry for 30 years. He is tall and short, thin and heavyset in addition to being handsome. He has one brown eye and one blue, hair is parted in the middle, left side dark and straight, right side brown and wavy.
>
> He has a burning desire to work with teenagers, and spends all his time with older folks. He smiles all the time with a straight face, because he has a sense of humor that keeps him seriously dedicated to his work. He makes 15 calls a day on church members, spends all his time evangelizing the unchurched, and is never out of the office (clipped).

In the same vein, we quote from the foreword of the book, *Some Preachers Do*, by Bertie Cole Bays:

> A preacher, Oswald, is a good mixer equipped with a loud speaker, a streamlined body, the thick skin of a mule, the patience of God, a bottle of oil, and a can of Flit.
>
> He is employed by an organized group of Christian people to preach two or three sermons on

Sunday, to conduct a midweek service, to marry
their children and to bury their dead; to encourage, to advise, to uplift, to warn, to lead and to love
them; to pray for them, and to stand by as the last
breath leaves the body of a loved one. Besides
these duties, he must be an all-around business
man and executive, so that the affairs of the
church may move smoothly and wax prosper-
ous.

Now a minister has no boss and so does not work
by rules and regulations. He can please himself, provided he does not displease some two or
three hundred, or seven or eight hundred,
more or less members of his congregation. He
can plan his work to suit himself, pray when he
chooses, study when he chooses—of course,
subject to constant interruption and demand
that he go here and there and do this and that
(Did he find Mrs. Jones' purse in church? If not,
will he please go and look and call Mrs. Jones'
daughter?). In returning to his sermon, he may
find six men and six grievances lined up at his
study door. A minister's time is his own! So in
order that you may use your time wisely, and
avoid certain pitfalls and mistakes and become
a figure in your denomination, I am going to
give you some advice concerning the work of the
ministry, ministerial etiquette, and your position in general.

You will have the poorest material of any profession on earth with which to work. The contrac-
tor can demand the best of materials; the physician, the purest of drugs; the jeweler, the most
flawless of stones; but the minister, working
with human nature, finds so much bad in the
best and so much unexpected good in the worst,
that the structure which he builds is so amazing a combination of weakness and of strength,

of solid timber and of worm-eaten boards, of
beauty and of hideous hypocrisy, that God alone
can distinguish the maze, trace the pattern,
and call it "good" or "bad."[2]

The concern of dealing with human needs. This
simply means that the pastor is dealing with more than a
"product." He is dealing with both the soul and spirit of
each person of the congregation. It was Joseph Parker
who said, "Every pew has at least one broken heart." In
this day of automation and computers a man is often
lonely and needs someone to care for him and love him. A
pastor who cares, and a church that cares, will go a long
way in meeting the spiritual needs of such a person. Remember, a pastor is a shepherd; he should have a shepherd's heart. He must look through the eyes of Christ and
have the same compassion and love for each member of
his congregation that Christ has.
C. It is a happy calling.
    It is important at this juncture that it be made clear
that the ministry is a happy calling. The foregoing para-
graphs may seem pessimistic, but mention of the difficult nature of the calling is only to impress upon the pastor that he can do nothing of himself. Once he draws away
from the difficulties, gets the proper perspective, and experiences the enabling of God's grace, and resources of
His strength, he will find himself not only succeeding but
happy in that success. In other words, His calling is His
enabling. Because the pastor has been called of God and
knows the enabling power of God, he will know the joy of
the Lord in that calling. "The joy of the LORD is your
strength" (Neh. 8:10).
    Representing the Lord as the pastor does, he is also
aware of the constant presence of the Lord. In Matthew
28:20 Christ has promised His presence. The union and
communion with Him in the vine-branch relationship

results in not only his joy but his full joy (John 15:11).

It is also a happy calling because of the results produced through service. As the farmer rejoices "bringing in the sheaves," so "we shall reap, if we faint not" (Gal. 6:9). Where there is sweat, the sweet will follow; and where there is rigor, there is sure reward. The pastor is a happy person because he is working in areas which have eternal dividends. It is understandable that anyone would like to know some exhilaration in having done a good job, however temporal results may be. But there is nothing quite like knowing that as the pastor invests his time in a project he is making eternal investments which will result in eternal dividends.

William Hogue aptly says:

And when all the monuments of human greatness shall have perished; when the grandest production of earth's philosophers, legislators, historians, poets and illustrious men shall have been destroyed; when the earth and the works that are therein shall be burned up, and the elements all melt with fervent heat; the influence of the faithful pastor will survive, the results of his toil and tears, his counsels and warnings, his preaching and praying, his study and visitation shall still remain, and those who were blessed and saved through his ministry "shall rise and call him blessed."[3]

D. It is a responsible calling.

We speak of the necessity of having a right relationship with the Lord. It cannot be emphasized too much that there needs to be a close walk with the Lord if the pastor is to be an effective servant for the Lord. Spurgeon quoted McCheyne as saying, "It is not so much great talents that God blesses as great likeness to Christ."

Spurgeon also said:

It will be in vain for me to stock my library, or organize societies, or project schemes, if I neglect
the culture of myself; for books, and agencies,
and systems are only remotely the instruments
of my holy calling; my own spirit, soul, and body
are my nearest machinery for sacred service;
my spiritual faculties, and my inner life are my
battle-axe and weapons of war.[4]

The need of prayer. The pastor, realizing his responsibility, ought to be a man of prayer. Select any man who is
truly successful in the ministry, as God deems success,
and it will be found that he is a man of constant interces-
sion before the throne. Did not our Lord spend many
nights in prayer as our example? Should the servant be
less faithful than his Master, particularly when he is
aware of the fact that the Master was sinless and for that
reason did not have all the same needs as the servant has?
Yet that communion through prayer was a vital necessity as He served the Father. Someone has said that it was so
easy and natural for Martin Luther to pray that sometimes even in company with his friends he would break
into petitions. There is no wonder that God used him in
the Great Reformation.

Hogue says of the Puritan Baxter:

He stained his study walls with praying breath;
and it was in his secret communings with God
that he acquired his distinguished piety, and
that divine unction which made his ministry so
eminently successful.[5]

The need of devotional study. It is only by coming into
contact with the written Word that the living Word will be
a day by day reality in the life of the pastor. He should un-

derstand that the people in the church have a right to regard him as an example of holiness. He does not become holy merely because he takes the position of a pastor. There is no spiritual change when he simply puts on the mantle or takes the shepherd's crook in hand. It is imperative that he be a holy man, a godly man, before he becomes a pastor. There is no miraculous transformation that takes place when men lay their hands on him in ordination. Someone has suggested that the stream seldom rises above its source. It is important therefore that the pastor not only be a student and preacher of the Word, but that his own personal life be exposed to the Word daily. This should result in a life of godliness and holiness. It was John Owen who said, "No man preaches a sermon well to others if he does not first preach it to his own heart." Spurgeon said:

> Abide under the shadow of the Almighty, dwell where Jesus manifests Himself, and live in the power of the Holy Ghost. Your very life lies in this. Whitefield mentions a lad who was so vividly conscious of the presence of God that he would generally walk the roads with his hat off. How I wish that we were always in such a mood. It would be no trouble to maintain earnestness then.[6]

The calling of a pastor is, indeed, a responsible calling.

I have found it helpful to keep a daily record of my devotional and Bible readings. A copy of the form used is reproduced at the end of this chapter (see Worksheet A). A similar systematic method will be of great value to any man in the work of the ministry.

Often in his Bible reading the pastor finds himself sermonizing and preparing for messages rather than feeding his own soul. This suggests a reason for keeping a record of where he is reading and for jotting down Scriptures that he would like to refer to later for research. However, the major purpose in reading the Bible is to feed one's own soul. In the form I have developed, the upper right-hand corner is used to list the chapters read in various parts of the Bible. I suggest that the pastor read some from each division regularly. It has been suggested that reading five Psalms and one chapter in Proverbs each day will take one through these two books every month, making a good spiritual diet. Indeed, one ought to be moving slowly through the historical and prophetic books of the Old Testament as well as the Gospels and epistles of the New Testament. While some make an effort to read the Bible through every year, it is important to set goals other than simply reading a certain number of chapters per day. Otherwise, one becomes occupied with covering ground and reads rather perfunctorily with more emphasis on getting through the material than applying it in one's own life.

The left-hand side of the form has a space for jotting down verses which can be used for hospital and counseling purposes. These can be followed up later and studied in more detail. I find it helpful to read the Bible with the intent of looking for specific truths. For example, as I read I may be looking for verses that speak of the Person and work of Christ. Another time the emphasis may be upon the promises of the Bible, or perhaps the manifestations of strength in service.

On the right-hand side are the letters S-P-E-C-S. The idea is to look for specific passages which will help spiritual growth:

S—a stumbling block to avoid

P—a promise to claim

E—an example to follow

C—a commandment to obey

S—a sin to avoid

Pastors, as well as lay people, need devotional verses that will "hit and fit."

On the back side of the page I allow space for sketching outlines, noting illustrations, and listing special material which can be researched later for sermon material (see Worksheet B). There is also space for a Daily Bible Reading Chart and Memory Work. It is important that pastors realize that the ministry is a most responsible calling and demands that a man of God be a godly man.

End Notes

[1] Hogue, *Homiletics and Pastoral Theology,* pp. 252–53.

[2] Bertie Cole Bays, *Some Preachers Do,* 3d ed. (Valley Forge, PA: Judson Press, 1953), foreword.

[3] Hogue, *Homiletics and Pastoral Theology*, p. 253.

[4] Spurgeon, *Lectures to His Students,* p. 15.

[5] Hogue, *Homiletics and Pastoral Theology*, p. 284.

[6] Spurgeon, *Lectures to His Students,* p. 293.

Date _____

DAILY BIBLE READING CHART

Memory Work: Personal Devotional Thoughts: Chapters read:

Historical _____
Poetic _____
Proverbs _____
Prophetic _____
Gospels _____
Epistles _____
Total _____

Scripture for Future Research:

Hospital and Counseling Verses:

New and Unnoticed: Hit and Fit:

S

P

The Work and Person of Christ: E

C

S

WORKSHEET A

Writing Ideas—Articles, Church Paper, etc., etc.	Illustrations
Verse Filing	Subject Filing

WORKSHEET B

CHAPTER THREE
The Pastor and People Relationship

In the scores of books on pastoral theology there seems to be very little written about the relationship between the pastor and his people. This is surprising in view of the fact that the pastor is a shepherd of the sheep, and the shepherd-sheep relationship should be very high on the scale of importance. A great many problems can be avoided by giving serious attention to this relationship.

What the Pastor Should be to His People

Concerned about their spiritual needs. This relationship can be improved and implemented two ways.

1. Through personal preparation. While some time in the last chapter was devoted to the necessity of a right spiritual relationship with the Lord, it may be added here that such a personal preparation will help the pastor to be all that he should be to his people. If the pastor is to be the spiritual leader of the church he must be that, not only because he has been placed there by appointment, but because he is entitled to that position by his deep commitment to the Lord. Most congregations consider their pastor the spiritual leader. The maintenance of this relationship depends on a right daily relationship with the Lord. The pastor should be concerned about the spiritual needs of the people in the church. The finest thing he can do for them is to be careful of his vertical relationship with the Lord. This will do the most good in stabilizing his hori-

zontal relationship with man.

2. Through pulpit preparation. Nothing should divert the pastor from the preparation he needs in order to do his best work in the pulpit. As important as other areas of pastoral life are, nothing is more important than the pulpit ministry. Such effectiveness in the pulpit depends on long, hard hours in the study. If the pastor is going to be all that he should be to his people, time should be spent getting messages ready that will speak to their hearts on the Lord's Day. One Christian psychologist, Dr. Henry Brandt, told a group of preachers that their best work in helping people in their needs was in the pulpit. Dr. Tim LaHaye refuses to counsel individuals unless they agree to come to the Sunday services where he is preaching. The point is, the greatest help to people in the church is through the pulpit ministry. This requires preparation!

Concerned with love for them and available when needed. While study hours should be regular, in an emergency the pastor may leave the desk. He should be available to his people twenty-four hours a day and willing to help them in any crisis or spiritual need. He should be one who can be depended upon to have an ear ready to listen and yet never betray a confidence.

Concerned and sympathetic with those in sorrow, a friend to the friendless. The pastor should be ready to minister to troubled hearts in the hour of bereavement. He should be a friend "that sticketh closer than a brother," ready to do all he can to relieve sorrow and meet the need with the Word of God.

What the Pastor Should be to His Boards and Church Leaders

It is important at this juncture to understand that it is sometimes difficult to draw the line between the work of the minister as a pastor and as an administrator. Such an integration of both the pastoral and business relationships needs the wisdom and direction of the Lord.

A leader, not a dictator. A true leader is able to lead the people without driving them. In some cases, the pastor makes it very clear that he is the dominant head and that the deacons have no say. The deacons are ignored as a board and considered significant only as long as they agree with the pastor. They are in effect "yes men," whose only function is to nod at the right time. Holy men will only chafe under such leadership. This generates friction and may result in unnecessary problems. While the pastor is not to be a "Casper Milquetoast," conforming to every idea and whim of the church boards, on the other hand he is not to be dictatorial and domineering.

I am not suggesting that the pastor is not to be a leader, for he is to be an elder that rules well (1 Tim. 5:17). He certainly should exercise strong and effective leadership among the men and in that position be respected by his fellow board members. However, if he is compelled to remind his boards that he is the leader, he is a failure. Genuine leadership should be recognized by the church and the officers. It would be ridiculous for the shepherd to keep repeating "I am your shepherd" as he leads the sheep. Leadership therefore is not something stated but something done.

In summary, the pastor is to be a shepherd—one who is able to use both the staff and the rod in a way that reflects a loving, caring heart. He should be neither spineless nor overbearing. He should take a sound Biblical position and exercise leadership as one interested in leading his flock to the Chief Shepherd. He should be bold but not bombastic. He should lead and comfort with the tender shepherd's heart and hand—just like his Lord.

Spiritual but not infallible. Woe is the man who feels that wisdom will die with him, and that his must be the last word on all subjects. Woe, too, is the man who has such a misconstrued view of himself as to consider himself infallible. Such a man, rather than being infallible, may have an extreme inferiority complex and may be trying to cover it rather than face questions regarding his judgment. A pastor who is willing to listen to his boards and not feel that he is being humiliated or rebuffed will be one greatly respected by his boards. A pastor should remember that to agree with his deacons in some areas does not lessen his image. One who is willing to admit that he made a mistake or to concede that others may know more in a given area than he does is not really losing but gaining. The boards will only seek to follow a pastor when they detect a genuineness in him and a desire to do the will of God. Nothing is worse than a man trying to be what he is not or seeking to assert himself in areas where he is uninformed. A pastor should not make a "mountain out of a molehill." The man who is constantly making big issues out of slight differences and turning small disagreements into large battlefields will soon find himself without a church.

A man should not try to imitate other pastors whose methodology may be unique and who may be dictatorial in their particular churches. Each individual has his own set of characteristics and abilities. To imitate some leading pastor or to seek to do things in a manner that is peculiar to him is to court danger. Again, the pastor should remember that he is to be a spiritual man; he should assert the kind of leadership that will be glorifying to the Lord.

Willing to improve constantly his relationship with his people. Many pastors would be profited by a course in public relations and in the simple psychology of working with people. Dale Carnegie has written two books that will be helpful: *How to Win Friends and Influence People* and *Public Speaking and Influencing Men in Busi-*

ness. A great deal of what he says is just plain good sense, and it will be good sense to learn some of his principles and apply them. While there are many differences between a pastor and an executive in the secular world, there are many similarities. Both men are dealing with people and the strengths and weaknesses of human nature. The Lord expects us to be "wise as serpents, harmless as doves" and to be down to earth in our human relations. A church board has a right to expect the leader to be spiritual, although not infallible, and ready and willing to lead his people, not drive them.

What the Pastor Should Recognize as a Major Hindrance

The danger of being a friend to the few. Among the major hindrances which may impair a man's ministry is one that deserves special attention. It is the danger of the pastor being a friend to the few and not the pastor of the entire congregation. It may seem trite but it is still true that "familiarity breeds contempt." A close relationship with a certain group in the church will hinder one's effectiveness in reaching others. I am not suggesting that the pastor should consider himself detached from his people or appear to be unaware of their needs. He should be concerned about the spiritual growth and requirements of all the people and have a loving consideration for them. He should, like the Lord, be sympathetic to all the problems of his congregation. The point I want to stress is that the pastor and his wife should not permit the cultivation of a "buddy" relationship with certain people or families in the congregation. When such a relationship is established with a few, the majority may conclude that they are on the outside and are not important. It will also decrease the respect of the "few" who have been taken into the inner circle. They will begin to look upon the pastor not as one who is their shepherd but as their special friend. For him to speak to them from the pulpit concerning sin and various areas which need correcting often offends them.

Intimate friendships in which the pastor is called by his first name seldom end the way they began. It has been observed that in some churches most of the people in the congregation address the pastor as "pastor," while others who seem to be in the inner circle consider him on a first-name basis. This is one of the early warnings that a relationship has been established that will ultimately cause difficulty.

The solution to the problem of being a friend to the few. There are a number of helpful solutions to the foregoing problem. I suggest that if there are doubts as to the wisdom of this precaution, the pastor take time to recall various church problems of which he has knowledge. Often he will find the very people who caused the problems were originally his bosom friends. While I regret that this is the case, it is the wisest decision to exercise care in these social areas.

1. Establish the principle of having no close personal friends in the congregation. This, of course, will take time because it is not something that is generally announced from the platform. If a situation of this kind already exists, it is difficult to disconnect yourself. It is often embarrassing and disruptive to the spirit of harmony. Therefore the pastor needs to be prayerfully cautious in dealing with the problem.

The pastor who is just beginning his ministry ought to make it his personal objective not to develop personal friends within the congregation. This can generally be accomplished by use of some of the following suggestions:

   a. Do not invite members to your home after services or during the week on an intimate friend basis.

The desire to do so seems to be very natural as members want to be friends and of course the pastor and his wife need friends. However, again I insist that the overall benefit of being a shepherd-pastor to all the people will be greater than the advantages gained by such practice. I am aware that this may seem contradictory to what many pastors practice. I feel very strongly, however, that this is the best policy. The only exception to this rule would be when official functions are held in the home; for example, when the whole board of deacons or the whole board of trustees is invited.

b. Do not "let your hair down" or discuss personal problems with your people. This is a general rule that ought to be observed at all times, not only in respect to the specific situation under consideration here. It is simply an abiding principle that one cannot deal with others' needs and problems by offering them problems of one's own. If the physician is going to help the patient, he cannot do it by discussing his own personal ailments. The shepherd called of God must remember that, while he is human and has needs, his relationship to his people must be as a pastor.

c. Be ultracareful in all relationships with those of the opposite sex. In this you must be both sensible and discreet. If you are guilty of anything, be guilty of being an extremist in your care to observe this rule. In your visitations you ought not to visit women when they are alone. It is best not to offer them a ride if, for example, you see them on the street alone.

It has been my experience that pastors react in different ways to the above suggestions. To a seminarian or budding pastor, the very idea of such caution seems to express a pride of rank and class that is offensive. It seems to him to widen the gap between the "clergy and the laity" and creates artificial barriers which are unhealthy for the church. But rather than setting barriers, we are trying to eliminate those that will hinder one's ministry. The pastor certainly ought to be a humble man with a heart for the people. He is not a pompous member of an elite clergy; rather, he is a shepherd who is careful to lay aside all personal "druthers," however gregarious he may be, for the good of the flock. When the pastor is needed, he certainly should be available and ready to help. He should be close to a phone twenty-four hours a day in case emergencies arise. He should pray for his flock, love them, disciple them and guide them like a "good shepherd." However, he also must exercise a care to prevent anything that will hinder the effectiveness of his ministry.

Again, I feel that the perils of ignoring this advice are many. In addition to resulting in a lack of unity among the people, it could cause problems of the flesh and make one vulnerable to the devices of Satan.

2. Establish the procedures for handling the personal problem of loneliness. While solutions to the problem of being a friend to the few have been given, the one area that has not been considered is the pastor's own needs. Assuming the foregoing advice is taken, the pastor may consider himself a very lonely person and in need of personal friendships.

First, let me say that it is better to be lonely and effective than to be a "hail fellow well met" who is failing in the ministry.

Ralph G. Turnbull talks about the chill of loneliness when he says:

The many demands now made upon a leader in the church are exacting. As it has been said—

he enters upon a high office and ends by running an office! This is the peril and danger of the
ministry, it is true. Whether a pastor, administrator, counselor, visitor, or preacher—the
minister has responsibilities which force him
into a lonely position. As he engages in these he
finds himself alone. He is a pastor and thus will
seek to shepherd the flock. Loneliness is inesca-
pable and the pastor has his share. His lot is
such that he is a man among men, and yet a man
set apart. His office and its function tend to iso-
late him, if not in a physical sense, in a spiritual
way. His thoughts and brooding over the life and
work of his congregation produce a feeling of
loneliness. He will talk about plans and programs with his officers and people, yet there
will always be a certain wistfulness and with-
drawal in reflecting upon the implications of
the work to be attempted. Who is sufficient for
these things? A pastor is then walled in and the
door is closed. This is a mark of our calling and
vocation. It cannot be otherwise. We are
men"set apart" by Christ. Our Lord has ordained us. We are not the same as others in the
church, however much we talk about it. Ministry and function imply separateness and therefore loneliness in spirit. As our Lord knew this
solitary way, so His servants follow Him still.[1]

Spurgeon, in his *Lectures to His Students,* has a
chapter entitled "The Minister's Fainting Fits." He
writes:

Our position in the church will also conduce to
this. A minister fully equipped for his work will
usually be a spirit by himself, above, beyond,
and apart from others. The most loving of his
people cannot enter into his peculiar thoughts,

cares and temptations. In the ranks, men walk shoulder to shoulder, with many comrades, but as the officer rises in rank, men of his standing are fewer in number. There are many soldiers, few captains, fewer colonels, but only one commander-in-chief. So, in our churches, the man whom the Lord raises as a leader becomes, in the same degree in which he is a superior man, a solitary man. The mountain-tops stand solemnly apart, and talk only with God as He visits their terrible solitudes.[2]

We feel the solution to such apartness and loneliness can be found in the following suggestions:

a. The pastor must be close to the Lord, spending time in His presence. Remember that He said, "Lo, I am with you alway, even unto the end of the age."

b. The pastor must have a close tie and relationship with his wife and family. Here he can share his burdens and enjoy a fellowship that will take away the sting of loneliness.

c. The pastor should have pastor friends with whom he can "let his hair down" and share his problems. However, here too he must be cautious; he must be careful always that in his relationships with others he does not betray the confidences of his people.

In summary, an efficient pastor must maintain a proper pastor-people relationship. Ignore this and as adept as he may be as an organizer and as gifted as he may be as a preacher, he can ruin his effectiveness as a pastor.

End Notes

[1] Ralph G. Turnbull, *A Minister's Obstacles* (Old Tappan, NJ: Fleming H. Revell Co., 1965), pp. 113, 115, 116.

[2] Spurgeon, *Lectures to His Students,* p. 136.

CHAPTER FOUR
In the Study

Next to the private closet of prayer, the most important and most sacred place to the pastor is his study. If the closet is the Holy of Holies, the study is the Holy Place. And, as in the Old Testament, the two are not fully separated; one is as vital as the other. Neglect of either will cause a man's ministry to falter and fail.

The Importance of Study Habits

Many pastors have never established regular study habits. Often the reason for this is that it was not done when they were starting out in the ministry; then the passing years find them in the same undisciplined mold. Common excuses for poor study habits might fall into one of the following categories:

The pastor who considers himself "not a scholar" and therefore not given to much study. The answer to this statement is not hard to find. Every pastor ought to be a teacher. The Scriptures say, "And he gave some, apostles; and some, prophets; and some, evangelists; and some, pastors and teachers" (Eph. 4:11). While the King James Version says "pastors and teachers," the original seems to bear out that the pastor is a pastor-teacher, and that he does not function properly until he assumes both responsibilities. Every pastor-teacher ought to be a man of the Book—a diligent student of the Word of God.

Sidlow Baxter well observes:

It needs to be shouted out loudly and again today, until it echoes throughout our evangelical churches; the pulpit (i.e., the Book and the Prophet) is the organic center of the local church! Going with that is the need for a new insistence that the minister shall really study the Book, so as to be proficient in expounding its "breadths, and lengths, and depths, and heights."[1]

The pastor who starts off impressively as a young gifted preacher and ends disappointingly because of the lack of spiritual and mental stimulation in the study. What can be said about the young man who starts off impressively but ends in disappointment? What is it along the way that has deterred him from being involved in the greatest business in the world? Why is it that the pace set in the earlier years slows to mere jogging in the path of the pastorate? Sometimes it is a spiritual problem. Sometimes the man has allowed himself to become indifferent to the real needs of his people. Sometimes his head is turned by material conditions, and he becomes more involved in monetary interests than spiritual.

More often than not it is a lack of real understanding of the role of the preacher. He is not properly motivated in his impressive start. The first few laps are energized by the intrigue or the fascinating nature of the new "occupation." But he is not fully aware that the continual feeding of the people requires constant replenishment of the storehouse. Thus he neglects the indispensable need— proper study habits.

The pastor who has a natural gift of gab and thinks it unnecessary to do a great deal of study. Interestingly, this so-called "gift of gab" may be a great disadvantage to a young man. The man who depends on his way with words and his ability to talk on any subject fluently without strenuous efforts in the study will have a shallow ministry and end in failure.

Wilson Hogue has written about the person who depends on wit, genius and inspiration, and fails to cultivate the mind, to dig in and study:

> To depend on wit, genius, or inspiration here, without continuously cultivating the mind and storing it with fresh funds of thought and knowledge, is to fail of permanent success, to insure inglorious defeat in one of the grandest enterprises which ever engaged the efforts of an intelligent being. It is to act the part of a fanatic or fool, and to deserve the failure and disgrace inevitably resulting from such a course. The Spirit of God never endorses mental slothfulness by inspiring the man who is too indolent to study and inform himself.[2]

The pastor who depends on the "barrel of sermons" or sermon outlines bought through subscription rather than on his own private study. An examination of many ministers' libraries, particularly those who have been in the ministry for a number of years, will prove enlightening. Often one finds a great storehouse of sermons preached by others and a "pantry" of canned illustrations, but hardly more. When a minister keeps preaching old sermons which he used years before—many of which are a resketching of sermons he has read or heard—it is no wonder that his ministry is unproductive. In his excellent book, *A Preacher's Portrait,* John Stott, speaking on this kind of preacher as a "babbler," says:

> This is the word which the Athenian philosophers used on the Areopagus to describe Paul. "What would this babbler say?" they asked with scorn (Acts 17:18). The Greek word is "spermologos," which means a "seed-picker." It is used

in its literal sense of seed-eating birds, and especially, I believe, by Aristophanes and Aristotle
of the rook. Metaphorically, it came to be applied
to a scavenger, a "guttersnipe," "one who
makes his living by picking up scraps, a rag-
picker." From this it was transferred to the gossip or chatterbox, "one who picks up retail
scraps of knowledge." The "babbler" trades in
ideas like secondhand merchandise, picking
up bits and pieces wherever he finds them. His
sermons are a veritable ragbag.[3]

*The pastor who gives the gospel message of "Four Things
God Wants You To Know" week after week with occa-
sional changes of the sermon arrangement.* Let it be understood, I do not minimize the need for presenting the
plan of salvation. It should be included in every sermon;
certainly reference should always be given to the gospel.
However, when the simple plan of salvation is given because there is a lack of real study and the minister finds
himself falling back on something he knows well, he is
being dishonest both with himself and his people. It is no
wonder that many people are starving in the pew and reflecting it in their daily lives.

The Importance of a Plan for Preparation of Study

Most Bible students will agree that a plan for study is
necessary. The idea of working in a specified place and
with definite study methods is vitally important. Have
you ever noted the manner in which various people pack
the trunk of their car? Those who have a system can pack
twice as much as those who have no system. Some just
throw their baggage and pile it high; others lay it out on
the ground and decide which suitcase or box should be
placed in the available space. This is also true when it
comes to planning and preparing to study. The pastor

must be methodical in his work, determining the best place for study, the best time for study and the availability of proper tools for such work.

Where to study. Most pastors will have a study either in their home or the church. We will consider the advantages and disadvantages of both.

1. The study in the home
   a. Advantages
      (1) It is readily available night and day. If a pastor decides to catch an extra hour in the evening or redeem a few minutes before dinner, he can go to his study and use it profitably.

      (2) It takes a minimum of personal preparation in getting ready to study. If the study is in the church, the pastor needs to shave and "dress up" because he will be in contact with the general public. On the other hand, if he studies at home, early in the morning he can dress casually. Shaving and dressing for public appearance can be done just before lunch. He can look his best, therefore, as he goes into the community for his pastoral calls.

      (3) It can be a quiet place away from the hustle and bustle of the general business of the church. This is particularly true if there are activities (club meetings, day school, etc.,) going on during the day at the church.
   b. Disadvantages
      (1) While the study at home is available night and day, it is not conducive to regular hours. It is much easier for an undisciplined person to remain in that state if he does not have regular stated hours to be at work away from his home.

      (2) When the study is at home it is difficult to distinguish between work hours and home hours.

If one is not careful, he will find himself puttering around the house and doing some of the chores which ordinarily a man would do after work hours. When plumbing needs to be done, or other repairs, it is often the first item of work for the day. It is also easier to be distracted by his children and wife. Unless there are some rather firm rules set down, it is particularly difficult when the children are younger and do not understand that Dad is at work, even though he has not left the house.

(3) While a study at home seems to be a disadvantage for the pastor, it is a disadvantage for the family as well. It is often difficult for them to live a normal life. When there is not a separate study in the church, people will come to the house for counseling. Suddenly the parsonage becomes an annex to the church and the family finds itself in a fish bowl, constantly under observation.

(4) When the church is large enough to have a staff, it is difficult to work with the staff when their offices are in the church and the pastor is operating at home. A good example is set by the pastor being in the office and helping get the staff off to their regular work.

2. The study in the church

  a. Advantages

    (1) It is much easier to establish regular hours of study when a pastor goes to work in the morning like any other worker in business. This regularity lends itself to a more disciplined study life.

    (2) It separates the home life from the church life and eliminates some of the disadvantages mentioned in the foregoing paragraphs.

  b. Disadvantages

(1) There is a temptation to get involved in extra-curricular activities of the church which are not related to the work in the study.

(2) There is a danger of becoming involved with administrative details, working with the staff in various problems and projects. Thus, the main business of the pastor in his study, which is to prepare himself to feed the flock, is neglected. Too often the study becomes an office; the pastor becomes an executive of "the corporation" and he is diverted from his major business of being a preacher and teacher of the Word.

(3) There is the possibility of frequent interruptions. The church is easily accessible to the general public and people may stop to see the pastor without prior notice or appointment. This may include members of the church, or a variety of enterprising businessmen who want to see the "chief executive."

Each pastor will have to weigh the advantages and disadvantages of both the home and the church for the study and make a decision accordingly. I have had a study in the church and another at home both at the same time, which has allowed me to "have my cake and eat it too." But every pastor does not have this advantage. When all is considered, it seems better to have the study in the church if the disadvantages can be overcome. To know them is the first step in being able to handle them. For example, if one is aware of the danger of becoming the executive in an office instead of the man of the Book in the study, he must deal with the problem. He can avoid much of the loss of time by budgeting his time to care for essential details and delegating the work load to others. Personal discipline and help from the secretary can eliminate many of the problems of disturbance.

If a church does not have a secretary, the pastor might announce that he is available only in an emergency situation during his study hours. Some may take offense at this and consider the pastor "removed from the needs of the congregation," but most of them will respect it, especially when they see the difference in his sermons.

If it is decided to keep the study in the home, I would suggest that some type of office be available for counseling purposes away from home. The pastor should take extra precautions to be in his place on time and to observe specific hours for his study.

How to study

1. Discipline in the study. Whether the study is at home or in the church, in either case it is possible to be undisciplined and unproductive. If a man's ministry is going to be more than a superficial one and involve the fresh dissemination of truth, it is going to require discipline in the study. This is particularly true if one is involved in expository preaching.

Stott well said:

> Expository preaching is a most exacting discipline. Perhaps that is why it is so rare. Only those will undertake it who are prepared to follow the example of the apostles and say, "It is not reason that we should leave the word of God, and serve tables ... we will give ourselves continually to prayer, and to the ministry of the word" (Acts 6:2, 4). The systematic *preaching* of the Word is impossible without the systematic *study* of it.[4]

A painstaking, thorough examination of the text therefore requires daily, dogged discipline in Bible study. It has been observed that to be a good preacher and teacher, one must be inaccessible during periods of study and sermon preparation. When there is discipline in this learning process there will be a bringing up of fresh, ample supplies of truth, both for one's own inspiration and for the help of others. When thinking in terms of discipline, the pastor must consider discipline in actual thinking as well as discipline with regard to time. He can have a well-scheduled plan for the day, but if he is not willing to apply himself in actual thought and meditation, he is just going through the motions and the day will end fruitless and unproductive.

In *Lectures to His Students,* Spurgeon says:

> Thinking is better than possessing books. Thinking is an exercise of the soul which both develops its powers and educates them. A little girl was once asked whether she knew what her soul was, and, to the surprise of all, she said, "Sir, my soul is my think." If this be correct some persons have very little soul. Without thinking, reading cannot benefit the mind, but it may delude the man into the idea that he is growing wise. Books are a sort of idol to some men. As the image with the Roman Catholic is intended to make him think of Christ, and in effect keeps him from Christ, so books are intended to make men think, but are often a hindrance to thought.[5]

We are not suggesting that books are not valuable. Indeed, Spurgeon had one of the finest libraries of the time and looked disdainfully upon ministers who felt that they should seek to learn without books. But what Spurgeon is saying in effect is that without discipline of thought, the availability of a fine study and a library well-stocked will be of little value. We must develop concentration; we must practice discipline and make ourselves work and think.

It was Donald Marquis who said, "If you make people think they are thinking, they will love you. If you really make them think, they will hate you. The reason for that, of course, is that we like to think that we are thinking because it is complimentary, but real thinking, hard thinking is work, and requires discipline."

J. K. Van Baalen said, "Nothing is easier than being busy; nothing is more difficult than hard work; and the hardest work is thinking."

2. Discipline in the daily schedule. Not only must there be discipline in study, but there must be discipline in the study. Now how is this to be done? The pastor can take good advice here even from those in the secular area. It must be remembered that basically people are lazy by nature. This is rather uncomplimentary, so much so that a great many might refuse to recognize it; but it is true, and the sooner the pastor is aware of it, the sooner he can do something about it. Sometimes this sin of slothfulness and laziness is not so apparent, particularly when the job or occupation is on a "self-employment" basis without a superior to whom the worker is responsible. In the end, of course, the pastor is accountable to the Lord and to the church, but it is easy to be lazy in the ministry and get away with it, at least for a time. The pastor can, therefore, learn from others who have had similar problems and find out what rules and principles were applied in helping them to be more disciplined in the study.

In an article, "Could You Write More?" by John Creasy in *The Writer* magazine, the author gives rules that apply to the pastor as well as the free-lance writer. He says:

There are a number of rules, mostly simple,

which I submit with the full knowledge that writers are above all things individualists, and that they will need to alter and amend these rules to suit their own individuality.

Rule 1. Work to rule, not to mood. Work *through* moods.

Rule 2. Regard yourself not as a man of remarkable but fragile talent which should be carefully nurtured, but as a hardy, hardened, tough working man.

Rule 3. Play golf (tennis, etc.) only as often as the ordinary working man, from business executive to garbage collector, plays.

Rule 4. Drill yourself to acquire neatness and system at the desk. *Everyone* can. The simple art of knowing where everything is can increase your output considerably.

Rule 5. If you have an armchair in your study, don't use it except between say, 2:00 and 2:30, and after 6:00 at night.

Rule 6. Be punctual. If you were going to an office to work for a boss, you would be. So be your own boss. When you are going to your study (or your corner of the living room table) be right on time. Just as nothing succeeds like success, so nothing works like work.

Rule 7. Surround yourself as with tall brick walls when you are working. Make it an absolute family rule that you must not be interrupted except in case of emergency. But when this rule is being applied, *work*. Your wife will respect it just as long as she is sure that it isn't a form of lazing without being interrupted.[6]

While John Creasy (now deceased) was a writer, he

was an example of one who put these rules into practice. "Since his first book in 1932 he has written 360 books (up to 1960) in addition to writing short stories, serials, countless articles and taking active part in politics and local affairs, lecturing, etc., etc. And he is still comfortably on the right side of 50."[7]

a. Suggested procedure for successful personal discipline.

(1) Set aside a certain time during the week, preferably on Monday, to outline the week's work (see Worksheet C). One hour applied sometime on Monday morning for planning for the week will prove most helpful. Standardized planning sheets will provide direction and order for notations. This weekly plan can be developed as the week progresses, but it will give a general idea of direction for the week. List the study hours, Monday through Saturday, and general calls that must be made. This, of course, will include emergency calls and other calls which must be made in a given area. Once again, while it is a general weekly plan, there may be special projects to accomplish. There is a miscellaneous column for anything which may be peculiar to the pastor's own work or ministry.

(2) In addition to the weekly planner there is value in using a daily record sheet (see Worksheet D). This can be an effective aid in budgeting the active pastor's time. Notice that on one side of the sheet there is a proposed daily schedule from 8 A.M. to 5 P.M., divided into fifteen-minute segments. This is not what has been done but what is proposed for that day. It should be filled out early in the day or on the previous evening.

On the right-hand side is the Diary and Data column for observations and check marks indicating what was actually done. Failure to adhere to the close schedule should not result in frustration. It must be flexible to allow for unforeseen events. The planning sheet does, however, give specific directions as to what needs to be done and helps to determine whether or not objectives have been accomplished.

The daily schedule is planned in fifteen-minute segments intentionally, since to schedule hour blocks can result in precious minutes drifting away. One must realize that there are twenty-four hours in each God-given day. Everyone has the same amount of time; it is how it is used that really matters.

Rossin, in his book, *Practical Study Methods for Students and Pastors,* says:

> Time is only a relative restriction upon the efforts of man. If there is just so much gas to lay in the tank, everything else being equal, the distance a car will travel depends upon the efficiency of the carburetor and the motor; or in other words, how much of the potential power in the fuel is utilized through efficiency.[8]

On the other side of the Daily Work Record (see Worksheet E) are divisions for recording progress in the study. The Daily Work Record will help in the organization of reading material for the day and will serve as an incentive to touch on various areas of study. The page can be duplicated on 8 1/2" x 11" paper. Reproduce enough sheets for a year and put them in a three-ring notebook.

On the left-hand side of the back of the Daily Record Sheet (Worksheet E) is a place for Devotional Passage, Prayer and Bible Reading.

Another section should be noted on the left-hand side which deals with Memory Work and Review. The writer strongly urges the pastor to learn a verse a day; there is a place for a review verse as well as a new verse. There is also a place for vocabulary and phrase review. It would be helpful to make it a habit to learn new words and phrases picked up in reading, and to review them occasionally.

There is also a place where one can designate Sermon Preparation. This can give one an idea, before the week is over, as to how much time is spent on each message, and later determine whether or not it should be increased. Here the morning and evening services are listed, the Sunday School, Wednesday preparation and special messages. Added to this, of course, would be radio and special writing assignments if one is involved in these ministries.

There is also an area for Reading, listing title of book, pages read and a brief comment as to whether or not it was found to be helpful or a blessing. Another area may be used for indicating any reading done in Theology: sermons, magazine articles, periodicals. There is also a section for listing Writing—church papers, weekly Sunday School papers, books or other material—and a section for Correspondence.

In the right-hand column there are areas for Calls and Counseling, Business Meetings and Boards, Unfinished Business, Work, etc.; also space for Today's Verse, Today's Word, Today's Promise and Health Workout.

I feel that such a record designed for the use of the pastor will be helpful in the work of the ministry.

(3) Write out messages. An excellent way to exercise discipline is to write out messages in their entirety. This was done by F. B. Meyer, J. H. Jowett and scores of others.

(a) It will help formulate thoughts more clearly. It has been well said that reading makes a man full, writing makes a man accurate.

(b) It will help in discipline of study and thought.

(c) It will be beneficial in improving writing skills.

(d) It will aid in future reference.

What to study. This of course, will depend upon the messages to be delivered on the Lord's Day. Regardless of where the pastor may be in sermon preparation, it is wise that he include in his schedule each day some of the following:

1. Theology. This can be from a periodical or from a theology book or set. Note the good selection of books on theology in the section, "The Minister's Library."

Spurgeon said to his students:

> Be well instructed in theology, and do not regard the sneers of those who rail at it because they are ignorant of it. Many preachers are not theologians, and hence the mistakes which they make. It cannot do any hurt to the most lively evangelist to be also a sound theologian, and it may often be the means of saving him from gross blunders.[9]

2. Biblical exegesis and exposition. One of these, of course, is analysis, and the other is synthesis. Both are important. A book-by-book approach in the pastor's preparation and preaching will result in the following:

a. It will keep the pastor alert and fresh in his preaching.

b. It will cause him to grow spiritually.

c. It will keep him off "hobby horses."

d. It will keep the people interested in the Word, not just the man; hence, they will be less likely to tire of his preaching. The Word is abiding; but a "bag full of tricks" or sermonettes will soon become stale.

e. It will help to develop a Biblical background for future messages.

f. It will help to develop a good library.

3. Biography. Both Biblical and contemporary bio-

graphical studies will be helpful in the life of the reader and as an aid in preaching.

4. Geography. The study of geography will help to visualize the location and topography of areas where Biblical events have taken place. It will make the Word clearer both to the student and to those to whom he ministers.

5. Miscellaneous reading. The pastor should always have a book handy for reading in spare moments. Most pastors read fewer than ten books a year. This is not to their credit. One a week would be much better. Someone has suggested that the newspaper be read "standing up," the idea being that one should not spend too much time with the morning news. Whether standing or sitting, do not get bogged down in reading that which is less important and fail in reading far more significant material. A news magazine a week and other secular works will prove helpful in keeping the pastor up on what is going on in the world. Form the habit—be always reading. This was the secret of Spurgeon. In the out-of-print autobiography of Spurgeon, Dr. Wright says:

> When I came to be Mr. Spurgeon's near neighbor, I found that his knowledge of all literature was wonderful. His power of reading was perhaps never equalled. He would sit down to five or six large books, and master them at one sitting. He sat with his left hand flat on the page at the left side of the book, and pushing his right hand up the page on the right side until the page projected a little, he turned it over with his finger, and proceeded to the next page. He took in the contents almost at a glance, reading by sentences as others read by words, and his memory never failed as to what he read. He made a point of reading a half-dozen of the hardest books every week, as he wished to rub his mind up against the strongest minds; and there was no skipping. I

several times had an opportunity of testing the thoroughness of his reading, and I never found him at fault.[10]

Sidlow Baxter said, "In my younger days we used to sing, 'Dare to be a Daniel,' but my song to you younger preachers today is 'Strive to be a Spurgeon.'"

We need a new generation of preachers who excel in preaching the doctrinal truths of the Word. Occasionally a young pastor will suggest that he is justified in preparing his messages on Saturday night because Charles Spurgeon did so. Also, Spurgeon prepared his Sunday evening service on Sunday afternoon. What he may not be aware of is that Spurgeon was an incessant reader—reading day and night. Actually as he was reading and searching the Word during the week he was being prepared by God to deliver the Lord's Day messages. Every preacher would do well to emulate Charles Spurgeon in this, rather than to imitate a man who prepared messages on the spur of the moment.

6. The Word of God itself. While listed last, this is not last in importance; rather, it is first. Dr. G. Campbell Morgan, prince among Bible expositors, stated that in the early part of his ministry there was a period when he read nothing but his daily mail and the four Gospels. This lasted for two years. Every day without break he read Matthew, Mark, Luke and John over and over and over again. This had a profound effect on his ministry, and it is no wonder that some of his best works are in consideration of the Gospels.

While we should read the entire Bible as stated earlier, for a good, healthy spiritual diet, intense concentration on specific books will be beneficial in our regular study hours. Naturally, one should distinguish between reading through the Bible for personal devotions and special hours of reading for study preparation.

When to study

1. In the early morning hours. This matter of when to study is just as personal and important as where to study. The advantages and disadvantages of different times are suggested, assuming that suitable hours be selected according to one's own physical makeup.

First, let us say that the pastor should spend from four to five hours, for at least five days a week, in his study. Hogue suggests that the best hours for study for most ministers are between eight o'clock in the morning and two o'clock in the afternoon. He quoted Dr. Murphy, who advises the pastor to study from eight o'clock to two o'clock with a recess of one hour. He breaks it down as follows: one hour of devotions before breakfast; five hours of study; two and a half hours of reading and correspondence, making ten hours a day for various duties in the office.

J. H. Jowett was convicted for not starting early enough. He writes:

> Enter your study at an appointed hour, and let that hour be as early as the earliest of your businessmen goes to his warehouse or his office. I remember in my earlier days how I used to hear the factory operative passing my house on the way to the mills, where work began at six o'clock. I can recall the sound of iron-clogs ringing through the street. The sound of the clogs fetched me out of bed and took me to my work. I no longer hear the Yorkshire clogs, but I can see and hear my businessmen as they start off early to earn their daily bread. And shall their minister be behind them in his quest of the Bread of Life? Shall he slouch and loiter into the day, shamed by those he assumes to lead, and shall his indolence be obtrusive in the service of the

sanctuary, when the hungry sheep look up and are not fed? Let the minister, I say, be as business-like as the businessman.[11]

Generalissmo Chiang Kai-shek started as a common soldier. Throughout his career he arose at dawn and worked from then until breakfast. When his rivals were doing nothing, he did his most important work.

Others of the secular world arose early; some, such as Daniel Webster, as early as four o'clock. John Milton started at four in the summer and "slept in" a little later in the winter, arising at five o'clock. He was busy until noon, and again from two until six he held forth. John Calvin started at six o'clock in the morning.

2. In the evening hours. Arthur Pink did a great deal of his work in the evening. So have many others. One disadvantage of the evening is that it pulls the pastor away from his family in the few hours that he is at home from church activities. For this reason, the morning seems best. It is important that regular hours be established for study and consistently observed.

The Pastor in the Library

Someone has suggested that the value of the books in the pastor's library should equal the amount he paid for his automobile. Needless to say, books are tools, and if the minister is going to do an adequate job in his study, it is important that he be properly equipped. A library should not be a status symbol, nor a collection of books to impress those who come to the study. Books should, on the other hand, be available tools, used as means to an end—to concisely and clearly present the Word of Truth to a hungry people. There are some pastors who look rather disdainfully on the buying of books and say that all they need is the Bible. Others will go beyond that in their intellectual pride and suggest that as long as they have in the original text and a handful of tools to help them in the original languages, other books such as commentaries on the text are unimportant. Perhaps the best answer to those who espouse this, or a similar philosophy, would be the wise words of Spurgeon:

> Of course you are not such a wise speaker as to think or say that you can expound the Scriptures without assistance from the work of the divine and learned men who have labored before you in the field of exposition. If you are of that opinion, pray remain so, for you are not worth the trouble of conversion, and like a little coterie who think with you, would resent the attempt as an insult to your infallibility. It seems odd, that certain men who talk so much of what the Holy Spirit reveals to themselves, should think so little of what He has revealed to others.[12]

The order of a pastor's library. I strongly recommend that the Dewey Decimal System be used in a pastor's library. This system is recommended because it is the one with which most of us are familiar in colleges and seminaries. It lends itself well to the cataloging of books, both religious and secular. It is universal and yet it is very practical. It also lends itself well to a vertical filing system and is helpful in the filing of articles and clippings.

With the Dewey Decimal System there is no limit as to how far one can go in expanding his library. The pastor who decides to use this system will find a number of volumes most helpful in implementing the system, such as *Building a Minister's Library* by Moyer and *Practical Study Methods for Students and Pastors* by Rossin and Ruschke.

Speaking of the importance of the pastor's library, Elgin S. Moyer, former librarian of the Moody Bible Institute, has stated:

It is impossible to overestimate the value or the importance of a good, effective, working library for the pastor. The better selection of books he is able to make for his library, the greater will be the promise of efficiency and success for his ministry.

A well-selected library is a storehouse of wealth for the active, growing pastor. It is the *sine qua non* for him if he is to maintain his intellectual keenness, his mental alertness, and his spiritual acumen. It will help him to keep abreast of the world's changing events. It will keep him in touch with the best thinking of his brother pastors and theologians. It will provide him with some of the best devotional literature of the past and of the present. It will clarify and purify his spiritual vision and will inspire him to greater and holier activity, and keep him in touch with the highest spiritual developments of the Christian world. It will acquaint him with the best thinking of the greatest scholars, and will challenge him to keep his eyes fixed constantly on the higher levels of devotional living and spiritual service. It will stimulate his thinking, develop his spirituality, and keep him growing.[13]

Recommended books for the pastor's library. Some preliminary observations ought to be made with regard to this recommended list.

1. This is not a selection of books exclusively for the scholar. Such a list would deal with some technical matter not included here; also some material which is strictly pastor-oriented and would not be of that much interest to a specialist in a given field.

2. This is not a selection of books for the layman. There are some books which deal primarily with the

ministry of the pastor which would be of no benefit to the layman beyond satisfying his curiosity.

3. These are always the first books in a pastor's library. They are books the pastor probably will have, or want to have, in the life span of his ministry.

4. This is not to suggest that other books are not good on these subjects, or that I am in full agreement with everything that is included in some of the volumes.

End Notes

[1] J. Sidlow Baxter, *Rethinking Our Priorities* (Grand Rapids: Zondervan Publishing House, 1974), p. 242.

[2] Hogue, *Homiletics and Pastoral Theology,* p. 292.

[3] John R. W. Stott, *The Preacher's Portrait* (Grand Rapids: William B. Eerdmans Publishing Co., 1961), p. 16.

[4] Ibid., pp. 30–31.

[5] Spurgeon, *Lectures to His Students,* p. 165.

[6] John Creasy, "Could You Write More?" *The Writer,* January 1960. Reprinted by permission of Harold Ober Associates Incorporated, p. 18.

[7] Ibid.

[8] Donald F. Rossin and Palmer Rushchke, *Practical Study Methods for Students and Pastors* (Rossin and Co., 1956), p. 14.

[9] Charles H. Spurgeon, *Second Series of Lectures to My Students* (London: Passmore and Alabaster, 1897), p. 24.

[10] Charles H. Spurgeon, *Autobiography,* edited and condensed from four original volumes by David Otis Fuller (Grand Rapids: Zondervan Publishing House, 1946), p. 143.

[11] Jowett, *Preacher: Life and Work,* p. 116.

[12] Charles H. Spurgeon, *Commenting on the Commentaries,* Lecture One (Grand Rapids: Kregel Publications, n.d.), p. 1.

[13] Elgin S. Moyer, *The Pastor and His Library* (Chicago: Moody Press, 1953), p. 12.

WEEKLY PLANNING SHEET

Week of ___April 5-10___

Hour	Monday	Tuesday	Wednesday	Thursday	Friday	Saturday	Sunday
8:00 A.M.	Devotions	Devotions	Devotions	Devotions	Devotions		
9:00 A.M.		Wed. message	Wed. message	S.S. lesson	Sunday messages	S.S. lesson	
10:00 A.M.		Memory work	Memory work	Memory work	Memory work	Memory work	S.S.
11:00 A.M.		Sunday sermon	Sunday sermon	Sunday messages	Writing	Sunday messages	Service
12:00 Noon		Lunch	Lunch	Lunch	Lunch	Sunday messages	
1:00 P.M.		Hospital calling	Counseling June Jones	Door-to-door evangelism	with pastors	Lunch	Lunch
2:00 P.M.		Hospital calling				Office and	
3:00 P.M.	D A	Hospital calling	Counseling Tim Knotts		Counseling	Hospital calls	Hospital calls
4:00 P.M.	Y	Dictation	Study time	Counseling Scotts	Telephone calls	T	Baptismal class
5:00 P.M.	O F		Study time			I	
6:00 P.M.	F	Visitation dinner				M E	Service
7:00 P.M.		Visiting	Prayer meeting	Trustees meeting	S.S. banquet	O	
8:00 P.M.		Deacons meeting				U T	
9:00 P.M.							

Miscellaneous Notes:
Baptism—Sunday night
Check on air schedules for trip to Calif. next week
Write birthday notes

WORKSHEET C

DAILY WORK RECORD

Name _____   Date _____

Proposed daily schedule	*Diary and Data on the day*
8:00 A.M. _____	_____
8:15 A.M. _____	_____
8:30 A.M. _____	_____
8:45 A.M. _____	_____
9:00 A.M. _____	_____
9:15 A.M. _____	_____
9:30 A.M. _____	_____
9:45 A.M. _____	_____
10:00 A.M. _____	_____
10:15 A.M. _____	_____
10:30 A.M. _____	_____
10:45 A.M. _____	_____
11:00 A.M. _____	_____
11:15 A.M. _____	_____
11:30 A.M. _____	_____
11:45 A.M. _____	_____
12:00 NOON _____	_____
12:15 P.M. _____	_____
12:30 P.M. _____	_____
12:45 P.M. _____	_____
1:00 P.M. _____	_____
1:15 P.M. _____	_____
1:30 P.M. _____	_____
1:45 P.M. _____	_____
2:00 P.M. _____	_____
2:15 P.M. _____	_____
2:30 P.M. _____	_____
2:45 P.M. _____	_____
3:00 P.M. _____	_____
3:15 P.M. _____	_____
3:30 P.M. _____	_____
3:45 P.M. _____	_____
4:00 P.M. _____	_____
4:15 P.M. _____	_____
4:30 P.M. _____	_____
4:45 P.M. _____	_____
5:00 P.M. _____	_____

* *

COMMENTS

Memory work (A)
Message preparation (B)
Filing (C)
Work out (D)
Writing (E)

Counseling and
Calling (F)
Correspondence (G)
Meetings (comm., etc.) (H)

WORKSHEET D

DAILY RECORD   Date _____

A. DEVOTIONAL PASSAGE,   1. CALLS AND COUNSELING
   PRAYER, BIBLE READING   TODAY:
   New Prayer Requests: a.
   Answers to Prayer: b.
   Bible Reading: c.
B. MEMORY WORK AND   d.
   REVIEW   2. BUSINESS MEETINGS, BOARDS,
   Verse Review   ETC.
   New Verse   _____
   Vocabulary   _____
C. SERMON PREPARATION   _____
   1. Sun. A.M._____   _____
   2. Sun. P.M. _____   3. UNFINISHED BUSINESS,
   3. S.S. _____   WORK, ETC.
   4. Wed. prep._____   _____
   5. Special messages _____   _____
D. READING   TODAY'S VERSE:
   1. Book _____
   Pages _____ to _____
   Comments _____
   _____   TODAY'S WORD:

   Book_____
   Pages_____ to _____   TODAY'S PROMISE AND QUOTE:
   Comments _____
   _____
   _____
   2. Theology   HEALTH WORKOUT:
   Book_____
   Pages _____ to _____
   3. Sermons Read_____
   _____

   4. Magazines, Periodicals
   _____
   _____
   _____

E. WRITING
   1. Articles _____
   2. Church Paper_____
   3. Books _____
   4. Other _____
F. CORRESPONDENCE

WORKSHEET E

Encyclopedias

There are a number of good encyclopedias on the market. Perhaps the two outstanding ones representing the liberal arts field and the field of sciences are:

New Encyclopedia Britannica, 30 vols. Chicago: Encyclopedia Britannica, 1976, in the area of liberal arts.

Encyclopedia Americana, 30 vols. New York: Americana Corp., 1966, in the area of sciences.

Both of these encyclopedias deal with the gamut of subjects, but they seem to have the emphases as indicated.

For easy reading, yet quite scholarly, I suggest:

The World Book Encyclopedia, 20 vols. Chicago: Field Enterprises Educational Corp., 1962. The World Book Yearbook updates the encyclopedia annually.

The Great Works of the Western World. Edited by Robert M. Hutchens, 54 vols. Chicago: Encyclopedia Britannica Inc., Wm. Benton Publishing Co., n.d.

I recommend this last set for personal reading and mental development. It is a rather expensive set, but it will be good to have in the ministry. The Syntopicon is particularly helpful as it has a unique way of classifying truth and facts referring to the various writers of the great books. It is not only good for reference but reading plans are available which would be most helpful to a pastor.

Dictionaries

I suggest *Webster's New International Dictionary* as an authority. At this present writing both the second and third editions are standard and are helpful. The second edition (which I prefer) does not include some of the newer words, and is somewhat more conservative in approach.

Webster's New International Dictionary of the English

Language, 2d edition. Springfield, MA: G. and C. Merriam Co., 1960.

Webster's New International Dictionary of the English Language, 3d edition. Springfield, MA: G. and C. Merriam Co., 1961.

Oxford Classical Dictionary. Edited by M. Cary, et al. Oxford: Clarendon Press, 1949. This book is excellent for the etymology of the English words.

Oxford English Dictionary. This is probably the greatest dictionary ever published. Originally published in twelve volumes, it is now available in one volume. You may need a magnifying glass to read the material, but it is *the* authority on the English language.

Bible Study and Methods

Baxter, James Sidlow. *Explore the Book.* Grand Rapids: Zondervan Publishing House, 1962.

Gaebelein, Arno C. *The Annotated Bible,* 9 vols. Chicago: Moody Press, 1971 (originally published in 1913).

Gray, James Martin. *Synthetic Bible Studies.* Westwood, NJ: Fleming H. Revell Co., 1959.

Jensen, Irving Lester. *Independent Bible Study.* Chicago: Moody Press, 1963. This book is excellent, particularly for students who want to study the Bible for themselves.

Morgan, G. Campbell. *Living Messages of the Books of the Bible.* Westwood, NJ: Fleming H. Revell Co., n.d.

The New Bible Commentary: Revised. Edited by Donald Guthrie, et al. Grand Rapids: Wm. B. Eerdmans Publishing Co., 1970.

Richards, Lawrence O. *Creative Bible Study.* Grand Rapids: Zondervan Publishing House, 1971. While I cannot agree with everything Richards has written, I feel that this is a worthwhile book to have, one which will help others study the Bible themselves.

Scroggie, William Graham. *Know Your Bible,* 2 vols. London: Pickering and Inglis, 1965.

_____. *The Unfolding Drama of Redemption.* London: Pickering and Inglis, 1953-71.

Spurgeon, Charles Haddon. *Commenting and Commentaries.* London: Banner of Truth Trust, 1960. This will be helpful for those interested in knowing what was available in Spurgeon's day, particularly among the Puritan writers, much of whose material has been reprinted today.

Unger, Merrill F. *Unger's Bible Handbook.* Chicago: Moody Press, 1966.

Bible Dictionaries and Encyclopedias

Dictionary of the Apostolic Church, 2 vols. New York: Charles Scribner's Sons, 1916-1922.

Dictionary of Christ and the Gospels, 2 vols. New York: Charles Scribner's Sons, 1967. This is an invaluable set and should be owned by every pastor.

Douglas, James Dixon. *New Bible Dictionary.* Grand Rapids: Wm. B. Eerdmans Publishing Co., 1962. This is perhaps the finest among Bible dictionaries available and has full articles on various subjects.

Hastings, James. *Dictionary of the Bible,* 5 vols. Edinburgh: T. and T. Clark, 1951. The revised edition was published in New York: Charles Scribner's Sons, 1963. The five-volume set includes areas of liberal theology.

Orr, James. *International Standard Bible Encyclopedia,* 5 vols. Grand Rapids: Wm. B. Eerdmans Publishing Co., 1939.

Tenney, Merrill C., ed. *Zondervan Pictorial Bible Dictionary.* Grand Rapids: Zondervan Publishing House, 1969. This is a fine dictionary for quick reference. I have two, one at home and one in my office.

Unger, Merrill F. *Unger's Bible Dictionary,* 3d edition. Chicago: Moody Press, 1961. A good, single volume dictionary.

Translations

Of translations there are many. Do not get carried away in this area. I preach and teach from the King James Version. The others listed are the most acceptable translations today.

Authorized King James Version. New York: Oxford Press, n.d.

New International Version—New Testament. Grand Rapids: Zondervan Publishing House, 1973.

New American Standard Version. Carol Stream, IL: Creation House, 1971.

Commentaries

Barnes, Albert. *Barnes' Notes on the New Testament.* Grand Rapids: Kregel Publications, 1966.

Clarke, Adam. *Adam Clarke's Commentary.* Grand Rapids: Baker Book House, 1967. There is now a one-volume edition of a former six-volume set. This is excellent as a commentary but be aware that it is Arminian in doctrine.

Erdman, Charles Rosenbury. *Commentaries on the New Testament Books,* 17 vols. Philadelphia: Westminster Press, 1916-1936.

Henry, Matthew. *Commentary on the Whole Bible,* 6 vols. Westwood, NJ: Fleming H. Revell Co. First published in 1708, this commentary is excellent, especially on the Old Testament. Spurgeon said that every pastor should read this on his knees.

Jamieson, Robert, A. R. Fausset, and Davis Brown. *A Commentary, Critical, Experimental and Practical on the Old and New Testaments,* 6 vols. Grand Rapids: Wm. B. Eerdmans Publishing Co., 1945. In my early ministry I used this set repeatedly.

Keil and Delitzsch. *Bible Commentary on the Old Testament,* 27 vols. Grand Rapids: Wm. B. Eerdmans Publishing Co., 1949. This is especially good for the scholar. The pastor must be careful to remember that his people, at least most of them, are not giraffes and that he will have to bring this material down to their understanding.

Lange, John Peter, ed. *Commentary on the Holy Scriptures,* 24 vols. Grand Rapids: Zondervan Publishing House, 1960. Originally published in 1866, this has been highly recommended by Wilbur Smith. It is excellent in that it gives fair treatment to almost any passage in Scripture.

Maclaren, Alexander. *Expositions of Holy Scripture,* 25 vols. New York: George H. Doran Co., n.d. Good, and highly recommended by many men.

The New Testament and Wycliffe Commentary, produced for Moody Monthly. New York: The Iversen-Norman Associates, 1971.

Parker, Joseph. *The People's Bible,* 28 vols. New York: Funk and Wagnalls, 1896. Reprinted, Grand Rapids: Baker Book House, 1956-61.

Robertson, Archibald Thomas. *Word Pictures in the New Testament,* 6 vols. Nashville: Broadman Press, 1930.

Simeon, Charles. *Expositor's Outlines of the Whole Bible,* 21 vols. Grand Rapids: Zondervan Publishing House, n.d.

Spence, H. D. M., and Joseph S. Exell, eds. *The Pulpit Commentary,* 23 vols. Grand Rapids: Wm. B. Eerdmans Publishing Co., 1963. This is one of the finest for the pastor. I wish I had purchased mine earlier. These are not simply books of canned sermons. These volumes provide both verse-by-verse exposition and homiletical outlines.

Stonehouse, N. B. *New International Commentary on the New Testament,* 17 vols. Grand Rapids: Wm. B. Eerdmans Publishing Co., 1951.

Vincent, Marvin R. *Word Studies in the New Testament,* 4 vols. Grand Rapids: Wm. B. Eerdmans Publishing Co., 1957.

Wuest, Kenneth S. *Wuest's Word Studies from the Greek New Testament,* 4 vols. Grand Rapids: Wm. B. Eerdmans Publishing Co., 1966.

Geography

Aharoni, Yohanan, and Michael Avi-Yonah, eds. *Macmillan Bible Atlas.* New York: Macmillan Co., 1968. One of the best Bible atlases available. It is a thorough and complete atlas, edited by two Jewish men.

Kraeling, Emil Gottlieb Heinrich, ed. *Rand McNally Bible Atlas.* New York: Rand MacNally and Co., 1956.

Pfeiffer, Charles Franklin, ed. *Baker's Bible Atlas.* Rev. ed. Grand Rapids: Baker Book House, 1973.

_____. *The Biblical World.* Grand Rapids: Baker Book House, 1966.

Pfeiffer, Charles F., and Howard F. Vos. *Wycliffe Historical Geography of Bible Lands.* Chicago: Moody Press, 1967. Excellent. I keep mine close to my desk at all times.

Thompson, William M. *The Land and the Book.* Grand Rapids: Baker Book House, 1966.

Concordances

Cruden, Alexander. *Cruden's Unabridged Concordance.* Grand Rapids: Baker Book House, 1953.

Strong, James. *Exhaustive Concordance of the Bible.* New York: Abingdon Press, 1890.

Young, Robert. *Analytical Concordance to the Bible.*
Grand Rapids: Wm. B. Eerdmans Publishing Co.,
1955.
    All three of these concordances are excellent; how-
ever, Young's is preferable if one is interested in seeing at
a glance how the word is used in the original. If, on the
other hand, one is interested in finding a verse with no
immediate interest in the Hebrew or Greek, Strong's
would serve better. Cruden's is not as complete as the other two.
Alexander, David, and Pat Alexander. *Eerdman's
    Handbook to the Bible.* Grand Rapids: Wm. B. Eerd-
    mans Publishing Co., 1973.
Clarke, Adam, ed. *Clarke's Bible Concordance.* Re-
    print. Grand Rapids: Kregel Publications, 1968.
Keach, Benjamin. *Preaching from the Types and Meta-
    phors of the Bible.* Reprint. Grand Rapids: Kregel
    Publications, 1972 . Although not actually a concor-
    dance, I feel this book belongs in this section.
Nave, Orville. *Nave's Topical Bible.* Chicago: Moody
    Press. Originally published in 1896.

Origin and Authenticity of the Bible
Can I Trust My Bible? a Symposium. Chicago: Moody
    Press, 1963.
Criswell, W. A. *Bible for Today's World.* Grand Rapids:
    Zondervan Publishing House, 1965.
_____. *Why I Preach that the Bible Is Literally True.*
    Nashville: Broadman Press, 1969.
Lloyd-Jones, David Martyn. *Authority.* London: Inter-
    Varsity Press, 1966.

Canonicity
Green, William Henry. *General Introduction to the Old
    Testament: The Canon.* London: John Murray,
    1899.

Harris, Robert Laird. *Inspiration and Canonicity of the Bible*. Grand Rapids: Zondervan Publishing House, 1957.

Lightner, Robert Paul. *The Saviour and the Scriptures*. Philadelphia: Presbyterian and Reformed Publishing Co., 1966.

Inspiration and Revelation

Custer, Stewart. *Does Inspiration Demand Inerrancy?* Nutley, NJ: Craig Press, 1968.

Gaussen, Francois Samuel. *Divine Inspiration of the Bible*. Reprint. Grand Rapids: Kregel Publications, n.d.

Pache, René. *Inspiration and Authority of Scripture*. Chicago: Moody Press, 1969.

Packer, James Innell. *God Speaks to Man: Revelation and the Bible*. Philadelphia: Westminster Press, 1966.

Urquhart, John. *The Inspiration and Accuracy of the Holy Scriptures*. London: Marshall Brothers, 1895.

Warfield, Benjamin Breckenridge. *The Inspiration and Authority of the Bible*. Philadelphia: Presbyterian and Reformed Publishing Co., 1958.

Young, Edward Joseph. *Thy Word Is Truth*. Grand Rapids: Wm. B. Eerdmans Publishing Co., 1957.

Prophetic Message

There are hundreds of good books written on the subject of the future events. Listed here are only two, both by the same author. I believe these two books are unexcelled on the subject.

Pentecost, J. Dwight. *Prophecy for Today*. Grand Rapids: Zondervan Publishing House, 1965.

_____. *Things to Come*. Findlay, OH: Dunham Publishing House, 1958.

Interpretation and Criticism of the Bible

Geisler, Norman L., and William Nix. *General Intro-duction to the Bible.* Chicago: Moody Press, 1968. One of the finest books on Biblical introduction to the Bible.

Horne, Thomas Hartawell. *An Introduction to the Criti-cal Study and Knowledge of the Holy Scriptures.* 5 vols. 8th ed. Grand Rapids: Baker Book House, 1970.

Hermeneutics

Berkhof, Louis. *Principles of Biblical Interpretation.* Grand Rapids: Baker Book House, 1950.

Pink, Arthur W. *Interpretation of the Scriptures.* Grand Rapids: Baker Book House, 1971.

Terry, Milton Spenser. *Biblical Hermeneutics.* Grand Rapids: Zondervan Publishing House, 1968.

Old Testament—General

Archer, Gleason L., Jr. *A Survey of Old Testament Intro-duction.* Chicago: Moody Press, 1964.

Bruce, F. F. *The Books and the Parchments.* Westwood, NJ: Fleming H. Revell Co., 1950.

Harrison, Roland Kenneth. *Introduction to the Old Tes-tament.* Grand Rapids: Wm. B. Eerdmans Publish-ing Co., 1969.

Ketcham, Robert T. *Old Testament Pictures of New Tes-tament Truth.* Des Plaines, IL: Regular Baptist Press, 1965.

Morgan, G. Campbell. *Living Messages of the Books of the Bible* (Genesis to Malachi). New York: Fleming H. Revell Co., 1912.

_____. *The Unfolding Message of the Bible.* Westwood, NJ: Fleming H. Revell Co., 1961.

Newell, William R. *Old Testament Studies.* Toronto: Evangelical Publishing Co., 1923.

Van Dooren, L. A. T. *Introducing the Old Testament.*

Grand Rapids: Zondervan Publishing House, 1967.

Old Testament—Specific

Genesis

Barnhouse, Donald Grey. *Genesis: A Devotional Commentary*. Grand Rapids: Zondervan Publishing House, 1970.

Candlish, Robert S. *Commentary on Genesis*. 2 vols. Grand Rapids: Zondervan Publishing House, n.d.

Gaebelein, Arno C. *The Book of Genesis*. New York: Our Hope, 1912.

Leupold, Herbert Carl. *Exposition of Genesis*. 2 vols. Grand Rapids: Baker Book House, 1942.

Mackintosh, Charles H. *Notes on the Book of Genesis*. Reprint. Neptune, NJ: Loizeaux Brothers, 1965.

Pink, Arthur W. *Gleanings in Genesis*. Chicago: Moody Press, 1922.

Thomas, W. H. Griffith. *Genesis: A Devotional Commentary*. Grand Rapids: Wm. B. Eerdmans Publishing Co., 1946.

Whitcomb, John Clement, Jr., and Henry M. Morris. *The Genesis Flood*. Philadelphia: Presbyterian and Reformed Publishing Co., 1962.

Exodus

Coates, C. A. *An Outline of the Book of Exodus*. Kingston-on-the-Thames: Stow Hill Bible and Tract Depot, n.d.

Mackintosh, Charles H. *Notes on the Book of Exodus*. New York: Loizeaux Brothers, 1959.

Morgan, G. Campbell. *The Ten Commandments*. New York: Fleming H. Revell Co., 1901.

Pink, Arthur W. *Gleanings in Exodus*. Chicago: Moody Press, n.d.

The Tabernacle

DeHaan, M. R. *The Tabernacle.* Grand Rapids: Zondervan Publishing House, 1955.

McGee, J. Vernon. *The Tabernacle: God's Portrait of Christ.* Wheaton, IL: Van Kampen Press (reprint from *Bibliotheca Sacra*), n.d.

Moorhead, W. G. *The Tabernacle, the Priesthood, Sacrifices and Feasts of Ancient Israel.* Grand Rapids: Kregel Publications, 1957.

Needham, George C. *Shadow and Substance.* Springfield, MO: Gospel Publishing House, 1950.

Ridout, Samuel. *Lectures on the Tabernacle.* New York: Loizeaux Brothers, 1945.

Slemming, C. W. *Made According to Pattern.* Wheaton, IL: Van Kampen Press, 1951.

_____. *These are the Garments.* London: Marshall, Morgan and Scott, n.d.

White, Frank H. *Christ in the Tabernacle.* London: S. W. Partridge & Co., 1914.

Leviticus

Bonar, Andrew Alexander. *A Commentary on the Book of Leviticus.* Grand Rapids: Zondervan Publishing House, 1959.

Ironside, H. A. *Lectures on the Levitical Offerings.* New York: Loizeaux Brothers, 1951.

Jukes, Andrew John. *The Law of the Offerings.* Grand Rapids: Kregel Publications, 1966.

Kellogg, Samuel Henry. *The Book of Leviticus.* New York: George H. Doran Co., n.d.

Mackintosh, Charles H. *Notes on Leviticus.* New York: Loizeaux Brothers, 1959.

Numbers

Bush, George. *Notes, Critical and Practical on the Book*

of Numbers. New York: Ivison, Phinney and Co., n.d.

Jensen, Irving Lester. *Numbers: Journey to God's Rest Land.* Chicago: Moody Press, 1964.

Mackintosh, Charles H. *Notes on the Book of Numbers.* New York: Loizeaux Brothers, 1959.

Deuteronomy

Coates, C. A. *An Outline of Deuteronomy.* Kingston-on-the-Thames: Stow Hill Bible and Tract Depot, n.d.

Mackintosh, Charles H. *Notes on Deuteronomy.* 2 vols. Neptune, NJ: Loizeaux Brothers, 1965.

Manley, George Thomas. *The Book of the Law.* Grand Rapids: Wm. B. Eerdmans Publishing Co., 1957.

Joshua

Armerding, Carl. *Conquest and Victory.* Chicago: Moody Press, 1967.

Blaikie, William Garden. *The Book of Joshua.* The Expositor's Bible. New York: A. C. Armstrong and Son, 1908.

Davis, John James. *Conquest and Crisis.* Grand Rapids: Baker Book House, 1969.

Gaebelein, Arno C. *Types in Joshua.* New York: Our Hope, n.d.

Ironside, H. A. *Addresses on the Book of Joshua.* New York: Loizeaux Brothers, 1950.

Pink, Arthur W. *Gleanings in Joshua.* Chicago: Moody Press, 1964.

Redpath, Alan. *Victorious Christian Living.* London: Pickering and Inglis, 1955.

Scroggie, William Graham. *The Land and the Life of Rest.* Glasglow: Pickering and Inglis, 1950.

Judges

Cundall, Arthur E., and Leon Morris. *Judges and Ruth.*

London: Tyndale Press, 1968.

Knapp, Christopher. *The Kings of Israel and Judah.* New York: Loizeaux Brothers, 1956.

Ridout, Samuel. *Lectures on the Books of Judges and Ruth.* New York: Loizeaux Brothers, 1958.

Ruth

DeHaan, M. R. *The Romance of Redemption.* Grand Rapids: Zondervan Publishing House, 1958.

Lawson, George. *Exposition of Ruth and Esther.* Evansville, IN: Sovereign Grace Publishers, 1960.

McGee, J. Vernon. *Ruth: The Romance of Redemption.* 2d ed. Wheaton, IL: Van Kampen Press, 1954.

Moorehouse, Henry. *Ruth, the Moabitess.* New York: Fleming H. Revell, Co., 1881.

1 and 2 Samuel

Blaikie, William Garden. *The First Book of Samuel.* The Expositor's Bible. London: Hodder and Stoughton, 1898.

_____. *The Second Book of Samuel.* The Expositor's Bible. New York: A. C. Armstrong and Son, 1908.

Crocket, William D. *A Harmony of the Books of Samuel, Kings and Chronicles.* Grand Rapids: Baker Book House, 1959.

Davis, John James. *The Birth of a Kingdom.* Old Testament Studies. Grand Rapids: Baker Book House, 1970.

1 and 2 Kings

Farrar, Frederic William. *The First Book of Kings.* The Expositor's Bible. New York: A. C. Armstrong and Son, 1908.

_____. *The Second Book of Kings.* The Expositor's Bible. New York: A. C. Armstrong and Son, 1908.

Thiele, E. R. *The Mysterious Numbers of the Hebrew*

Kings. Rev. ed. Grand Rapids: Wm. B. Eerdmans Publishing Co., 1965.

Whitcomb, John Clement, Jr. *Solomon to the Exile: Studies in Kings and Chronicles*. Grand Rapids: Baker Book House, 1971.

1 and 2 Chronicles

Bennett, W. H. *The Book of Chronicles*. The Expositor's Bible. New York: Hodder and Stoughton, n.d.

Ezra, Nehemiah and Esther

Adeny, Walter F. *Ezra, Nehemiah and Esther*. New York: Hodder and Stoughton, n.d.

Ironside, H. A. *Notes on the Books of Ezra, Nehemiah and Esther*. New York: Loizeaux Brothers, 1951.

McGee, J. Vernon. *An Exposition on the Book of Esther*. Wheaton, IL: Van Kampen Press, 1951.

Redpath, Alan. *Victorious Christian Service*. Westwood, NJ: Fleming H. Revell Co., 1958.

Thomas, W. Ian. *If I Perish ... I Perish*. Grand Rapids: Zondervan Publishing House, 1966.

Turnbull, Ralph G. *The Book of Nehemiah*. Grand Rapids: Baker Book House, 1968.

Poetical Books

Job

Blair, J. Allen. *Living Patiently*. Neptune, NJ: Loizeaux Brothers, 1966.

Cox, Samuel. *Commentary on the Book of Job*. London: C. Kegan Paul and Co., 1880.

Morgan, G. Campbell. *The Book of Job*. Analyzed Bible. London: Hodder and Stoughton, 1909.

Psalms

Chappell, Clovis Gillham. *Sermons from the Psalms*.

Nashville: Cokesbury Press, 1931.

Evans, William. *The Shepherd Psalm*. Chicago: Moody
Press, 1921.

Gaebelein, Arno C. *The Book of Psalms*. New York: Our
Hope, 1939.

Ironside, H. A. *Studies in the Psalms*. New York: Loizeaux Brothers, 1952.

Jowett, John Henry. *Springs in the Desert*. New York:
George H. Doran Co., 1924.

Ketcham, Robert T. *I Shall Not Want*. Chicago: Moody
Press, 1953.

King, Guy Hope. *All Through the Day*. London: Church
Book Room Press, 1948.

Lloyd-Jones, David Martyn. *Faith on Trial*. Grand Rapids: Wm. B. Eerdmans Publishing Co., 1965.

Maclaren, Alexander. *The Psalms*. 3 vols. The Expositor's Bible. London: Hodder and Stoughton, 1893.

Scroggie, William Graham. *The Psalms*. Westwood,
NJ: Fleming H. Revell Co., 1948 (formerly four volumes).

Spurgeon, Charles Haddon. *Treasury of David*. 6 vols.
Grand Rapids: Zondervan Publishing House, 1963.

Proverbs

Bridges, Charles. *An Exposition of Proverbs*. Evansville,
IN: Sovereign Grace Book Club, 1959.

Ironside, H. A. *Notes on the Book of Proverbs*. New York:
Loizeaux Brothers, n.d.

Wardlow, Ralph. *Lectures on the Book of Proverbs*. 3
vols., n.d.

Song of Solomon

Ironside, H. A. *Song of Solomon*. New York: Loizeaux
Brothers, 1933.

Rust, Argeretta. *An Exposition of the Song of Solomon*.
Argeretta Rust, 1950.

Ecclesiastes

Bridges, Charles. *An Exposition of the Book of Ecclesiastes*. London: Banner of Truth Trust, 1960.

Cox, Samuel. *The Book of Ecclesiastes*. New York: A. C. Armstrong and Son, n.d.

Jennings, Frederick Charles. *Old Groans and New Songs*. New York: Loizeaux Brothers, 1946.

Prophetic Books

Alexander, Joseph Addison. *Commentary on the Prophecies of Isaiah*. Grand Rapids: Zondervan Publishing House, 1974.

Baron, David. *The Servant of Jehovah*. London: Marshall, Morgan and Scott, 1922.

Boutflower, Charles. *The Book of Isaiah*. London: SPCK, 1930.

Ironside, H. A. *Expository Notes on the Book of the Prophet Isaiah*. New York: Loizeaux Brothers, 1952.

Jennings, Frederick Charles. *Studies in Isaiah*. Neptune, NJ: Loizeaux Brothers, 1966.

Kelly, William. *An Exposition of the Book of Isaiah*. 4th ed. London: C. A. Hammond Co., 1947.

Morgan, G. Campbell. *The Prophecy of Isaiah*. 2 vols. London: Hodder and Stoughton, 1910.

Redpath, Alan. *Faith for the Times*. Studies in Prophecy of Isaiah. Old Tappan, NJ: Fleming H. Revell Co., 1972.

Young, Edward Joseph. *The Book of Isaiah*. 2 vols. Grand Rapids: Wm. B. Eerdmans Publishing Co., 1965.

Jeremiah and Lamentations

Erdman, Charles Rosenbury. *The Book of Jeremiah and Lamentations*. Westwood, NJ: Fleming H. Revell Co., 1955.

Ironside, H. A. *Notes on the Prophecy and Lamentation*

of Jeremiah. New York: Loizeaux Brothers, 1952.

Jensen, Irving Lester. *Jeremiah: The Prophet of Judgment.* Chicago: Moody Press, 1966.

Morgan, G. Campbell. *Studies in the Prophecy of Jeremiah.* London: Oliphants, 1963.

Ezekiel

Blackwood, Andrew Watterson. *The Other Son of Man: Ezekiel/Jesus.* Grand Rapids: Baker Book House, 1966.

Feinberg, Charles Lee. *The Prophecy of Ezekiel.* Chicago: Moody Press, 1969.

Gaebelein, Arno C. *The Prophet Ezekiel.* New York: Our Hope, 1918.

Ironside, H. A. *Expository Notes on Ezekiel the Prophet.* New York: Loizeaux Brothers 1949.

Daniel

Anderson, Robert. *Daniel in the Critic's Den.* London: James Nisbet, 1902.

DeHaan, M. R. *Daniel, the Prophet.* Grand Rapids: Zondervan Publishing House, 1967.

Gaebelein, Arno C. *The Prophet Daniel.* Grand Rapids: Kregel Publications, 1955.

Ironside, H. A. *Lectures on Daniel the Prophet.* New York: Loizeaux Brothers, 1953.

Kelly, William. *Notes on Daniel.* Loizeaux Brothers, 1952.

Lang, George Henry. *The Histories and Prophecies of Daniel.* 4th ed. London: Paternoster Press, 1950.

Larkin, Clarence. *The Book of Daniel.* Philadelphia: Clarence Larkin, 1929.

Leupold, Herbert Carl. *Exposition of Daniel.* Minneapolis: Augsburg Publishing House, 1961.

Luck, G. Coleman. *Daniel.* Chicago: Moody Press, 1958.

McClain, Alva J. *Daniel's Prophecy of the Seventy*

Weeks. 7th ed. Grand Rapids: Zondervan Publishing House, 1940.

Stevens, W. C. *The Book of Daniel.* Los Angeles: Bible House of Los Angeles, 1949.

Strauss, Lehman. *The Prophecies of Daniel.* Neptune, NJ: Loizeaux Brothers, 1969.

Walvoord, John F. *Daniel: The Key to Prophetic Revelation.* Chicago: Moody Press, 1971.

Whitcomb, John Clement, Jr. *Darius the Mede: A Study in Historical Identification.* Grand Rapids: Wm. B. Eerdmans Publishing Co., 1959.

Wilson, Robert Dick. *Studies in the Book of Daniel.* Grand Rapids: Baker Book House, 1972.

Wood, Leon J. *A Commentary on Daniel.* Grand Rapids: Zondervan Publishing House, 1972.

Minor Prophets

Barnes, Albert. *Notes on the Minor Prophets.* 2 vols. Grand Rapids: Baker Book House, 1968.

Feinberg, Charles Lee. *Major Messages of the Minor Prophets.* 5 vols. New York: American Board of Missions to the Jews, 1947-1952.

Freeman, Hobart E. *Introduction to the Old Testament Prophets.* Chicago: Moody Press, 1968.

Gaebelein, Frank E. *Four Minor Prophets.* Chicago: Moody Press, 1970.

Ironside, H. A. *Notes on the Minor Prophets.* New York: Loizeaux Brothers, 1909.

Morgan, G. Campbell. *Voices of Twelve Minor Prophets.* London: Pickering and Inglis, n.d.

Pusey, Edward Bouverie. *The Minor Prophets: A Commentary, Explanatory and Practical.* 2 vols. Grand Rapids: Baker Book House, 1961.

Hosea

Feinberg, Charles Lee. *Hosea: God's Love for Israel.* The

Major Messages of the Minor Prophets. New York: American Board of Missions to the Jews, 1947.

Morgan, G. Campbell. *Hosea: The Heart and Holiness of God.* Westwood, NJ: Fleming H. Revell Co., 1934.

Joel

Di Gangi, Mariano. *The Book of Joel.* Grand Rapids: Baker Book House, 1970.

Feinberg, Charles Lee. *Joel, Amos and Obadiah.* New York: American Board of Missions to the Jews, 1948.

Amos

Feinberg, Charles Lee. *Amos: The Righteousness of God.* New York: American Board of Missions to the Jews, 1948.

Howard, J. K. *Amos Among the Prophets.* Grand Rapids: Baker Book House, 1967.

Kelley, Page H. *The Book of Amos.* Grand Rapids: Baker Book House, 1966.

Obadiah

Feinberg, Charles Lee. *Obadiah: Doom Upon Edom.* New York: American Board of Missions to the Jews, 1948.

Gaebelein, Frank E. *The Servant and the Dove.* New York: Our Hope, 1946.

Hillis, Don W. *The Book of Obadiah.* Grand Rapids: Baker Book House, 1968.

Watts, J. D. *Obadiah: A Critical Exegetical Commentary.* Grand Rapids: Wm. B. Eerdmans Publishing Co., 1969.

Jonah

Banks, William L. *Jonah: The Reluctant Prophet.* Chicago: Moody Press, 1966.

Feinberg, Charles Lee. *Jonah: God's Love for all Nations*. New York: American Board of Missions to the Jews, 1951.

Martin, Hugh. *The Prophet Jonah: His Character and Mission to Nineveh*. London: Banner of Truth Trust, 1958.

Micah

Bennett, T. Miles. *The Book of Micah*. Grand Rapids: Baker Book House, 1968.

Feinberg, Charles Lee. *Micah: Wrath upon Samaria and Jerusalem*. The Major Messages of the Minor Prophets. New York: American Board of Missions to the Jews, 1951.

Nahum

Feinberg, Charles Lee. *Nahum: Judgment on Nineveh*. American Board of Missions to the Jews, 1951.

Maier, Walter A. *The Book of Nahum*. St. Louis: Concordia Publishing House, 1959.

Habakkuk

Feinberg, Charles Lee. *Habakkuk: Problems of Faith*. The Major Messages of the Minor Prophets. New York: American Board of Missions to the Jews, 1951.

Lloyd-Jones, David Martyn. *From Fear to Faith*. London: InterVarsity Press, 1964.

Zephaniah

Feinberg, Charles Lee. *Habakkuk, Zephaniah, Haggai, and Malachi*. New York: American Board of Missions to the Jews, 1951.

Haggai

Feinberg, Charles Lee. (See under Zephaniah.)
Wolff, Richard. *The Book of Haggai.* Grand Rapids: Baker Book House, 1967.

Zechariah

Baron, David. *The Visions and Prophecies of Zechariah.* Fincastle, VA: Scripture Truth Book Co., 1962.
Feinberg, Charles Lee. *God Remembers.* Wheaton, IL: Van Kampen Press, 1950.
_____. *Zechariah: Israel's Comfort and Glory.* New York: American Board of Missions to the Jews, 1952.
Leupold, Herbert Carl. *Exposition of Zechariah.* Grand Rapids: Baker Book House, 1971.
Luck, G. Coleman. *Zechariah.* Chicago: Moody Press, 1957.
Meyer, F. B. *The Prophet of Hope. Studies in Zechariah.* Fort Washington, PA: Christian Literature Crusade, 1952.
Unger, Merrill F. *Zechariah: Prophet of Messiah's Glory.* Grand Rapids: Zondervan Publishing House, 1963.

Malachi

Logsdon, S. Franklin. *Malachi: Will A Man Rob God?* Chicago: Moody Press, 1961.
Morgan, G. Campbell. *Wherein Have We Robbed God?* New York: Fleming H. Revell Co., 1898.

New Testament—General

Greek Language Tools

Abbot-Smith, George. *Manual Greek Lexicon of the New Testament.* 3d ed. New York: Charles Scribner's Sons, 1937.

Bullinger, Ethelbert William. *A Critical Lexicon and Concordance to the English and Greek New Testament*. London: Lamp Press, 1957.

Kittle, Gerhard, ed. *Theological Dictionary of the New Testament*. 9 vols. 5th ed. Grand Rapids: Wm. B. Eerdmans Publishing Co., 1972.

Liddell, Henry George, and Robert Scott. *Greek-English Lexicon*. Oxford: Clarendon Press, 1966.

Moulton, William Fidian, and A. S. Geden. *Concordance to the Greek Testament*. 4th ed. Edinburgh: T. and T. Clark, 1963.

Robertson, Archibald Thomas. *Grammar of the Greek New Testament in the Light of Historical Research*. Nashville: Broadman Press, 1934.

Trench, Richard Chenevix. *Synonyms of the New Testament*. Grand Rapids: Wm. B. Eerdmans Publishing Co., 1953.

Vine, William Edwyn. *Expository Dictionary of the New Testament Words*. London: Oliphants, 1963.

Introduction to New Testament

Burton, Ernest Dewitt, and Edgar Johnson Goodspeed. *Harmony of the Four Gospels, Synoptic*. New York: Charles Scribner's Sons, 1917.

Gromacki, Robert G. *New Testament Survey*. Des Plaines, IL: Regular Baptist Press, 1974.

Jukes, Andrew. *The Characteristic Differences of the Four Gospels*. London: Pickering and Inglis, n.d.

Robertson, Archibald Thomas. *Harmony of the Gospels*. New York: Harper and Brothers, 1922.

_____. *Studies in the New Testament*. Nashville: Broadman Press, 1949.

Scroggie, William Graham. *A Guide to the Gospels*. London: Pickering and Inglis, 1962. Highly recommended. This book is one of the most outstanding works on the Gospels.

Tenney, Merrill C. *New Testament Survey*. Grand Rapids: Wm. B. Eerdmans Publishing Co., 1961.

_____. *New Testament Times*. Grand Rapids: Wm. B. Eerdmans Publishing Co., 1965.

Thiessen, Henry Clarence. *Introduction to the New Testament*. Grand Rapids: Wm. B. Eerdmans Publishing Co., 1943.

Wuest, Kenneth S. *The New Testament*. 4 vols. Grand Rapids: Wm. B. Eerdmans Publishing Co., 1961.

The Life of Christ

Edersheim, Alfred. *The Life and Times of Jesus the Messiah*. 2 vols. New York: Randolph and Co., n.d.

Harrison, Everett F. *A Short Life of Christ*. Grand Rapids: Wm. B. Eerdmans Publishing Co., 1968.

Hastings, James. *Dictionary of Christ and the Gospels*. 2 vols. Edinburgh: T. and T. Clark, 1906.

Shepard, J. W. *The Christ of the Gospels*. Grand Rapids: Wm. B. Eerdmans Publishing Co., 1939.

Stalker, James. *Life of Jesus Christ*. New York: Fleming H. Revell Co., 1880.

Vos, Howard F. *The Life of Our Divine Lord*. Grand Rapids: Zondervan Publishing House, 1958.

Matthew

Broadus, John A. *An American Commentary on the New Testament*. Vol. 1. Philadelphia: American Baptist Publishing Society, 1886.

English, E. Schuyler. *Studies in the Gospel According to Matthew*. New York: Loizeaux Brothers, 1960.

Erdman, Charles Rosenbury. *The Gospel of Matthew*. Philadelphia: Westminster Press, 1920.

Gaebelein, Arno C. *The Gospel of Matthew*. New York: Loizeaux Brothers, 1910. This is an excellent treatment of Matthew from the dispensational viewpoint.

Hendriksen, William. *Exposition of the Gospel According to Matthew*. Grand Rapids: Baker Book House, 1973.

Ironside, H. A. *Notes on Matthew*. New York: Loizeaux Brothers, 1948.

Lloyd-Jones, David Martyn. *Studies on the Sermon on the Mount*. 2 vols. Grand Rapids: Wm. B. Eerdmans Publishing Co., 1959.

Morgan, G. Campbell. *The Gospel According to Matthew*. New York: Fleming H. Revell Co., 1929.

Pink, Arthur W. *An Exposition of the Sermon on the Mount*. Grand Rapids: Baker Book House, 1951.

Ryle, J. C. *Expository Thought on the Gospels*. 5 vols. Grand Rapids: Zondervan Publishing House, 1951. This set of books is both scholarly and practical.

Thomas, W. H. Griffith. *Outline Studies in the Gospel of Matthew*. Grand Rapids: Wm. B. Eerdmans Publishing Co., 1961.

Mark

Blaiklock, Edward Musgrove. *Mark: The Man and His Message*. Chicago: Moody Press, 1967.

English, E. Schuyler. *Studies in the Gospel According to Mark*. New York: Our Hope, 1943.

Morgan, G. Campbell. *The Gospel According to Mark*. Westwood, NJ: Fleming H. Revell Co., 1927.

Ironside, H. A. *Notes on Mark*. New York: Loizeaux Brothers, 1948.

Robertson, Archibald Thomas. *Studies in Mark's Gospel*. Nashville: Broadman Press, 1958.

Scroggie, William Graham. *The Gospel of Mark*. London: Marshall, Morgan and Scott, n.d.

Swete, Henry Barclay. *The Gospel According to St. Mark*. Grand Rapids: Wm. B. Eerdmans Publishing Co., 1956.

Wuest, Kenneth S. *Mark in the Greek New Testament.* Grand Rapids: Wm. B. Eerdmans Publishing Co., 1950.

Luke

Barclay, William. *The Gospel of Luke.* Philadelphia: Westminster Press, 1953. The reader should exercise care with Barclay as he tends to have liberal leanings. However, the background material on the original language is both interesting and useful for preachers and teachers.

Darby, J. N. *The Man of Sorrows.* London: Pickering and Inglis, n.d.

Erdman, Charles Rosenbury. *Gospel of Luke.* New Century Bible. New York: Thomas Nelson and Sons, 1966.

Godet, Frederic Louis. *A Commentary on the Gospel of St. Luke.* Grand Rapids: Zondervan Publishing House, 1957.

Hobbs, Hershel H. *An Exposition of the Gospel of Luke.* Grand Rapids: Baker Book House, 1966.

Kelly, William. *An Exposition of the Gospel of Luke.* London: Pickering and Inglis, n.d.

Liddon, Henry Parry. *The Magnificat.* 3d ed. London: Longman's Green and Co., 1898.

Morgan, G. Campbell. *The Gospel According to Luke.* New York: Fleming H. Revell Co., 1931.

Plummer, Alfred. *A Critical and Exegetical Commentary on the Gospel According to St. Luke.* International Critical Commentary. Edinburgh: T. and T. Clark, 1896.

Robertson, Archibald Thomas. *Luke the Historian in the Light of Research.* New York: Charles Scribner's Sons, 1936.

Stonehouse, N. B. *The Witness of Luke to Christ.* Grand Rapids: Wm. B. Eerdmans Publishing Co., 1951.

Thomas, W. H. Griffith. *Outline Studies in the Gospel of Luke*. Grand Rapids: Wm. B. Eerdmans Publishing Co., 1950.

John

Gaebelein, Arno C. *The Gospel of John*. Wheaton, IL: Van Kampen Press, 1936.

Godet, Frederic Louis. *Commentary on the Gospel of John*. 2 vols. Reprint. Grand Rapids: Zondervan Publishing House. First published in English in 1893.

Hendriksen, William. *A Commentary on the Gospel of John*. 2 vols. Grand Rapids: Baker Book House, 1953.

Hobbs, Hershel H. *An Exposition of the Gospel of John*. Grand Rapids: Baker Book House, 1968.

Ironside, H. A. *Addresses on the Gospel of John*. New York: Loizeaux Brothers, 1942.

Kelly, William. *An Exposition of the Gospel of John*. London: T. Weston, 1898.

Macaulay, Joseph Cordner. *Devotional Studies in St. John's Gospel*. Grand Rapids: Wm. B. Eerdmans Publishing Co., 1954.

Morgan, G. Campbell. *The Gospel According to John*. Westwood, NJ: Fleming H. Revell Co., 1933.

Morris, Leon. *Dead Sea Scrolls and St. John's Gospel*. London: Westminster Chapel, 1960.

_____. *The Gospel According to John*. Grand Rapids: Wm. B. Eerdmans Publishing Co., 1971.

Moule, Handley Carr Glyn. *The High Priestly Prayer*. London: The Religious Tract Society, 1907.

Pink, Arthur W. *Exposition of the Gospel of John*. 3 vols. Grand Rapids: Zondervan Publishing House, 1945.

Plummer, Alfred. *The Gospel According to St. John*. Cambridge: University Press, 1889.

Rainsford, Marcus. *Our Lord Prays for His Own*. Chicago: Moody Press, 1950.

Robertson, Archibald Thomas. *The Divinity of Christ in the Gospel of John.* New York: Fleming H. Revell Co., 1916.

Scroggie, William Graham. *St. John, Introduction and Notes.* New York: Harper and Brothers, 1931.

Tenney, Merrill C. *John: The Gospel of Belief.* Grand Rapids: Wm. B. Eerdmans Publishing Co., 1948.

Thomas, W. H. Griffith. *The Apostle John: Studies in His Life and Writings.* Grand Rapids: Wm. B. Eerdmans Publishing Co., 1953.

Acts

Alexander, Joseph Addison. *Commentary on the Acts of the Apostles.* Grand Rapids: Zondervan Publishing House, 1956.

Bruce, F. F. *Commentary on the Book of Acts.* Grand Rapids: Wm. B. Eerdmans Publishing Co., 1954.

Gaebelein, Arno C. *The Acts of the Apostles.* New York: Loizeaux Brothers, 1961.

Ironside, H. A. *Lectures on the Book of Acts.* New York: Loizeaux Brothers, 1965.

Jensen, Irving Lester. *Acts: An Inductive Study.* Chicago: Moody Press, 1968.

Kelly, William. *An Exposition of the Acts of the Apostles.* London: C. A. Hammond Co., 1952.

Laurin, Roy L. *Acts: Life in Action.* Findlay, OH: Dunham Publishing Co., 1962.

Lenski, R. C. H. *The Interpretation of the Acts of the Apostles.* Minneapolis: Augsburg Publishing House, 1934.

Macaulay, Joseph Cordner. *A Devotional Commentary on the Acts of the Apostles.* Grand Rapids: Wm. B. Eerdmans Publishing Co., 1946.

Morgan, G. Campbell. *The Acts of the Apostles.* New York: Fleming H. Revell Co., 1924.

_____. *The Birth of the Church.* Old Tappan, NJ: Fleming H. Revell Co., 1968.

Rackham, Richard Belward. *The Acts of the Apostles.* Grand Rapids: Baker Book House, 1964.

Ryrie, Charles Caldwell. *The Acts of the Apostles.* Chicago: Moody Press, 1961.

Scroggie, William Graham. *The Acts of the Apostles.* London: Marshall, Morgan and Scott, 1931.

Thomas, W. H. Griffith. *Outline Studies in the Acts of the Apostles.* Grand Rapids: Wm. B. Eerdmans Publishing Co., 1956.

Woodbridge, Charles J. *A Study of the Book of Acts.* Grand Rapids: Baker Book House, 1955.

Miracles

Habershon, Ada Ruth. *The Study of the Miracles.* Grand Rapids: Kregel Publications, 1957.

Laidlow, John. *The Miracles of Our Lord.* Grand Rapids: Baker Book House, 1956.

Taylor, William M. *The Miracles of Our Saviour.* London: Hodder and Stoughton, 1891.

Trench, Richard Chenevix. *Notes on the Miracles of Our Lord.* London: Pickering and Inglis, 1953.

Wallace, Ronald S. *Many Things in Parables, and the Gospel Miracles.* Grand Rapids: Wm. B. Eerdmans Publishing Co., 1963.

Parables

Arnot, William. *The Parables of Our Lord.* London: Thomas Nelson and Sons, 1893.

Habershon, Ada Ruth. *The Study of the Parables.* Grand Rapids: Kregel Publications, 1957.

Hunter, Archibald MacBride. *Interpreting the Parables.* Philadelphia: Westminster Press, 1960.

Morgan, G. Campbell. *The Parable of the Father's Heart.* New York: Fleming H. Revell Co., 1949.

_____. *The Parables of the Kingdom.* London: Hodder and Stoughton, 1907.

Swete, Henry Barclay. *The Parables of the Kingdom.* London: Macmillan Co., 1920.

Trench, Richard Chenevix. *Notes on the Parables of Our Lord.* London: Pickering and Inglis, 1953.

Romans

Archer, Gleason L., Jr. *The Epistle to the Romans.* Grand Rapids: Baker Book House, 1959.

Barnhouse, Donald Grey. *Exposition of Bible Doctrine Taking the Epistles to the Romans as the Point of Departure.* 10 vols. Grand Rapids: Wm. B. Eerdmans Publishing Co., 1952-1963.

Bruce, F. F. *The Epistle of Paul to the Romans.* Tyndale New Testament Commentaries. Grand Rapids: Wm. B. Eerdmans Publishing Co., 1963.

Erdman, Charles Rosenbury. *The Epistle to the Romans.* Philadelphia: Westminster Press, 1925.

Godet, Frederic Louis. *Commentary on St. Paul's Epistle to the Romans.* Grand Rapids: Zondervan Publishing House, n.d.

Haldane, Robert. *Exposition of the Epistle to the Romans.* Reprint. London: Banner of Truth Trust. First published in 1835; again in 1839.

Harrison, Norman B. *His Salvation.* Minneapolis: The Harrison Service, 1926.

Hodge, Charles. *Commentary on the Epistles to the Romans.* Reprint. Grand Rapids: Wm. B. Eerdmans Publishing Co., 1950.

Ironside, H. A. *Lectures on the Epistle to the Romans.* New York: Loizeaux Brothers, 1951.

Laurin, Roy L. *Where Life Begins.* Findlay, OH: Dunham Publishing Co., 1948.

Liddon, Henry Parry. *Explanatory Analysis of St.*

Paul's Epistle to the Romans. Grand Rapids: Zondervan Publishing House, 1961.

Lloyd-Jones, David Martyn. *The Plight of Man and the Power of God.* Grand Rapids: Wm. B. Eerdmans Publishing Co., 1966.

_____. *Romans: Assurance.* London: Banner of Truth Trust, 1971.

_____. *Romans: Exposition of Chapters 3:20 to 4:25.* Grand Rapids: Zondervan Publishing House, 1971.

Luther, Martin. *Lectures on Romans.* Translated by Wilhelm Pauck. Philadelphia: Westminster Press, 1961.

McGee, J. Vernon. *Reasoning through Romans.* 2 vols. Los Angeles: Church of the Open Door, n.d.

Moule, Handley Carr Glyn. *Romans.* Cambridge Bible for Schools and Colleges. Cambridge: University Press, 1879.

Murray, John. *The Epistle to the Romans.* 2 vols. New International Commentary on the New Testament. Grand Rapids: Wm. B. Eerdmans Publishing Co., 1959-65.

Newell, William R. *Romans, Verse-by-Verse.* Chicago: Moody Press, 1938.

Stifler, James Madison. *The Epistle to the Romans.* Chicago: Moody Press, 1960.

Thomas, W. H. Griffith. *St. Paul's Epistle to the Romans.* Grand Rapids: Wm. B. Eerdmans Publishing Co., 1946.

Wuest, Kenneth S. *Romans in the Greek New Testament.* Grand Rapids: Wm. B. Eerdmans Publishing Co., 1956.

1 Corinthians

Barclay, William. *The Letters to the Corinthians.* 2d ed. Philadelphia: Westminster Press, 1956.

Brown, John. *The Resurrection of Life: An Exposition of First Corinthians 15*. Edinburgh: Oliphants, 1852.

Bruce, F. F. *I and II Corinthians*. New Century Bible. London: Oliphants, 1971.

Godet, Frederic Louis. *Commentary on the First Epistle of St. Paul to the Corinthians*. Translated by A. Cousins. Grand Rapids: Zondervan Publishing House, 1957.

Hodge, Charles. *An Exposition of the First Epistle to the Corinthians*. Grand Rapids: Wm. B. Eerdmans Publishing Co., 1965.

Ironside, H. A. *Addresses on the First Epistle to the Corinthians*. New York: Loizeaux Brothers, 1952.

Laurin, Roy L. *Where Life Matures*. Findlay, OH: Dunham Publishing Co., 1950.

Luck, G. Coleman. *First Corinthians*. Chicago: Moody Press, 1958.

Morgan, G. Campbell. *The Corinthian Letters of Paul*. Westwood, NJ: Fleming H. Revell Co., 1956.

Morris, Leon. *The First Epistle of Paul to the Corinthians*. Tyndale New Testament Commentary. Grand Rapids: Wm. B. Eerdmans Publishing Co., 1958.

Redpath, Alan. *The Royal Route to Heaven: Studies in I Corinthians*. London: Pickering and Inglis, 1960.

Robertson, Archibald Thomas, and Alfred Plummer. *A Critical and Exegetical Commentary on the First Epistle of St. Paul to the Corinthians*. 2d ed. Edinburgh: T. and T. Clark, 1914.

Scroggie, William Graham. *The Love Life: A Study of I Corinthians 13*. London: Pickering and Inglis, n.d.

Zodhiates, Spiro. *To Love Is To Live*. Grand Rapids: Wm. B. Eerdmans Publishing Co., 1967.

2 Corinthians

Denney, James. *Epistle to the Corinthians*. The Expositor's Bible. London: Hodder and Stoughton, 1898.

Hodge, Charles. *An Exposition on the Second Epistle to the Corinthians*. Grand Rapids: Wm. B. Eerdmans Publishing Co., 1953.

Ironside, H. A. *Addresses of the Second Epistle to the Corinthians*. Neptune, NJ: Loizeaux Brothers, 1954.

Kelly, William. *Notes on the Second Epistle to the Corinthians*. London: G. Morrish, n.d.

Laurin, Roy L. *Where Life Endures*. Findlay, OH: Dunham Publishing Co., 1955.

Luck, G. Coleman. *Second Corinthians*. Chicago: Moody Press, 1959.

Redpath, Alan. *Blessings Out of Buffetings*. New York: Fleming H. Revell Co., 1965.

Galatians

Barclay, William. *Flesh and Spirit: An Examination of Galatians 5:19-23*. Nashville: Abingdon Press, 1962. The finest exposition of this Galatians passage that I have ever read or studied. Useful for preaching material.

Brown, John. *An Exposition of the Epistle of Paul the Apostle to the Galatians*. Evansville, IN: Sovereign Grace Book Club, 1957.

Cole, Robert Alan. *The Epistle of Paul to the Galatians*. Tyndale New Testament Commentaries. Grand Rapids: Wm. B. Eerdmans Publishing Co., 1865.

DeHaan, M. R. *Galatians*. Grand Rapids: Zondervan Publishing House, 1960.

Eadie, John. *Commentary on the Epistle of Paul to the Galatians*. Grand Rapids: Zondervan Publishing House, n.d.

Girdlestone, Robert Baker. *St. Paul's Epistle to the Galatians*. London: The Religious Tract Society, 1912.

Harrison, Norman B. *His Side Versus Our Side: God's Great Antithesis*. Minneapolis: The Harrison Service, 1940.

Hendriksen, William. *Exposition of Galatians*. New Testament Commentary. Grand Rapids: Baker Book House, 1968.

Hogg, C. F., and William Edwyn Vine. *The Epistle to the Galatians*. London: Pickering and Inglis, 1959.

Lightfoot, Joseph Barber. *The Epistle of St. Paul to the Galatians*. Grand Rapids: Zondervan Publishing House, 1966.

Luther, Martin. *Commentary on the Epistle to the Galatians*. London: James Clarke and Co., 1953.

Ramsay, William Mitchell. *A Historical Commentary on St. Paul's Epistle to the Galatians*. Grand Rapids: Baker Book House, 1965.

Sayles, George. *Grace in Galatians*. New York: Gospel Publishing House, 1912.

Stott, John Robert Walmsey. *The Message of Galatians*. London: InterVarsity Press, 1968.

Strauss, Lehman. *Devotional Studies in Galatians and Ephesians*. Neptune, NJ: Loizeaux Brothers, 1957.

Tenney, Merrill C. *Galatians: The Charter of Christian Liberty*. Grand Rapids: Wm. B. Eerdmans Publishing Co., 1954.

Vos, Howard F. *Galatians: A Call to Christian Liberty*. Chicago: Moody Press, 1971.

Wuest, Kenneth S. *Galatians in the Greek New Testament*. Grand Rapids: Wm. B. Eerdmans Publishing Co., 1944.

Ephesians

Bruce, F. F. *The Epistle to the Ephesians*. Westwood, NJ: Fleming H. Revell Co., 1961.

Chafer, Lewis Sperry. *The Ephesian Letter*. Findlay, OH: Dunham Publishing Co., 1935.

Eadie, John. *Commentary on the Epistle to the Ephe-*

sians. Grand Rapids: Zondervan Publishing House, n.d.

Gore, Charles. *St. Paul's Epistle to the Ephesians*. London: John Murray, 1902.

Harrison, Norman B. *His Very Own: Paul's Epistle to the Ephesians*. Chicago: Moody Press, 1930.

Hendriksen, William. *Exposition of Ephesians*. New Testament Commentary. Grand Rapids: Baker Book House, 1967.

Hodge, Charles. *A Commentary on the Epistle to the Ephesians*. Grand Rapids: Wm. B. Eerdmans Publishing Co., 1966.

Ironside, H. A. *In the Heavenlies: Practical Expository Addresses on the Epistle to the Ephesians*. Neptune, NJ: Loizeaux Brothers, 1955.

Kent, Homer A., Jr. *Ephesians: The Glory of the Church*. Chicago: Moody Press, 1971.

Ketcham, Robert T. *God's Provision for Normal Christian Living* (Eph. 6). Chicago: Moody Press, 1960.

Lloyd-Jones, David Martyn. *God's Way of Reconciliation* (Eph. 2). Grand Rapids: Baker Book House, 1972.

Meyer, F. B. *Ephesians—Key Words of the Inner Life*. Grand Rapids: Zondervan Publishing House, 1953.

Moule, Handley Carr Glyn. *Ephesian Studies: Lessons in Faith and Walk*. 2d ed. Grand Rapids: Zondervan Publishing House, n.d.

Paxson, Ruth. *The Wealth, Walk and Warfare of the Christian*. Westwood, NJ: Fleming H. Revell Co., 1939.

Pellegrin, Harold F. *The Epistle of Paul the Apostle to the Ephesians*. Grand Rapids: Zondervan Publishing House, 1937.

Scroggie, William Graham. *Paul's Prison Prayers*. London: Pickering and Inglis, n.d.

Strauss, Lehman. *Devotional Studies in Galatians and Ephesians*. New York: Loizeaux Brothers, 1957.

Talbot, Louis T. *Ephesians, An Exposition*. Chicago: Van Kampen Press, 1937.

Wuest, Kenneth S. *Ephesians and Colossians in the Greek New Testament*. Grand Rapids: Wm. B. Eerdmans Publishing Co., 1952.

Philippians

Adams, James Russell. *The Courier of God's Grace*. Westwood, NJ: Fleming H. Revell Co., 1948.

Blair, J. Allen. *Living Victoriously*. Grand Rapids: Wm. B. Eerdmans Publishing Co., 1956.

Eadie, John. *Commentary on the Greek Text of the Epistle of Paul to the Philippians*. Reprint. Grand Rapids: Zondervan Publishing House. First published in 1859.

Erdman, Charles Rosenbury. *The Epistle of Paul to the Philippians*. Philadelphia: Westminster Press, 1932.

Harrison, Norman B. *His in Joyous Experience*. Minneapolis: The Harrison Service, 1926.

Hendriksen, William. *A Commentary on the Epistle to the Philippians*. New Testament Commentary. Grand Rapids: Baker Book House, 1962.

Ironside, H. A. *Notes on Philippians*. New York: Loizeaux Brothers, 1922.

Jowett, John Henry. *The High Calling: Meditations on St. Paul's Letter to the Philippians*. London: Andrew Melrose, 1909.

Kelly, William. *Philippians and Colossians*. Oak Park, IL: Bible Truth Publications, n.d.

King, Guy Hope. *Joy Way*. London: Marshall, Morgan and Scott, 1954.

Laurin, Roy L. *Philippians: Where Life Advances.* Chicago: Van Kampen Press, 1954.

Martin, Ralph P. *The Epistle of Paul to the Philippians.* Tyndale New Testament Commentaries. Grand Rapids: Wm. B. Eerdmans Publishing Co., 1959.

Meyer, F. B. *The Epistle to the Philippians.* Grand Rapids: Baker Book House, 1952.

Moule, Handley Carr Glyn. *Philippian Studies: Lessons in Faith and Love.* Grand Rapids: Zondervan Publishing House, n.d.

Plummer, Alfred. *A Commentary on St. Paul's Epistle to the Philippians.* London: Robert Scott, 1919.

Rees, Paul Stromberg. *The Adequate Man.* Westwood, NJ: Fleming H. Revell Co., 1959.

Robertson, Archibald Thomas. *Paul's Joy in Christ: Studies in Philippians.* Revised and edited by W. C. Strickland. Nashville: Broadman Press, 1959.

Strauss, Lehman. *Devotional Studies in Philippians.* New York: Loizeaux Brothers, 1959.

Tenney, Merrill C. *Philippians: The Gospel at Work.* Grand Rapids: Wm. B. Eerdmans Publishing Co., 1956.

Vincent, Marvin R. *A Critical and Exegetical Commentary on the Epistle to the Philippians and to Philemon.* International Critical Commentary. New York: Charles Scribner's Sons, 1897.

Walvoord, John F. *Philippians: Triumph in Christ.* Chicago: Moody Press, 1971.

_____. *To Live Is Christ.* Findlay, OH: Dunham Publishing Co., 1961.

Wuest, Kenneth S. *Philippians in the Greek New Testament.* Grand Rapids: Wm. B. Eerdmans Publishing Co., 1942.

Colossians

Eadie, John. *Commentary on the Epistle of Paul to the*

Colossians. Grand Rapids: Zondervan Publishing House, 1957.

English, E. Schuyler. *Studies in the Epistle to the Colossians.* New York: Our Hope, 1944.

Harrison, Everett F. *Colossians: Christ All-Sufficient.* Chicago: Moody Press, 1971.

Hendriksen, William. *Exposition of Colossians and Philemon.* New Testament Commentary. Grand Rapids: Baker Book House, 1964.

Ironside, H. A. *Lectures on the Epistle to the Colossians.* Neptune, NJ: Loizeaux Brothers, 1955.

King, Guy Hope. *Crossing the Border, An Expositional Study of Colossians.* London: Marshall, Morgan and Scott, 1957.

Lincoln, William. *Lectures on the Epistle to the Colossians.* Scotland: John Ritchie, n.d.

Maclaren, Alexander. *Colossians and Philemon.* The Expositor's Bible. New York: A. C. Armstrong and Son, 1908.

Moule, Handley Carr Glyn. *Colossians and Philemon Studies: Lessons in Faith and Holiness.* Grand Rapids: Zondervan Publishing House, n.d.

Nicholson, Bishop William Rufus. *Popular Studies in Colossians.* Reprint. Edited by James M. Gray. Grand Rapids: Kregel Publications. Formerly published under the title of *Oneness in Christ.*

Robertson, Archibald Thomas. *Paul and the Intellectuals: The Epistle to the Colossians.* Revised and edited by W. C. Strickland. Nashville: Broadman Press, 1959.

Thomas, W. H. Griffith. *Christ Pre-eminent.* Chicago: Bible Institute Colportage Assn., 1923.

Vine, William Edwyn. *The Epistle to the Philippians and Colossians.* London: Oliphants, n.d.

The Pastoral Epistles

Erdman, Charles Rosenbury. *The Pastoral Epistles of Paul*. Philadelphia: Westminster Press, 1923.

Gaebelein, Frank E. *Philemon: The Gospel of Emancipation*. Wheaton, IL: Van Kampen Press, 1939.

Greene, J. P. *The Pastoral Epistles*. Nashville: Broadman Press, 1915.

Guthrie, Donald. *The Pastoral Epistles*. Grand Rapids: Wm. B. Eerdmans Publishing Co., 1957.

Hendriksen, William. *Exposition of the Pastoral Epistles*. New Testament Commentary. Grand Rapids: Baker Book House, 1968.

Hiebert, David Edmond. *First Timothy*. Chicago: Moody Press, 1957.

_____. *Second Timothy*. Chicago: Moody Press, 1958.

Ironside, H. A. *Timothy, Titus and Philemon*. Neptune, NJ: Loizeaux Brothers, 1955.

Kelly, William. *An Exposition of the Two Epistles to Timothy*. London: C. A. Hammond Co., 1948.

Kent, Homer A., Jr. *The Pastoral Epistles: Studies in I and II Timothy and Titus*. Chicago: Moody Press, 1958.

King, Guy Hope. *A Leader Led (I Timothy)*. London: Marshall, Morgan and Scott, 1951.

_____. *To My Son (II Timothy)*. Fort Washington, PA: Christian Literature Crusade, 1944.

Moule, Handley Carr Glyn. *The Second Epistle to Timothy*. London: The Religious Tract Society, 1905.

Scroggie, William Graham. *A Note to a Friend: Paul to Philemon*. London: Hulbert Publishing Co., n.d.

Vine, William Edwyn. *The Epistles to Timothy and Titus: Faith and Conduct*. Grand Rapids: Zondervan Publishing House, 1965.

_____. *The Epistles to Timothy*. London: Pickering and Inglis, 1925.

Wuest, Kenneth S. *The Pastoral Epistles in the Greek New Testament*. Grand Rapids: Wm. B. Eerdmans Publishing Co., 1952.

1 and 2 Thessalonians

Denny, James. *The Epistle to the Thessalonians*. The Expositor's Bible. New York: A. C. Armstrong and Son, 1908.

Eadie, John. *A Commentary on the Greek Text of the Epistles of Paul to the Thessalonians*. Edited by William Young. London: Macmillan Co., 1877.

Ellicott, Charles John. *Commentary on the Epistle of St. Paul to the Thessalonians*. Grand Rapids: Zondervan Publishing House, 1957.

Erdman, Charles Rosenbury. *The Epistles to the Thessalonians*. Philadelphia: Westminster Press, 1935.

Hendriksen, William. *Exposition of I and II Thessalonians*. New Testament Commentary. Grand Rapids: Baker Book House, 1964.

Hiebert, David Edmond. *The Thessalonian Epistles*. Chicago: Moody Press, 1971.

Hogg, Charles Frederick, and William Edwyn Vine. *The Epistles to the Thessalonians*. London: Pickering and Inglis, 1959.

Ironside, H. A. *Addresses on Thessalonians*. New York: Loizeaux Brothers, 1947.

Kelly, William. *The Epistles of Paul to the Thessalonians*. London: C. A. Hammond Co., 1953.

Lincoln, William. *Lectures on Thessalonians*. Scotland: John Ritchie, n.d.

Morris, Leon. *The First and Second Epistles to the Thessalonians*. New International Commentary on the New Testament. Grand Rapids: Wm. B. Eerdmans Publishing Co., 1959.

Walvoord, John F. *The Thessalonian Epistles*. Findlay, OH: Dunham Publishing Co., 1955.

Woodring, H. C., and Robert J. Little. *The Thessalonian Epistles*. Oak Park, IL: Emmaus Bible School, 1962.

Hebrews

Anderson, Sir Robert. *The Hebrew Epistle in the Light of the Type*. London: Pickering and Inglis, n.d.

Barclay, William. *The Letter to the Hebrews*. Philadelphia: Westminster Press, 1957.

Brown, John. *An Exposition of the Epistle of the Apostle Paul to the Hebrews*. Reprint. London: Banner of Truth Trust. First published in 1862.

Bruce, F. F. *The Epistle to the Hebrews*. New International Commentary on the New Testament. Grand Rapids: Wm. B. Eerdmans Publishing Co., 1964.

English, E. Schuyler. *Studies in the Epistle to the Hebrews*. Traveler's Rest, SC: Southern Bible Book House, 1955.

Erdman, Charles Rosenbury. *The Epistle to the Hebrews*. Philadelphia: Westminster Press, 1934.

Ironside, H. A. *Epistle to the Hebrews and Titus*. New York: Loizeaux Brothers, 1932.

Kent, Homer A., Jr. *The Epistle to the Hebrews*. Grand Rapids: Baker Book House, 1972.

Lenski, R. C. H. *The Interpretation of the Epistle to the Hebrews and of the Epistle of James*. Columbus, OH: Wartburg Press, 1946.

Morgan, G. Campbell. *God's Last Word to Man*. New York: Fleming H. Revell Co., 1936.

_____. *The Triumphs of Faith*. New York: Fleming H. Revell Co., 1944.

Murray, Andrew. *The Holiest of All*. New York: Fleming H. Revell Co., 1965.

Newell, William R. *Hebrews Verse-by-Verse*. Chicago: Moody Press, 1947.

Owen, John. *An Exposition of the Epistle to the Hebrews.* 4 vols. Wilmington: Sovereign Grace Publishing Co., n.d.

_____. *Hebrews: The Epistle of Warning.* Grand Rapids: Kregel Publications, 1968.

Pettingill, William. *Into the Holiest.* Findlay, OH: Fundamental Truth Publications, 1939.

Pink, Arthur W. *An Exposition of Hebrews.* 3 vols. Grand Rapids: Baker Book House, 1954.

Ridout, Samuel. *Lectures on the Epistle to the Hebrews.* New York: Loizeaux Brothers, n.d.

Saphir, Adolph. *The Epistle to the Hebrews.* 2 vols. New York: Gospel Publishing House, n.d.

Seiss, Joseph Augustus. *Lectures on Hebrews.* Grand Rapids: Baker Book House, 1954.

Steen, J. C. *Christ Supreme.* Scotland: John Ritchie, n.d.

Stibbs, Alan M. *So Great Salvation: The Meaning and Message of the Letter to the Hebrews.* Exeter, England: Paternoster Press, 1970.

Thomas, W. H. Griffith. *Hebrews: A Devotional Commentary.* Grand Rapids: Wm. B. Eerdmans Publishing Co., 1962.

_____. *Let Us Go On.* Grand Rapids: Zondervan Publishing House, 1954.

Vine, William Edwyn. *The Epistle to the Hebrews.* Grand Rapids: Zondervan Publishing House, 1952.

Wuest, Kenneth S. *Hebrews in the Greek New Testament.* Grand Rapids: Wm. B. Eerdmans Publishing Co., 1947.

James

Dale, R. W. *The Epistle of James.* London: Hodder and Stoughton, 1895. Out of print.

Gaebelein, Frank E. *Practical Epistle of James: Studies in Applied Christianity.* Great Neck, NY: Doniger and Raughley, 1955.

Ironside, H. A. *Notes on James and Peter*. Neptune, NJ: Loizeaux Brothers, 1947.

Johnstone, Robert. *Lectures, Exegetical and Practical, on the Epistle of James*. Grand Rapids: Baker Book House, 1954.

King, Guy Hope. *A Belief that Behaves*. Fort Washington, PA: Christian Literature Crusade, 1941.

Robertson, Archibald Thomas. *Studies in the Epistle of James*. Revised and edited by Heber F. Peacock. Nashville: Broadman Press, 1959.

Stevenson, Herbert F. *James Speaks for Today*. Westwood, NJ: Fleming H. Revell Co., 1966.

Strauss, Lehman. *James, Your Brother: Studies in the Epistle of James*. New York: Loizeaux Brothers, 1956.

Tasker, Randolph Vincent Greenwood. *The General Epistle of James*. Tyndale New Testament Commentaries. Grand Rapids: Wm. B. Eerdmans Publishing Co., 1960.

Zodhiates, Spiros. *The Behavior of Belief*. Grand Rapids: Wm. B. Eerdmans Publishing Co., 1970.

1 and 2 Peter

Blair, J. Allen. *Living Faithfully*. New York: Loizeaux Brothers, 1961.

Brown, John. *Expository Discourses in the First Epistle of the Apostle Peter*. 3 vols. Marshalltown, DE: National Foundation for Christian Education, n.d.

English, E. Schuyler. *The Life and Letters of St. Peter*. New York: Our Hope, 1942.

Green, Edward Michael Bankes. *Second Epistle General of Peter and the General Epistle of Jude*. Tyndale New Testament Commentaries. Grand Rapids: Wm. B. Eerdmans Publishing Co., 1968.

Ironside, H. A. *Expository Notes on the Epistles of James and Peter*. New York: Loizeaux Brothers, 1947.

Jowett, John Henry. *The Epistles of St. Peter.* Grand Rapids: Kregel Publications, 1970.

Kelly, William. *The Epistles of Peter.* London: C. A. Hammond Co., n.d.

Leighton, Robert. *A Practical Commentary upon the First Epistle General of Peter.* Grand Rapids: Kregel Publications, 1972.

Meyer, F. B. *Peter: Fisherman, Disciple, Apostle.* London: Marshall, Morgan, and Scott, 1953.

_____. *Tried by Fire.* New York: Fleming H. Revell Co., n.d.

Nieboer, J. *Practical Expositions of I and II Peter.* 2 vols. North East, PA: Our Daily Walk Publications, 1951, 1952.

Robertson, Archibald Thomas. *Epochs in the Life of Simon Peter.* New York: Charles Scribner's Sons, 1933.

Stibbs, Alan M. *The First Epistle General of Peter.* Grand Rapids: Wm. B. Eerdmans Publishing Co., 1959.

Thomas, W. H. Griffith. *The Apostle Peter: Outline Studies in His Life, Character and Writings.* Grand Rapids: Wm. B. Eerdmans Publishing Co., 1950.

Westwood, Tom. *Peter's Epistles.* Glendale, CA: Westwood Co., n.d.

Wolston, W. T. P. *Simon Peter, His Life and Letters.* Edinburgh: J. K. Sauter and Co., 1926.

Wuest, Kenneth S. *First Peter in the Greek New Testament.* Grand Rapids: Wm. B. Eerdmans Publishing Co., 1942.

_____. *In These Last Days.* Grand Rapids: Wm. B. Eerdmans Publishing Co., 1954.

1, 2, 3 John

Bruce, F. F. *The Epistles of John.* London: Pickering and Inglis, 1970.

Cameron, Robert. *First Epistle of John, or God Revealed in Life, Light and Love.* No Address: A. J. Rowland, 1899.

Candlish, Robert S. *The First Epistle of John.* Grand Rapids: Zondervan Publishing House, n.d.

Cotton, John. *An Exposition of First John.* Evansville, IN: Sovereign Grace Publications. 1962.

Findlay, George G. *Fellowship in the Life Eternal.* Grand Rapids: Wm. B. Eerdmans Publishing Co., 1955.

Ironside, H. A. *Addresses on the Epistles of John and an Exposition on the Epistle of Jude.* 2d ed. New York: Loizeaux Brothers, 1954.

Kelly, William. *An Exposition of the Epistles of John the Apostle.* London: T. Weston, 1905.

King, Guy Hope. *The Fellowship.* London: Marshall, Morgan, and Scott, 1954.

Laurin, Roy L. *Life at Its Best.* Findlay, OH: Dunham Publishing House, 1946.

Plummer, Alfred. *The Epistles of St. John.* Cambridge: University Press, 1894.

Steele, Daniel. *Half Hours with St. John's Epistles.* Chicago: Christian Witness Co., 1908.

Strauss, Lehman. *The Epistles of John.* New York: Loizeaux Brothers, 1962.

Vine, William Edwyn. The Epistles of John. Grand Rapids: Zondervan Publishing House, n.d.

Westcott, Brooke Foss. *The Epistles of St. John.* Grand Rapids: Wm. B. Eerdmans Publishing Co., 1966.

Jude

Coder, S. Maxwell. *Jude: The Acts of the Apostates.* Chicago: Moody Press, 1958.

McIntire, Carl. *The Epistle of the Apostasy.* Collingswood, NJ: Christian Beacon Press, 1958.

Revelation

Barnhouse, Donald Grey. *Revelation: God's Last Word.* Reprint. Grand Rapids: Zondervan Publishing House, 1971.

Blanchard, Charles A. *Light on the Last Days.* Chicago: Moody Press, 1913.

Criswell, W. A. *Expository Sermons on Revelation.* Grand Rapids: Zondervan Publishing House, 1961-66.

DeHaan, M. R. *Revelation.* Grand Rapids: Zondervan Publishing House, 1967.

Gaebelein, Arno C. *The Revelation: An Analysis and Exposition of the Last Book of the Bible.* New York: Loizeaux Brothers, 1961.

Ironside, H. A. *Lectures on the Book of Revelation.* New York: Loizeaux Brothers, 1955.

Kelly, William. *Lectures on the Book of Revelation.* London: G. Morrish, n.d.

Larkin, Clarence. *The Book of Revelation.* Philadelphia: Clarence Larkin Estate, 1919.

Lincoln, William. *Lectures on the Book of Revelation.* New York: Fleming H. Revell Co., n.d.

Morgan, G. Campbell. *The Letters of Our Lord: A First Century Message to Twentieth Century Christians.* London: Pickering and Inglis, 1961.

Morris, Leon. *The Revelation of St. John.* Grand Rapids: Wm. B. Eerdmans Publishing Co., 1969.

Newell, William R. *The Book of Revelation.* Chicago: Moody Press, 1935.

Ottman, Ford C. *The Unfolding of the Ages.* Fincastle, VA: Scripture Truth Book Co., 1967.

Ramsay, William Mitchell. *Letters to the Seven Churches of Asia.* Grand Rapids: Baker Book House, 1963.

Ryrie, Charles Caldwell. *Revelation*. Chicago: Moody Press, 1968.

Scott, Walter. *Exposition of the Revelation of Jesus Christ*. 4th ed. London: Pickering and Inglis, n.d.

Scroggie, William Graham. *The Great Unveiling*. Edinburgh: author, 1920.

Seiss, Joseph Augustus. *The Apocalypse*. Grand Rapids: Zondervan Publishing House, 1964.

_____. *Letters to the Seven Churches*. Grand Rapids: Baker Book House, 1956.

Smith, Jacob Brubaker. *A Revelation of Jesus Christ*. Edited by J. Otis Yoder. Scottsdale, PA: Herald Press, 1961.

Strauss, Lehman. *The Book of the Revelation*. Neptune, NJ: Loizeaux Brothers, 1965.

Swete, Henry Barclay. *The Apocalypse of St. John*. Grand Rapids: Wm. B. Eerdmans Publishing Co., n.d.

Trench, Richard Chenevix. *Commentary on the Epistles to the Seven Churches in Asia*. 6th ed. London: Kegan Paul, Trench, Trubner and Co., 1897.

Walvoord, John F. *The Revelation of Jesus Christ*. Chicago: Moody Press, 1966.

Doctrinal Theology

While there are scores of good books on theology, I suggest the following to be helpful to the pastor.

Bancroft, Emery H., arranger and compiler. *Christian Theology*. Grand Rapids: Zondervan Publishing House, twelfth printing, 1974.

Buswell, James Oliver, Jr. *A Systematic Theology of the Christian Religion*. 2 vols. Grand Rapids: Zondervan Publishing House, 1962.

Calvin, John. *The Institutes of the Christian Religion*. Grand Rapids: Wm. B. Eerdmans Publishing Co., 1953.

Chafer, Lewis Sperry. *Major Bible Themes.* Grand Rapids: Zondervan Publishing House, 1926.

_____. *Systematic Theology.* 8 vols. Dallas: Dallas Seminary Press, 1948.

Evans, William. *The Great Doctrines of the Bible.* Revised ed. Chicago: Moody Press, 1964.

Henry, Carl F., ed. *Contemporary Evangelical Thought.* Grand Rapids: Baker Book House, 1968.

Hodge, Alexander Archibald. *Outlines of Theology.* New York: R. Carter and Brothers, 1860.

Hodge, Charles. *Systematic Theology.* 3 vols. Grand Rapids: Wm. B. Eerdmans Publishing Co., 1960.

Lightner, Robert Paul. *Neo-Evangelicalism.* Des Plaines, IL: Regular Baptist Press, 1965.

_____. *Neo-Liberalism.* Des Plaines, IL: Regular Baptist Press, 1959.

Machen, J. Gresham. *Christianity and Liberalism.* Grand Rapids: Wm. B. Eerdmans Publishing Co., 1923.

Pentecost, J. Dwight. *Things Which Become Sound Doctrine.* Westwood, NJ: Fleming H. Revell Co., 1965.

Shedd, William Greenough Thayer. *Dogmatic Theology.* 3 vols. Grand Rapids: Zondervan Publishing House, 1969.

Strong, Augustus Hopkins. *Systematic Theology.* Valley Forge, PA: Judson Press, 1907.

Thiessen, Henry Clarence. *Introductory Lectures in Systematic Theology.* Grand Rapids: Wm. B. Eerdmans Publishing Co., 1949.

The Godhead

Bickersteth, Edward Henry. *The Trinity.* Grand Rapids: Kregel Publications, 1965.

Phillips, John Bertram. *Your God Is Too Small.* New York: Macmillan Co., 1967.

Stone, Nathan J. *Names of God in the Old Testament.* Chicago: Moody Press, 1944.

God, the First Person

Strauss, Lehman. *The First Person.* Neptune, NJ: Loizeaux Brothers, 1967.

God, the Holy Spirit

Bickersteth, Edward Henry. *The Holy Spirit: His Person and Work.* Grand Rapids: Kregel Publications, 1959.

Criswell, W. A. *The Holy Spirit in Today's World.* Grand Rapids: Zondervan Publishing House, 1906.

Moule, Handley Carr Glyn. *Veni Creator.* London: Hodder and Stoughton, 1895.

Murray, Andrew. *The Spirit of Christ.* Fort Washington, PA: Christian Literature Crusade, 1964.

Owen, John. *The Holy Spirit, His Gifts and Power.* Grand Rapids: Kregel Publications, 1960.

Pache, René. *The Person and Work of the Holy Spirit.* Chicago: Moody Press, 1954.

Pentecost, J. Dwight. *The Divine Comforter.* Westwood, NJ: Fleming H. Revell Co., 1963.

Pink, Arthur W. *The Holy Spirit.* Grand Rapids: Baker Book House, 1970.

Ridout, Samuel. *The Person and Work of the Holy Spirit.* New York: Loizeaux Brothers, n.d.

Ryrie, Charles Caldwell. *The Holy Spirit.* Chicago: Moody Press, 1965.

Swete, Henry Barclay. *The Holy Spirit in the New Testament.* Grand Rapids: Baker Book House, 1964.

Thomas, W. H. Griffith. *The Holy Spirit of God.* Grand Rapids: Wm. B. Eerdmans Publishing Co., 1950.

Torrey, R. A. *The Person and Work of the Holy Spirit.* Grand Rapids: Zondervan Publishing House, 1968.

Unger, Merrill F. *The Baptizing Work of the Holy Spirit.*

Wheaton, IL: Scripture Press, 1953.

Walvoord, John F. *The Holy Spirit.* Findlay, OH: Dunham Publishing Co., 1965.

Sovereignty of God

Pink, Arthur W. *The Sovereignty of God.* Grand Rapids: Baker Book House, 1959.

Christology—Person and Work of Jesus Christ

Anderson, Robert. *The Lord from Heaven.* Grand Rapids: Kregel Publications, 1965.

Guthrie, Donald. *Jesus the Messiah.* Grand Rapids: Zondervan Publishing House, 1972.

Owen, John. *The Glory of Christ.* Chicago: Moody Press, 1949.

Walvoord, John F. *Jesus Christ Our Lord.* Chicago: Moody Press, 1969.

Christology—Atonement

Lightner, Robert Paul. *The Death Christ Died: A Case for Unlimited Atonement.* Des Plaines, IL: Regular Baptist Press, 1967.

Marsh, Frederick Edward. *Why Did Christ Die?* Grand Rapids: Zondervan Publishing House, n.d.

Christology—Life of Christ

Feinberg, Charles Lee. *Is the Virgin Birth in the Old Testament?* Whittier, CA: Smith Publishing Co., 1967.

Machen, J. Gresham. *Virgin Birth of Christ.* Grand Rapids: Baker Book House, 1967.

Morgan, G. Campbell. *The Crises of the Christ.* London: Pickering and Inglis, 1963.

_____. *The Teaching of Christ.* London: Pickering and Inglis, n.d.

Sanders, John Oswald. *The Incomparable Christ.* Chicago: Moody Press, 1971.

Scroggie, William Graham. *Tested by Temptation*. London: Pickering and Inglis, 1956.

Smith, Wilbur M. *A Treasury of Great Sermons on the Resurrection*. Grand Rapids: Baker Book House, 1970.

Spurgeon, Charles Haddon. *Christ's Words from the Cross*. Grand Rapids: Zondervan Publishing House, 1965.

_____. *Twelve Sermons on the Passion and Death of Christ*. Grand Rapids: Baker Book House, 1971.

_____. *Twelve Sermons on the Resurrection*. Grand Rapids: Baker Book House, 1968.

Stalker, James. *The Life of Jesus Christ*. Westwood, NJ: Fleming H. Revell Co., 1949.

Stewart, James Stuart. *The Life and Teaching of Jesus Christ*. New York: Abingdon Press, n.d.

Whyte, Alexander. *The Walk, Conversation and Character of Jesus Christ our Lord*. Grand Rapids: Zondervan Publishing House, 1953.

Salvation

Baxter, James Sidlow. *God So Loved*. Grand Rapids: Zondervan Publishing House, 1960.

_____. *His Part and Ours*. Grand Rapids: Zondervan Publishing House, 1964.

Chafer, Lewis Sperry. *Grace*. Grand Rapids: Zondervan Publishing House, 1965.

_____. *He that Is Spiritual*. Grand Rapids: Zondervan Publishing House, 1965.

_____. *Salvation*. Grand Rapids: Zondervan Publishing House, 1965.

Ryle, J. C. *Holiness: Its Nature, Hindrances, Difficulties, and Roots*. Grand Rapids: Kregel Publications, 1956.

Ryrie, Charles Caldwell. *The Grace of God*. Chicago: Moody Press, 1963.

Schaeffer, Francis A. *True Spirituality*. Wheaton, IL: Tyndale House Publishers, 1971.

Strombeck, John Frederick. *Shall Never Perish*. 9th ed. Moline, IL: Strombeck Foundation, 1964.

Thomas, W. Ian. *The Mystery of Godliness*. Grand Rapids: Zondervan Publishing House, 1964.

Spirit Beings

Barnhouse, Donald Grey. *The Invisible War*. Grand Rapids: Zondervan Publishing House, 1965.

Chafer, Lewis Sperry. *Satan: His Motives and Methods*. Grand Rapids: Zondervan Publishing House, 1964.

Gaebelein, Arno C. *The Angels of God*. Grand Rapids: Zondervan Publishing House, 1969.

Lockyer, Herbert. *The Mystery and Ministry of Angels*. Grand Rapids: Wm. B. Eerdmans Publishing Co., 1958.

Pentecost, J. Dwight. *Your Adversary the Devil*. Grand Rapids: Zondervan Publishing House, 1969.

Unger, Merrill F. *Demons in the World Today: A Study of Occultism in the Light of God's Word*. Wheaton, IL: Tyndale House Publishers, 1971.

Eschatology

Blackstone, William E. *Jesus Is Coming*. Westwood, NJ: Fleming H. Revell Co., 1908.

Gaebelein, Arno C. *The Conflict of the Ages*. London: Pickering and Inglis, 1933.

Harrison, William K. *Hope Triumphant: Studies in the Rapture of the Church*. Chicago: Moody Press, 1966.

Pache, René. *The Future Life*. Chicago: Moody Press, 1962.

Pentecost, J. Dwight. *Things to Come*. Findlay, OH: Dunham Publishing Co., 1958.

Smith, Wilbur M. *The Biblical Doctrine of Heaven*. Chicago: Moody Press, 1968.

Walvoord, John F. *The Millennial Kingdom*. Findlay, OH: Dunham Publishing Co., 1965.

_____. *The Return of the Lord*. Grand Rapids: Zondervan Publishing House, 1955.

The pastor may have several shelves of books of miscellaneous works. In this section of my library I have J. Edward's works; the complete works of John Owen; the works of C. H. Mackintosh and the works of J. N. Darby.

There should be spacious allowance for books on sermons, especially some of the classics. I have hundreds of volumes that deal with sermons and try to get through at least one sermon a day if possible.

The pastor's library should have an ample section of devotional material. It is heartwarming and stimulating to expose his mind to the devotional discoveries of others.

Books on prayer should be read with an examination of his own life.

There should be sections on expository preaching, homiletics, church history, biographies, church administration and pastoral theology.

The pastor should be aware of some excellent books written on the subject of the minister's library which give far more exhaustive lists than are given here, such as the following:

Barber, Cyril J. *The Minister's Library*. Grand Rapids: Baker Book House, 1974. This book treats the subject of a minister's library extensively. Dr. Barber provides a comprehensive list of books that may be used by the evangelical pastor. Accompanying each entry is the Dewey Decimal Number, which makes this volume extremely valuable.

Annotated Bibliography. Compiled by the Faculty of Western Conservative Baptist Seminary, Portland, Oregon, 1973.

Profitable Bible Study. Compiled by Wilbur M. Smith. 2d
   revision. No address, W. A. Wilde Co., 1964.

Pamphlets and Paperbacks

As mentioned before, my library has been organized
according to the Dewey Decimal System. Pamphlets,
however, do not lend themselves to such a system. My library has nearly three thousand pamphlets or small paperback books. I have numbered them from one to three
thousand and then run a cross index on them. The index
is according to author, subject, title and sequence.

I have emphasized the pastor's library, but it should
be remembered that books can never be a substitute for
the power of the Holy Spirit in the life of the pastor. The
man of God, with the Spirit's enduing, can have his life
greatly enriched and blessed by reading good books—
with the Word of God having first place always.

CHAPTER FIVE
The Pastor as an Administrator

What is administration? Arthur Merrihew Adams defines it as "working with and through people to get things done." The idea is one of executive management. The executive head of the church is generally the pastor. Some do not prefer the word "executive," but this is precisely what the pastor is. However, if he is *only* the executive and an administrator, both he and the church are in real danger.

The word *executive* comes from two Latin words: "Ex," meaning "out," and "sequi," which means to follow up to the end. Thus it means to carry out or follow through to completion. The pastor as administrator or executive, therefore, works with and through people to get things done. He takes the proper leadership in following up each objective to the end that God might be glorified.

Administration, then, involves planning programs and seeing them through to the end. It involves the leading of the church staff, the church officers, and various committees in the church, as well as the general membership.

Marks of a Good Administrator

An administrator loves people. It is important that the pastor does not see administration as simply administering the cogs in a machine. A good pastor-administrator will be found working with and through people and loving them.

An administrator is able to put people to work in worthwhile areas. The pastor needs to recognize that the church is a called-out assembly, expected to fulfill the Great Commission. This involves training and evangelism. As administrator he will give direction and leadership to accomplish these goals.

An administrator maintains a correct balance and perspective in his service. Adams, in his book *Pastoral Administration,* points out that there is a danger of a pastor seeing himself as an orator. He is "in jeopardy of posing and vain display, a love of the sound of his voice, an illusion that saying something is equivalent to doing it."[1]

As a counselor he risks the danger of considering himself a psychiatrist, and as an administrator the pastor is in danger of becoming more interested in programs than he is in people. Balance! Balance! Balance! That is the needed quality of the pastor in every area of his service and administration.

An administrator makes proper use of his time. He must be disciplined in this respect; otherwise he is likely to get bogged down in any one of the many executive responsibilities.

Donald A. Laird and Eleanor C. Laird in the book, *The Techniques of Getting Things Done,* have listed the work habits of many successful men as follows:

> The world's producers outstripped other people because they had productive work habits, habits that helped them do superior work easily. Whether or not they were born with genius, they nevertheless worked like geniuses and got geniuses' results. Not many of them stood at their work, but they all *had certain essential work habits* that are worth reviewing.

1. They had the habit of planning their work not only for tomorrow but also for goals in the future. They worked for a purpose; that purpose carried them through hardships and over obstacles.

2. They had the habit of working on *things that counted*. They avoided enticing distractions. They knew that the steam that blows the whistle does not turn the wheel. They worked with foresight.

3. They had the habit of saying *no* to things that would not help them produce. They kept on the main highway; *off the detours*.

4. They had the habit of reading books and magazines that would help in their work.

5. They kept *priming their heads* with ideas, facts, and inspiration.

6. They had the habit of *doing the unpleasant job first*. They did not paralyze present activity by letting past work hang over their heads.

7. They had the habit of *making themselves work*. They kept their effort alive.

8. They had the habit of *deciding trifles quickly*. They did not putter around trying to make up their minds what to do next.

9. They had the habit of *starting vigorously* and promptly, often early in the morning. They did not let the grass grow under their feet.

10. They had the habit of working like craftsmen. By working for quality, they got more done and received more satisfaction than if they had pushed for quantity.

11. They had the habit of using both hands, the habit of doing *two things at once*. They used each minute before it had disappeared forever. Doing nothing was the most annoying thing in the world to them.

12. They had the habit of *getting others to help*

them. They *trained others* to be extra hands, eyes, and heads for them.

13. They had the habit of working for more than money. Pride in a job well done, in accomplishment, was more rewarding to them than a big bank account.

14. They had the habit of *taking on more work.* They kept expanding their abilities and achievements. They caught up on work quickly, could take on more work easily. They kept out of ruts by broadening the high roads. They put pressure on themselves to do or sink.

15. They had the habit of requiring production from themselves, of not accepting their own alibis. They *cracked the whip over themselves* instead of feeling sorry for their lot in life.[2]

An administrator is efficient and careful in his planning. Someone has suggested that "planning" is the process of determining a course of action. Adams lists six stages in planning.

1. Clarification of purpose.
2. Analysis of the situation.
3. Development of possible lines of action.
4. Decision.
5. Outlining a program in detail.
6. Preparing a pattern of action.[3]

Whether it is the pastor's personal life or his work in the church, it should be obvious that planning is necessary. "God is not the author of confusion, but of peace" (1 Cor. 14:33). The Lord Himself made it clear that we are to think ahead in our planning.

For which of you, intending to build a tower, sitteth not down first, and counteth the cost, whether he have sufficient to finish it? Lest haply, after he hath laid the foundation, and is not able to finish it, all that behold it begin to mock him, Saying, This man began to build, and was not able to finish. Or what king, going to make war against another king, sitteth not down first, and consulteth whether he be able with ten thousand to meet him that cometh against him with twenty thousand? Or else, while the other is yet a great way off, he sendeth an ambassage, and desireth conditions of peace (Luke 14:28-32).

Unless a Christian plans properly he will often find himself reacting to problems and fighting fires. How many pastors go from one fire to the other, dealing with problems and situations which perhaps would never have taken place if there had been proper planning? This kind of activity results in frantic frustration. The whole tenor and tone of Scripture talks about both motivation and objectives in service. Paul said, "Know ye not that they which run in a race run all, but one receiveth the prize? So run, that ye may obtain" (1 Cor. 9:24). We are seeking to obtain, not "as one that beateth the air" (v. 26). The pastor's course should be deliberate, well-planned and thought through. Purposes need to be clarified, a proper analysis should be made, and lines of action should be developed. This is true in any area of Christian service. Possibly the greatest difficulty in churches today is the lack of a definite plan. The pastor needs to plan his work and work his plan. Paul did this when he started churches in major cities.

An administrator is able to delegate work to others. When Moses was under extreme pressure, his father-in-law approached him and said, "What is this thing that thou doest to the people? Why sittest thou thyself alone, and all the people stand by thee from morning unto even?" (Exod. 18:14).

His father-in-law saw something that even Moses did not see—that he was not going to be able to endure the pressure without help. Moses' answer is quite typical of the average pastor: "Because the people came unto me to enquire of God" (v. 15).

Surely Moses was doing a good work. He was doing God's work; and he felt that there were no other alternatives. It was a good work, and yet it was not. What he was doing was good, but the manner in which it was being done was far from good. His father-in-law answered, "The thing that thou doest is not good. Thou wilt surely wear away, both thou, and this people that is with thee: for this thing is too heavy for thee: thou are not able to perform it thyself alone" (vv. 17, 18). Jethro then proceeded to instruct Moses to delegate authority and to let them share in the responsibility.

Moses' reaction was a wise one. "And Moses chose able men out of all Israel, and made them heads over the people, rulers of thousands, rulers of hundreds, rulers of fifties, and rulers of tens. And they judged the people at all seasons: the hard causes they brought unto Moses, but every small matter they judged themselves" (Exod. 18:25, 26).

Apparently with all the wisdom that Moses acquired in Egypt, he needed this very simple course in administration.

Andrew Blackwood says of these verses in Exodus:

These words from Exodus might well hang on the study wall as a motto. If the young man reads them day after day, in the spirit of humility and of prayer, he may begin to mend his ways. The words of Jethro suggest the following observations:

1. Many a pastor today has no broad plan for the field.

2. He does not seek advice from men who excel in his line.

3. He tries to do everything himself as though he alone knew how.

4. He consumes time and energy on details; no statesman!

5. He lives on his nerves, and gets on other people's nerves.

6. He does not delegate responsibility to his teammates.

7. He does not discover and enlist new leaders.

8. He does not let strong men work in their own ways.

9. He does not inspire loyalty to the kingdom.

10. He does not gain a reputation for knowing how to lead.[4]

Jethro encouraged Moses to use the available manpower in order that the work of God might be accomplished. The principle of *delegating authority* is well-known in the field of business. Bernard Baruch made it clear that he would never do anything that he could get someone else to do.

Dwight L. Moody is quoted as saying, "It is better to get ten men to work than to do the work of ten men." Successful churches are built by pastors who are willing to apply the "Jethro principle."

Ordway Tead in his book *The Art of Leadership* writes:

In this connection, it is important for the leader in many cases to know how to make use of technical experts. He should be able to select experts shrewdly, to stimulate them to their best work and to use their findings judiciously without being overborne by them. The expert, it has been wisely said, should be on tap and not on top. And the good leader can greatly extend his area of effective work if he learns how to draw on experts while still keeping technical opinions in subordination to his own more inclusive and therefore truer perspective of what he and his group are trying to do.[5]

The pastor who puts his people to work and exerts the necessary leadership in seeing them through their various areas of service in the church will be a successful pastor.

An administrator is decisive in his work. Again Ordway Tead has written a wise word:

Ultimately the leader has to get results. There must be action and accomplishment. The group objective must be measurably realized. This is vital. To cut across indecision with decision, to galvanize indifference into enthusiastic performance, to translate doubt of possibilities into the swing of going actuality—to effect these transitions is the leader's peculiar prerogative and duty. . . . In a word, the demand is that the leader should take human experience in hand and resolutely make it eventuate in the direction he believes it should take. Dangers of his arbitrariness, of stubbornness, of too great rigidity of method there will be—real dangers to be guarded against. But the world waits, when it places individuals in positions of headship, upon their readiness to act—forcefully, vigorously, effectively, and rightly if possible—but to act so that the rest of us may with a certain relief throw off the incubus of vacillation and act too.[6]

Types of Administrative Responsibilities

General administration. By this we simply mean the general planning of the activities of the church, which involves direction and correlation; the overall blueprint of the church's program. Here, administration involves reviewing the major priorities in the church, its objectives, and the ways and means for achieving its goals. This involves *planning,* and it is the general overview that is vital here. Some of the specific areas of planning are:

1. Group planning by various committees as outlined in the bylaws and constitution.
2. Long-range planning including a one-year, two-year and even ten-year overall plan, showing the general direction of the church.
3. Planning for definite events such as evangelistic services, prophetic conferences, family conferences and missionary conferences.
4. The general long-range building program of the church.

Educational administration. This area includes Sunday School, Sunday evening training meetings, women's and men's fellowships, Awana clubs, home Bible study ministries, responsibilities to educational institutions such as local Christian day schools, colleges and seminaries. While there is need for specific details in these areas, it should be remembered that the general direction of the church ought to be spelled out by the pastor and various committees designated to assume responsibility as overseers on their specific projects.

Financial administration. Often the pastor is expected to be a financial wizard. More often than not he is not an expert in this area, for his training has not been along this line. Therefore, extra effort should be made to become more knowledgeable in the area of finance. One helpful book is *How to Carry Out God's Stewardship Plan* by Truman Dollar (Thomas Nelson, publisher, New York, 1975). Seminars on church finances are frequently available. Also the pastor should not be reluctant to learn from his own congregation. In many churches there are businessmen or certified public accountants (CPAs) who would be only too happy to help in these areas. A lot of listening and learning on the part of the pastor, especially the young pastor, will bring helpful dividends in future pastorates.

The detailed area of church finances can be dealt with more fully in a book strictly on church administration. Yet, because this is so crucial in the pastor's work, it will be helpful to list a number of principles regarding the subject.

1. Principles vital to churches of every size.

a. Dedicated personnel. Often when one thinks of the administration of the church finances, he thinks of a group of businessmen who have a greater financial acumen than spiritual. Frankly, this kind of thinking is often the basis for some of the greatest problems. The men involved, specifically the trustees, ought to be men of high Christian character, meeting the requirements set forth for deacons in 1 Timothy and Titus. If the trustees are considered as a non-Biblical, nondescript board with no standing or standards as far as the Scriptural context is concerned, the church is inviting problems. Therefore, the board of trustees, the treasurer, the financial secretary and the finance committee should be Spirit-filled believers, aware that the business part of the church requires spiritual insight as much as other areas of the ministry.

b. Officers in the business department. Officers in the business area of the church are designated in the bylaws and the constitution. The minimum of officers required to handle the church's finances efficiently are: trustees, church treasurer, financial secretary, a finance committee, and, if possible, a budget committee. If a church is incorporated, trustees are required by law. In larger churches a business manager may be hired as well as appropriate bookkeepers.

2. The financial budget. Every church ought to have a budget, the purpose of such being as follows:

a. It is a guide to the official board and the membership of the church as to where the church is going in its financial obligations for a fiscal year.

b. It is a means of measuring the progress of the church in its program of giving. Thus it can be used to challenge the people to increase their support of missions and other vital ministries.

c. It helps to eliminate impulsive, spur-of-the-moment decisions regarding the spending of funds.

d. It is a means of encouraging and urging a program of organized giving and tithing. When the people have the budget before them, they can rise to the challenge and prayerfully consider what increase God would have them make. A church budget will help the church members plan an increase of their giving into their own personal budgets.

3. The budget committee. Members of this committee are often specified in the bylaws and the constitution, but the budget committee should be comprised of the following officers: representatives of the board of deacons, Sunday School superintendent, Christian education director, trustees (two or three), the custodian, missionary committee chairman.

4. Procedure in church budgets. H. Linamen in his fine book, *Business Handbook for Churches,* says re-

garding the "Preparation of the Budget":

> The steps in the preparation of the budget will
> vary from one situation to another depending
> largely upon whether a budget has been in use
> formerly and the amount of information avail-
> able. If the church has previously used a bud-
> get, the following procedure might be followed:
> 1. *Estimate the anticipated income.*
> a. Collect income data from preceding two to four
> years. Trends in giving and relationships be-
> tween past pledges and budgeted income should
> be noted.
> b. Consider factors which may be expected to affect
> future income such as:
> Economic conditions. What are the business fore-
> casts for the coming year? Is information availa-
> ble concerning possible strikes? What are the
> trends in the cost of living? Will there be any new
> places of employment?
> Changes in membership. Is there any evidence
> indicating that present members may move or
> that new members will be coming into the congre-
> gation? How many of the younger members will be
> accepting positions and be in a position to contrib-
> ute a larger amount? What would be the effect of
> death or retirement of current members?
> Nature of the stewardship program. Has there
> been any change in the religious education pro-
> gram of the church which should be expected to af-
> fect giving?
> List the estimated sources of income and the
> amount expected from each. This represents the
> amount of income that is anticipated for the pur-
> pose of paying expenses.
> 2. *Estimate the expenses in terms of the anticipat-
>   ed needs of the congregation.*
> a. Ask the person responsible for each phase of the

church's work to submit a detailed statement indicating the estimated costs of the items required to carry out this program for the coming year. This list should represent the composite thinking of all the people in his department. There is a tendency for people to ask for more than is expected so evidence supporting the need for each of the items might well be included. In addition, the list should be arranged in the order of priority. Then, if adjustments have to be made in order to keep budgeted expenditures within anticipated income, the order of elimination will have already been determined.

b. Ask the treasurer to supply comparative information concerning the budget and actual expenditures for two to four of the most recent years and for the current year to date. A suitable form for assembling this type of information should be made. The data should indicate trends in spending and suggest whether the requests under 2a are realistic.

c. Divide the budget committee into study groups for the purpose of analyzing the information in 2a and 2b. For purpose of study and analysis, the Park Place Church of God, Anderson, Indiana, divides its budget into these phases: giving beyond operating expenses; salaries; religious education; upkeep and maintenance of buildings; publicity; stewardship, and general supplies for equipment; and robes, music and supplies for worship.

Each study group should recommend to the committee the amount it feels should be allowed for each expense that falls within its sphere of responsibility.

Care should be exercised so that the same classification of expenses is used for the budget and the accounting system. A general classification such as miscellaneous is meaningless and should be avoided.

d. Have the entire committee act upon the recommendations of the individual study groups. It may become necessary to trim certain items to keep the proposed budget within the expected income.

3. *Submit the proposed budget to the board of trustees.*

4. *Present the proposed budget to the entire congregation for adoption during the regular business meeting.*

The budget should be printed, or duplicated, and mailed to each member at least a week before the scheduled meeting. This gives each person an opportunity to study the budget so that he can ask questions and vote upon it intelligently. The vote on the budget should be by secret ballot. Three choices might be given: to accept; to reject; to accept with suggested modifications, which should be noted on the ballot. Although the suggestions might not affect the current budget, they should be noted by the budget committee for the following year. Those who plan the budget desire to know the specific points that do not meet the approval of individual members of the congregation.[7]

Administration Involves Working with People

We will consider first the pastor's relationship with the staff and then his relationship with the boards.

A. The church staff.

In order for a pastor to administrate properly he should be aware, not only of his responsibility as a pastor in relation to the staff, but of the various duties of the staff and their function in the overall church program.

The pastor. It is important to understand the pastor's role as an administrator in relationship to other members of the staff. The success of the staff in a church will depend to a great degree on his ability to lead them, to coordinate their activities, and to establish the kind of rapport with them which will promote a working relationship. There are a number of self-evaluation questions the pastor should consider which will help to put his relationship to the staff in the proper perspective. Some of them are as follows:

1. Am I aware of my place in the church with respect to my responsibility of leadership? That is, do I know that I am responsible for the leadership of the staff, or do I simply feel that I am one among the others, and the leadership should come from some other place?

2. Have I, as an administrator, weighed properly the function of each member of the staff? Is the staff member aware, as a result of my help and counsel, of his responsibilities and limitations?

3. Is there an understanding as to the "chain of command" between me and the staff?

4. Am I aware that this is more than a "boss" relationship, but rather a coordinator relationship, exerting strong leadership?

5. Are assignments made to members of the staff logically and clearly?

6. Is there a right and proper respect and appreciation for each member of the staff?

7. Are goals being set and periodically reviewed?

8. Have I established and properly implemented the calendar of activities of the church?

9. Is there proper oversight of members of the staff relative to their performance? Is there a rapport established between me and the staff members so that both the progress and difficulties can be considered without embarrassment?

10. Is there fairness on my part with respect to each member of the staff?

11. Is there a desire on the part of the members of the staff to respond to my leadership, and a desire on my part to help sympathetically with the particular functions of the staff members?

The custodian. Possibly the second person hired within a church, at least on a part-time basis, is the custodian. The custodial activities can vary as much as those of any other staff member, and perhaps in some cases much more, depending on the size of the church. Basically, the job of the custodian is to open and close the church for all major activities, to keep it clean and in good repair, and to be responsible for the maintenance of equipment, building and grounds. One of the problems faced by the custodian is in the fact that he has as many "bosses" as there are church members. This is unfortunate and should be corrected when it occurs. The custodian ought to be responsible to the pastor, or to someone appointed by the board of trustees. The pastor is the reasonable choice because he is on the premises more than the others, and he can be the liaison between the custodian and the trustees. While this may seem to bog the pastor down with mundane things, the benefits of the custodian being considered a part of the staff and responsible to the pastor far outweigh the liabilities. It is helpful if the pastor can set aside some time during the week, preferably in the morning hours, to sit down with the custodian, hear him out, and go over some of the activities of the week and any changes or adjustments which must be made.

The secretary. It is very difficult to understand how a church with a membership of over one hundred and fifty to two hundred manages to survive without a secretary. It is my judgment that a good secretary is indispensable to the proper function of the church. In many ways she can lighten the burden of the pastor as she manages the office, which is the hub of all church activities. The question often arises as to whether she is secretary to the church or to the pastor. In most cases it will be a combination of serving in both capacities. In all cases there should be some awareness of her responsibility to the pastor as the administrator. A good relationship between the pastor and the secretary is vital for the proper functioning of the local church. The employing should not be done impulsively but only after prayer and careful consideration. Often there are members of the church who do secretarial work and feel themselves qualified for such a function. It will be the better part of wisdom to act slowly with regard to this, even at the expense of being criticized. There are some who think the secretary is hardly more than an answering service and someone to talk to rather than someone who is working officially in the office. This is totally unsatisfactory. While a secretary often works as a receptionist, she is far more than this. A secretary should be a Spirit-filled Christian, loyal to the pastor and the church. She must be one who will hold confidences. Perhaps there is no area in church work in which a person should be more versatile. She ought to be skilled in office procedures and personal relationships. She will be called upon to operate the mimeograph machine, take dictation, write and type letters, and do a multitude of other jobs, too many to enumerate here.

Miss Daisy Lewie, the secretary of Temple Baptist Church, Tacoma, Washington, compiled the following list from her many years of experience:

a. Assist the pastor in all areas that he requires.
b. Greet the public.
   (1) By receiving and making telephone calls.

(2) By receiving and assisting visitors to the office.
c. Handle the mail.
(1) Sort the incoming mail and route each piece to the proper person.
(2) See that outgoing mail is properly addressed, stamped and mailed.
d. Take and transcribe dictation.
e. Keep a yearly church calendar.
(1) Check each day to be sure all appointments are kept.
(2) Check each day to be sure specified duties are performed.
f. Prepare publicity on church activities.
g. File correspondence and other material.
h. Mimeograph weekly church bulletin, mailings to the church membership, materials for various church groups.
i. Keep records.
(1) Those related to church membership.
(2) Those related to church activities.
(3) Those related to bookkeeping.

Many demands are made upon the church secretary, but she should do her best in serving the church, realizing that everything she does should be "With good will doing service, as to the Lord, and not to men" (Eph. 6:7).

Minister of visitation. The minister of visitation could be a man or a woman; the choice depends upon the visitation goals the church has in view. The work involves the following fields:

1. Calling on the sick and shut-ins. Often the minister of visitation will not only be helpful in giving spiritual counsel to individuals who are shut-ins but will also carry cassette tapes of the morning and evening services for them to hear.
2. Door-to-door visitation. This involves church and Sunday School visitation on a door-to-door

basis to enlist children and adults for the Sunday School and for the bus program.

3. New convert visitation. The worker will follow up new converts, particularly children, and seek to enroll them in a class to help them grow and walk in the Christian faith.

4. Follow-up visitation. This is a follow-up call on a person who has attended the church.

It is my feeling that a church which reaches the four or five hundred mark in membership should have a full-time visitation minister. This person will share the visitation responsibilities with the pastor. He may also launch out in special areas, particularly among retired people and young people.

Minister of youth. Paul Plew, minister of music and youth at Temple Baptist Church, Tacoma, Washington, has provided job descriptions for these ministries.

My philosophy of a youth director is that he be concerned primarily with the youth from Junior High through College age. He will assist and be concerned with younger ages such as in the Awana programs, VBS and camp programs; however, these groups will be more directly the field of concern for the Christian education director. The responsibilities of the minister of youth will include:

a. Personal study and evaluation of youth activities within the church; personal reading concerning trends in youth and youth-related literature.

b. Overseeing of youth groups already in action such as Junior High youth group, Senior High youth group and College/Career age; working with sponsors of all younger groups and starting new groups when none exist.

c. Planning with the workers of various youth groups for socials, retreats, Christian service assignments and other activities.

d. Working with youth sponsors to plan more effective programs and larger outreach; to have a planned system in mind whereby the youth take part extensively in their own program under proper leadership; to have the programs graded to the mature Christian, the young Christian and the unbeliever.

e. Having the minister of youth's office open regularly to young people for rap sessions, counsel, etc.

f. Having weekly Bible studies with young people in their homes; having sing-ins after services and other activities which will promote fellowship.

g. Visiting young people when necessary.

h. Promoting, with God's leading, the avenues of worship, fellowship, instruction and service in the life of a Christian young person.

Minister of music. Responsibilities will include:

a. Evaluation of entire music program.

b. Planning and instituting a graded-choir system.

   (1) Beginner choir—ages 4-5.

   (2) Primary choir—ages 6-8.

   (3) Junior choir—ages 9-12.

   (4) Youth and teen choir.

   (5) Adult choir.

c. Instituting other groups such as women's chorus, men's chorus, octets and ensembles within the different choirs, especially the adult choir.

d. Implementing a useful instrumental program.

e. Planning and rehearsing for full concerts on special occasions; i.e., Christmas, Easter, Thanksgiving, Spring, Patriotic.

f. Working with soloists and small ensembles who will sing for services and on radio; hearing them and helping them in the areas needed; being responsible for tape music library and all recording sessions.

g. Planning and conducting congregational singing for all services of the church.

h. Correlating music with value for the Sunday School, youth training programs and other agencies within the church.

i. Teaching a course related to music in the church as the need may demand, such as hymnology, conducting (for congregational singing), etc.

j. Helping individual choir members who may desire to improve their musical skills in voice, piano or organ; also orchestral instruments where possible.

k. Setting up a music council to assist the overall music program; revamping music library and music room.

l. Working closely with the pastor and correlating music with the message and mood of the service.

m. Setting up a schedule of personal practice time for special numbers within the church and for own improvement.

Christian education director. A Christian education director in the church can be simply a planner, which is certainly falling short of what he should be doing, or he can be an organizer who will exert leadership and implement plans. The Christian education director must be a self-motivator. He is a key individual in the developing and instituting of most programs within the church. In this capacity he will be directly responsible to the pastor and will work with him and other members of the staff in all church affairs. Some of his specific responsibilities are as follows:

a. Outline responsibilities and goals for committees and organizations.

b. Explain Christian workers' standards for those who are involved in areas of service in the church.

c. Aid in the enlistment of workers for service in the church.

d. Assist in setting goals and initiating programs for:

(1) Sunday School

(2) Training Hour

(3) Awana program

(4) Vacation Bible School

(5) Good News Clubs

(6) Library

(7) Camp ministries

(8) Audiovisuals

(9) Leadership education

(10) Athletics

(11) Classes for handicapped; mentally limited, deaf, etc.

(12) Classes for new believers and new members

(13) Junior church program

e. He will draft and define job descriptions for all of those in leadership.

(1) Sunday School superintendent

(2) Assistant to the Sunday School superintendent

(3) Vacation Bible School workers

(4) Training hour workers

(5) Librarian

(6) Awana workers

(7) Others involved in the educational programs of the church

f. He will lead the Christian education committee which is composed of the heads of the educational departments of the church.

g. He will be responsible for looking over the curriculum to see what best fits the needs of the church.

Assistant pastor. The assistant pastor's function is primarily to help carry the load of the pastor in his counseling and visitation work as well as in some of the preaching. In some churches the calling of an assistant pastor has presented problems between him and the pastor. This should not be. Two reasons for these unpleasant experiences may be briefly stated. First, there may be a failure to mark out the definite responsibilities and limitations of the assistant pastor. Second, there may be a failure on the part of the pastor to exert the type of leadership that is necessary. There is no reason why the assistant pastor should be a threat to the pastor as long as there is an understanding between them as to where his responsibility begins and ends.

B. The boards.

There are some very important areas that should be considered with regard to a pastor-board relationship.

The first relates to humility. The pastor should not assume the position of a dictator or lord over the board. He should pray for divine leadership; he should be considerate of each member of the board and work with them in a spirit of humility.

The second relates to tact. The pastor should be careful to exercise good common sense in approaching members of the board in outlining their work and when corrections are to be made. When differences occur and suggestions for change are given, they should be given in a spirit of helpfulness rather than destructive criticism.

The third consideration relates to conviction. There ought to be a spirit of both sincerity and conviction in the presentation of all matters or projects. Boards are not interested in proposals that have not been thought through and are offered in a "let's try it and see" attitude. There should be absolute conviction in one's mind that what is proposed is going to succeed as God enables.

In his book, *Building Better Churches,* G. S. Dobbins says:

> Let action rest on conviction, not on mere consent. Depend more on honest, intelligent prayer than upon human wisdom and shrewd practice. Base decisions, policies, courses of action on facts, not guesses, rumors, gossip, sentimental wishes. Keep uppermost always the eternal value of the individual. Cultivate the spirit of incurable optimism.[8]

The fourth suggestion is in reference to wisdom in leading the board to decisive action. In his book, *Church Management,* William H. Leach suggests a number of techniques which a minister can use to get the desired action through the proper board. He lists them as follows:

> 1. Never suggest a cold proposition. Any program that is worthwhile is worth warming before it is formally presented. If a man has sufficient strength, he might put through a new program unheard before the meeting, but it would not be fair to the program itself.
> 2. When you have a program to suggest, mention it long before the time it is introduced.
> 3. Get the sponsors for it before it is introduced. Let someone else introduce the subject. If no one is sufficiently interested to sponsor the matter, probably it should not be introduced anyway.
> 4. Do not ask for passage as a personal favor. If you do, you may get it. A board of honest men and women should never be asked to vote except to express their own convictions. The minister who makes the personal loyalty appeal is unfair to the proposition he proposes. If it is reasonable and he used the right technique, he can almost

surely get support. The personal favor appeal is too elementary.

5. Do not ask for a decision on any important matter until you know how it shall be put into effect.[9]

End Notes

[1] Arthur Merrihew Adams, *Pastoral Administration* (Philadelphia: Westminster Press, 1964), p. 15. Used by permission.

[2] Donald A.Laird and Eleanor C. Laird, *The Techniques of Getting Things Done* (NY: McGraw-Hill Book Co., 1957). Used by permission.

[3] Adams, *Pastoral Administration,* pp. 32-35.

[4] Andrew Watterson Blackwood, *Pastoral Leadership* (Nashville: Abingdon Press, 1949), p. 31. Used by permission.

[5] Ordway Tead, *The Art of Leadership* (NY: McGraw-Hill Book Co., 1935), p. 119. Used by permission.

[6] Ibid., pp. 120-122.

[7] J. H. Linamen, *Business Handbook for Churches* (Anderson, IN: Warner Press, 1958), pp. 122-125.

[8] G. S. Dobbins, *Building Better Churches* (Nashville: Broadman Press, n.d.), pp. 422-423.

[9] William H. Leach, *Handbook of Church Management* (Englewood Cliffs, NJ: Prentice-Hall, 1958), pp. 175-176. Used by permission.

CHAPTER SIX
The Pastor and His Time

One of the greatest frustrations in a pastor's life is the proper use of time. A poll of pastors revealed that the average minister puts in more than seventy hours each week. Leslie B. Flynn writes:

> Members of one congregation were asked to indicate on a questionnaire how many hours they felt their pastor should devote per week to each of the following tasks: preparing sermons, personal interviews, administrating the affairs of the church, committee meetings, budget planning and promotion, community activities, youth groups, comforting the bereaved, and advising those contemplating matrimony. Totals on the answers averaged eighty-two hours per week. One member proposed two hundred hours. (A week has only 168 hours.)[1]

The question is simple : how can the pastor get everything done that he should do? If anyone needs to study ways and means of getting things done and the proper utilization of time to do them, it is the pastor. Yet, pastors seem to be some of the most unorganized people in the world. Many probably have never had a lesson in college or seminary or read a book on time management. We need to consider several areas of time management where pastors could do a better job.

Activity Is not always Productivity

First, we need to agree that activity should not be regarded necessarily as productivity. Looking busy and keeping busy are not the same as being productive. The Foreign Legion saying, "When in doubt, gallop," is not the answer. I know many pastors who carry work home every evening and never seem to have a spare minute for their families or for just enjoying life. The story is told of a certain pastor who brought work home in his briefcase every night. His little daughter noticed it and asked her mother about it.

"Why does Daddy come home every night with so many books and things?" she asked.

"Well," answered her mother, "Daddy has so much work, he can't get it all done at the office."

"Why don't they put him in a slower class?" the little daughter inquired.

Good question! Looking busy, and telling others how hard you work, and never taking a day off does not always mean that you are overworked. It could mean that you are not as efficient in your use of time as you could be.

In the Office

Let's start with the office, or study. One writer suggests that we need to group our daily work into five categories: Important and Urgent, Important, but not Urgent, Urgent but not Important, Busy Work and Wasted Time. Take a moment and think this through. For a pastor there are many important and urgent areas. But would you agree that much of our time is in busy work?

One poet said it this way:

I've dusted my desk and I've wound up my
  watch,
I've tightened (then loosened) my belt by a notch.
I've polished my glasses, removed a small
  speck,

I've looked at my check stubs to check on a check.
I've searched for my tweezers and pulled out a
  hair,
I've opened a window to let in some air.
I've straightened a picture, I've swatted a fly,
I've shifted the tie clip that clips down my tie.
I've sharpened each pencil till sharp as a dirk. . .
I've run out of reasons for not starting work.

Richard Armour

Busy work is often put before the urgent and important. Edwin Bliss writes:

There are many tasks that are marginally
worth doing but are neither urgent nor important. We often do them ahead of more important
things because they are *diversionary*—they
provide a feeling of activity and accomplishment while giving us an excuse to put off tack-
ling those Category 2 tasks which have a far
greater benefit.
One aerospace executive, for example, told me
of coming to his office the previous Saturday
morning to do some work he had been postpon-
ing. He decided to organize the materials on his
desk. Having done so, he decided that while he
was at it he might as well straighten up the desk
drawers. He spent the rest of the morning reor-
ganizing drawers and files.
"I left the office feeling vaguely disappointed
that I hadn't accomplished what I went in for"
he said, "but I consoled myself with the thought
that I had been busy doing worthwhile things. I
was playing games with myself—working on
low-priority tasks, to give myself an excuse for
further delay on the far more essential task I
originally had assigned myself."[2]

Planning Your Day

So, when you come into your office in the morning, it should not be "hit or miss" and "where shall I begin." Rather, you must plan your work and work your plan. If you begin in a flurry of activity without planning your work, someone will do it for you. Remember, "He who rides a tiger can never dismount." So, if you start at it hard and heavy without having a plan, you might go home at night feeling tired but having been anything but productive.

We addressed the issue of study time in another part of this book. The need of hours designated for study is unquestionable. However, a great deal of a pastor's time will involve "office" chores—handling mail, working with committees, dealing with financial issues and solving the multitudinous problems in his day-to-day work as the "chief administrator" of the church and shepherd of the flock.

Identifying Time-Wasters

Ted Engstrom and R. Alec Mackenzie take a hard look at the most obvious "time-wasters" in the office:

Twenty-five heads of Christian organizations meeting in Chicago at a management seminar were asked to list the greatest time-robbers they faced. The following, not arranged in any particular order, were included in their list:

Misplaced items
Visitors (drop ins)
Unanticipated interruptions
Commuting
Long letters
Waiting for people
Failure to delegate
Mediocre personnel (instruction required)

Lack of preparation (conferences, etc.)
Correspondence delays (shuffling papers)
Reading material not relevant to job
Unnecessary correspondence (outgoing)
Telephone interruptions
Poor organization
Coffee breaks
Procrastination
Routine detail[3]

Procrastination: A Major Time-Waster

As much as we hate to admit it, procrastination—putting off the work—is one of our major problems. Pastors are like everyone else and often have a chronic case of the "I'm gonnas." Did you know that there is a National Procrastination Club? However, the members have never met! Guess why?

Procrastination is costly. Dale Carnegie remarked that we all dream of some magical rose garden over the horizon and don't enjoy the roses that are blooming outside our window. How many reading this book have always wanted to write a book? Chances are the desire will continue, but you will keep putting it off. Well has one said, "Procrastination is an immobilizer that blocks fulfillment." For the procrastinator, tomorrow never comes, only frustration and regret. But it doesn't have to be that way. There are ways to overcome it and be fruitful and productive. Let's consider some of them.

1. Acknowledge that you are a "put-it-off-er" and that you are going to do something about it.

2. Once you have planned your work—and established your goals—break the project down into smaller tasks and take them one at a time. A book begins with the first page. A jogging program begins with the first two hundred yards. A special effort in the church begins with its first presentation to a friend.

3. Set aside special blocks of time (however small) to work on your project. Get it on your calendar and don't cancel it (or put it off!).

4. Start it. If you are writing a book, get behind the typewriter, put your fingers on the keys—and press. It sounds silly, but it is so important. Begin! Start! Commence! Every writer will tell you that this is one of the most successful ways to overcome procrastination.

5. Work through moods. Control them; don't let them control you. Begin to work whether you feel like it or not. Soon you will be "on a roll" and doing the things you put off for so long.

Delegating

The subject of delegating has already been touched on in chapter 5, but it bears repeating because it has been one of the greatest helps to me in the ministry. Remember the clarity of the Scriptures on this subject: God gave pastors to perfect the saints for the work of the ministry (Eph. 4:12).

In his excellent book, *Working Smart*,[4] Michael Le-Boeuf lists reasons why the average person does not delegate. While he is not approaching the subject as it relates to the pastor, the reasons are still most appropriate.

1. "We believe it is a sign of weakness." Somehow we feel that as grown-up pastors who have trained for this work, we would be showing signs of inability if we asked someone to do something we could do ourselves. Here we usually don't practice what we preach. After all, we are but one member in the Body of Christ. How terrible to have "the ear" or "the mouth" in the Body seek to do what other members were designed to do in exercising their gifts.

2. "We believe it is immoral." The idea here is that we are to be working ourselves. It seems immoral to ask someone to do what we "get paid" to do. But remember, it

is our responsibility to equip others to work with us, not just for us.

3. "We want to do the job ourselves." After all, we can probably do it better. While this may be true, and while it is also true that showing another person how to do the job is time-consuming, you are in reality duplicating yourself. When I learned I could teach one hundred others to visit on Monday night, I discovered that I was multiplying myself one hundredfold and getting more done for the Lord.

4. "Fear of losing control." Now we come to the "nitty gritty" of the problem. This, I believe, is the major reason for not delegating. It is absurd to think we could lose our job to someone we ask to speak on a Wednesday night or to a group we ask to help visit. This fear is a classic sign of insecurity, and we need to spend time in prayerful thought over this weakness. Many churches are moving at a slow pace, and the pastors are wearing themselves out, because of such insecurities. What a beautiful thing it is to see gifted men and women in the church function in their gifts, led by a pastor who is more interested in the ministry of the church and glorifying Christ than he is in being in control.

So whether it is work in the office, chairmanship of a committee, involvement in evangelism or any other function, you will be more productive and make better use of your time if you learn to delegate.

One time expert put it this way:

The four steps in good executive administration are: analyze, organize, deputize, and supervise. Restating these points: survey the problem, design a plan, assign competent helpers, then call to accountability. With reference to the third step, sometimes in business when personnel is needed for a job, an executive will

often look for a man with unused ability, perhaps finding someone with not-so-obvious
qualifications. Sometimes a task is delegated to
a man with a weakness purposely to develop a
potential skill. One leader says, "Tell him
where to get information, challenge him, but let
the worker expend initiative and carry the
ball." . . . In deputizing his helpers the pastor
should inspire, motivate and create enthusiasm.[5]

The most obvious person to delegate to is a secretary.
This person should probably be the first employee hired
in the church after the pastor. I have known pastors who
waited for years before hiring a full-time secretary, and
as a result the progress of the church was slower than it
might have been. Delegating responsibilities to members of the board and other committees is also important.
Sharing the work of evangelism with other members of
the church is very Scriptural and will bring great dividends. Giving individuals in the church an opportunity
to exercise their gifts brings optimum performance, resulting in health and growth in the body. At the same
time, such delegation releases the pastor to give leadership in the many areas of service and worship in the
church.

End Notes

[1] Leslie B. Flynn, *How to Save Time in the Ministry*
(Grand Rapids: Baker Book House, 1975), p. 7. Used by
permission.

[2] Edwin C. Bliss, *Getting Things Done* (NY: Charles
Scribner's Sons, 1980), pp. 20-21. Used by permission.

[3] Ted W. Engstrom and R. Alec Mackenzie, *Managing Your Time* (Grand Rapids: Zondervan Books), p. 194.
Used by permission.

[4] Michael LeBoeuf, *Working Smart* (NY: Warner
Books), n.p. Used by permission.

[5] Flynn, *How to Save Time,* n.p.

CHAPTER SEVEN
The Pastor and the Computer

There is no question about it, this is the computer age. While our message is an old and reliable one, and even our methods are Biblically based, it is certainly reasonable to apply new technologies that will help us in the ministry. I have been involved in using a computer for several years. While I am not an expert, I find myself using my P.C. (personal computer) to great advantage. If a computer is viable for your particular situation, you need to consider some ways this modern convenience can be of help to you as a pastor.

Help in Writing

There are several good computer programs that will aid the pastor in his many writing responsibilities. Assuming that you can type (and if you can't, you can buy a program which, with the use of the computer, will help you learn), the P.C. will be invaluable in writing personal reports, messages, devotionals and any other kind of work that would ordinarily be done on the typewriter. While the faithful old typewriter is still valuable and useful, the computer will save you much time. Every pastor should have a computer just for the word processing system alone. I use the Word Perfect system, which has been most helpful. For example, this system has an outlining program which makes sermon outlining fast and easy. The text column feature is excellent for newsletters, inventory lists or any text that needs to be arranged in columns. Of course, the Word Perfect editing ability and the built-in speller with 100,000-plus word dictionary are very helpful. The thesaurus helps find the right word and displays synonyms and other words that point to similar ideas. Word Perfect does the searching and work. These are convenient and useful features.

Database Software

Those who want to go one step further will find some kind of a database software to be helpful. Database software is basically used to store information. It is designed so that you can set up a database according to your particular needs and store names, dates, prices—anything you want to file and of which you want to keep track. The material can be located within seconds. Again, like word processing, there are many such programs available at a whole range of prices. I would suggest that any person interested in buying database software consider various options in price and sophistication. I use the Nutshell Information Finder from Leading Edge. It is a rather simple, easy-to-use system and meets all my present needs. I file my books on this system. I still use the Dewey decimal system, but with the database I can bring up in seconds any book according to its title, subject or author. Pastors thinking of listing their books should consider such a system in place of a card index file. Other uses of this kind of system include keeping track of your sermons, Scripture memory work, calling files, inventories and financial accounts. There is no end to potential applications both in your personal life and in church business. A great many of the more expensive church software programs might be unnecessary if one learned to use a database system to meet his own personal and church needs. Information can be formatted in any way desirable, with layouts that are convenient and flexible.

Computers in the Study

The computer can help you in your study. One program that is most useful is The Word Processor. This company has several good Bible study tools which will be a help to the average pastor. The Word Processor gives you access to every verse and word in the Bible and allows you to call up that verse or word in seconds. It will search for a word or a phrase, create permanent concordances on any subject and even print any and all Bible text related to that subject. For example, I "asked" the program to find all references in the New Testament to the Holy Spirit. It did so in minutes and then spilled them out on my printer. If, on the other hand, you want to work within a certain range of Scripture (e.g., the book of Romans), you set the range and the program stays within those confines. An additional feature includes a place for a personal commentary on any verse in the Bible.

Another "tool" from the same people is The Greek Transliterator. "The text of the King James New Testament, with Strong's reference numbers assigned to the English words and with programs for searching for Greek words to show their English translations or for English words to show their Greek origins."[1]

These programs are not to be used as crutches. Rather, they are time-savers; that is, they eliminate some routine time-consuming work, such as looking up passages, so that you are free for quality concentration and study.

Overhead Transparencies

Space will permit discussion of only one more program that can be used by the pastor, a program for designing overhead transparencies. Many of us have spent hours designing transparencies to be used in our teaching ministries. To eliminate some of those hours, I have been using a program called Fontasy, a system of on screen fonts and drawings. Over 275 fonts are available. You can draw or print using the many features and designs available. Then, when the lettering or drawing is printed, this copy can be used to make transparencies. (Transparencies cannot be made directly on Fontasy.) The beauty of this program is that you can make beautiful, professional-looking transparencies in minutes instead of hours. Of course the program can be used also for signs, invitations, newsletters, pie charts, greeting cards and other programs requiring layouts. My principle use of the program, however, is for my overhead projector, and it has proved invaluable.

Once you purchase a computer and begin to use it you will find multitudinous uses for it. For example, there is a program I use for my personal calendar and in which I can store information concerning special dates. In one program, in addition to a calendar there is a time clock, a note pad (which can be used for taking notes, even when you are in another program), a calculator and a phone dialer. Information from outside sources (libraries, news lines, etc.) can be brought in with the use of a telephone line, providing you have a modem. The possibilities are endless for accessing libraries throughout the world to aid you in your work.

Yes, we are living in a computer world. It is surprising how many people are afraid of computers. To be sure, nothing will ever take the place of hard study and deep meditation and prayer. There are some areas in our lives and in our studies that cannot be helped by shortcuts. But, like any other tool, the computer can be a help or a hindrance. One thing is sure, it is here to stay, and those who use it wisely will find that it is a friend.

End Notes

[1]From a brochure, Bible Research Systems, Austin, Texas.

CHAPTER EIGHT
The Way the Pastor Looks and Feels

This chapter deals with the "outward man," the person everybody sees. In other words, we are about to deal with the physical rather than the strictly spiritual. The fact is, however, that if we do not feel right physically, it could affect our work for the Lord. The claim that what is on the inside is most important is certainly valid. Christ spoke of those who were proper on the outside but had sinful hearts. However, it should not be an "either-or" matter. It is refreshing to find a person, living in a day-by-day close relationship with Christ, who emphasizes the spiritual but at the same time takes good care of his body.

The Way You Feel

It is true that some of the greatest pastors have had lifelong infirmities. Sometimes these weaknesses made them stronger spiritually. More often than not, the infirmity was not the result of neglect of the body. God in His sovereignty has not assured us of good health, but no one can deny that we need to do all we can to be in good physical condition so that we are able to function to our maximum in our work.

The Way You Look

In general, how would you describe what preachers look like? If you answer that they are fat, frumpy little fellows, I for one don't feel flattered. The way you look depends on what you put into your body, what you do with your body and what you wear on your body. Contrary to popular opinion, these are important factors in the ministry, and we should consider them one by one.

The Way You Eat

In his excellent book, *The Aerobics Program for Total Well-Being,* Kenneth H. Cooper gives eight basic principles for establishing a healthy balance in one's eating habits.

> 1. Strike a 50-20-30 percentage balance among the three main food types. To keep your energy at peak levels, your daily intake of calories should be distributed so that about 50 percent come from complex carbohydrates, 20 percent from protein, and 30 percent from fats.
> 2. ... I recommend that you still eat most of your calories before supper, with a 25-30-45 percentage approach (25 percent of your calories at breakfast, 30 percent at lunch, and 45 percent at dinner).
> 3. Do your aerobic exercise at the end of the day, just before the evening meal, to depress the appetite and thus enhance weight loss and maintain your ideal weight.
> 4. Develop a healthy fear of obesity, which may be a more mysterious killer than many people today suspect.
> 5. Avoid an imbalance in your eating in the direction of consuming too few calories. This mistake can be deadly, especially for those who engage in very strenuous and prolonged aerobic exercise.
> 6. Know the scientific formula for determining your ideal weight.
> 7. Learn the formula for determining the number of calories you need to take in each day to

maintain your ideal weight.

8. If you're overweight, establish a P.E.P. (Positive Eating Plan) diet to get yourself off the "roller-coaster effect" of constant weight gain and weight loss.[1]

I recommend that our readers get this book and "devour" it because it emphasizes a balanced program in exercise, diet and emotional health.

Someone has said that people who say they are on a diet are "wishful shrinkers." It is true that most of us at one time or another have decided that enough was enough and started on a crash diet, only to find ourselves falling back into the same eating habits and often putting on more weight. Breaking through the "pound barrier" is tough. It requires more than a half-serious attempt. If temperance (self-control) is a fruit of the Spirit (Gal. 5:22, 23), then it is proper that we ask the Lord to help us keep our weight under control. It is hardly a good testimony for us to preach about the need to shun tobacco and liquor when we are not watching our food intake. Consistency in this matter of respect for the "temple of the Holy Spirit" will be a testimony to the world that we are serious about the body God has given us (1 Cor. 6:19).

Exercise

Every Christian minister who wants not only to feel good but to be at "peak performance" in his day-to-day living ought to be involved in some kind of exercise program. An hour and a half per week in some kind of aerobic exercise program could give you more energy, help you control your weight, increase your productivity and even help you in stressful situations so common to the pastor. Add to this list protection from dreaded heart disease and you have more than enough reasons for such an investment. What is aerobic exercise? Let's turn again to our expert for help.

Aerobic exercises refer to those activities that require oxygen for prolonged periods and place such demands on the body that it is required to improve its capacity to handle oxygen. As a result of aerobic exercise, there are beneficial changes that occur in the lungs, the heart, and the vascular system. More specifically, regular exercise of this type enhances the ability of the body to move air into and out of the lungs; the total blood volume increases; and the blood becomes better equipped to transport oxygen.... Aerobic exercises usually involve endurance activities which don't require excessive speed. In fact, when recommending various kinds of aerobic exercise, I always stress that it's better to use long, slow distances (or "L.S.D.") than it is to rely on short, fast bursts of energy.[2]

There is a whole range of exercises that can have an aerobic effect, including walking, running, swimming, handball, racquetball and tennis. The idea is sustained exercise. I have been involved in a scheduled exercise program for over a year. My routine includes jogging at least two miles three to four times a week and playing tennis about twice a week, generally on the days I do not jog. The difference in the way I feel is most encouraging. Some of my friends find walking more exhilarating. One problem, of course, is that some exercise (such as walking or playing doubles tennis) takes a little longer for the aerobic effect. However, these exercises are still beneficial. The details for figuring out the "aerobic points" for different exercises and times must be left for other reading. (Again, I would suggest Cooper's book.) Nor will we consider all the benefits. I do, however, want to emphasize one benefit that I feel in itself is reason enough for a pastor to start exercising. I speak of the "stress reduction factor." Frankly, this was the main reason I started my routine. I came home at night "stressed out" as a result of the pressures and demands of the day. It is not a matter of "rolling your burdens on the Lord." The fact is, we have bodies and they are under pressure. Those of us with pressure jobs ought to be aware of ways of coping with these pressures more effectively. Cooper writes:

> I've taught many of my keyed-up executives, both men and women, to exercise at the end of the day as a means of "burning up" the stress physiologically, the way nature meant for it to be handled. Why should exercise at the end of the day be such a great benefit in reducing stress and anxiety levels? . . . For one thing, it's likely that increasing the metabolism helps you dissipate the effect of the accumulated adrenal secretions that are still readying you for a fight or flight response. If you're keyed up from a high level of these hormones, your body is chemically out of balance, and you can't hope to achieve a relaxed feeling of well-being until that situation is corrected. Exercise apparently acts as nature's waste-removal process and helps your body return to a more relaxed state of equilibrium.[3]

I can personally testify that often at the end of the day, after I have jogged two or three miles and showered, I feel as though I were just starting the day, and I am ready to attack the responsibilities of the evening schedule. I would urge all Christian workers to give serious consideration to an exercise program.

Some Help in Getting Started

Here are some suggestions to help you in your own routine.

1. Set a certain hour every day for exercise.
2. Find a partner who will exercise with you. Sometimes it is helpful having someone to whom you are accountable.
3. Keep a record of how much you exercise and total it every week. This is my practice and I find it helpful and encouraging. (I log it on my computer!)
4. Share the results with others such as your wife or friends in the office. Sometimes a public commitment to a program will help you stick to it.
5. Do not be discouraged if you miss a day or so. Keep at it and be "religious" in your commitment to be in good shape.

You will feel better, look better, preach better and become a good example for others to follow.

The Way You Dress

When we discuss the importance of dress, it seems contrary, again, to what we have been taught about the real person and the danger of emphasizing the outward appearance. But, whether we like it or not, many first impressions about us come from the way we look. William Thourlby, in his book *You Are What You Wear,* stresses:

> When you step into a room, even though no one in that room knows you or has seen you before, they will make ten decisions about you based solely on your appearance. They may make many more, but you can be assured that they will make these:
> 1. Your economic level
> 2. Your educational level
> 3. Your trustworthiness
> 4. Your social position
> 5. Your level of sophistication
> 6. Your economic heritage
> 7. Your social heritage

8. Your educational heritage
9. Your success
10. Your moral character[4]

You may find yourself resenting what you have just read. But before you begin preaching against it, let me add that while such conclusions may be unfair and incorrect we should make sure that the way we look does not stand in the way of our message.

In his excellent work *Dress for Success,* John T. Molloy has researched the impressions that are made by what we wear. In one section, "How 100 Top Executives Described Successful Dress," he writes: "I asked several series of questions of 100 top executives in either medium-sized or major American corporations. The first series was to establish the most up-to-date attitudes on corporate dress."[5]

Some of the questions he asked these men, after showing them pictures of a variety of clothing, included these:

> "Would a number of men at your firm have a much better chance of getting ahead if they knew how to dress?" Ninety-six said yes, four said no.
> Another question was: "If there were a course in how to dress for business, would you send your son?" All 100 answered in the affirmative.
> "Do you think employee dress affects the general tone of the office?" was asked with a 100% yes response.
> Another question was, "Would you hold up the promotion of a man who didn't dress properly?" Seventy-two said yes, twenty-eight answered in the negative.[6]

Again, the way we look speaks volumes to people and we cannot ignore it.

We will take time to touch on various areas of the pastor's wardrobe in the hope that you will do more serious study on this subject.

Suits

Most pastors wear a suit every day. While I am aware that many pastors do not have the finances to invest in several suits, it is important to choose the right material and colors of the suits you are going to wear. Have you ever seen a pastor wearing a shiny, purple polyester suit that is too small for him, with a garish tie to match? While it is tempting to consider the psychological impact of various colors and patterns on different people, I will leave that to your further study. I would simply suggest that you find a salesman you can trust and buy most of your suits from one store. If you are fortunate enough to have four or five suits of good quality and you keep them clean and pressed, you will feel good and look good in them. Generally you should wear suits, not sport coats. Also, you probably should wear a dress shirt and tie, not a sport shirt. Be careful not to wear wide ties when thin ones are in. Practice on various kinds of knots in your ties—the Windsor, the Half-Windsor, the Four-in-Hand knot. Ask around: you will get help in how to tie them. Molloy states: "The tie is probably the single most important denominator of social status for a man in the United States today. Show me a man's ties and I will tell you who he is, or who he is trying to be."[7]

Again, if you bristle a little when you hear that a tie is a symbol of respectability and responsibility, just remember, it does matter how you look. What do you think Paul meant when he said, "I am made all things to all men, that I might by all means save some" (1 Cor. 9:22)? Certainly that verse has been ripped out of context, and it does not mean that we are at liberty to go anywhere or do anything if it gives us the opportunity to witness. Paul is not saying that the end justifies the means. Instead, he seems to be saying that he is willing to conform to the customs of the Jew and to any cultural expectation in order to reach the lost. He is speaking of conformity without compromise. It is simply adaptation to custom, a principle that would be applied on the mission field. Applied to the subject of dress, the principle is to make an effort not to stand out like a Christmas tree, or like a peculiar fellow. We should not be drawing attention to ourselves with poorly chosen clothes. A rather good practice is to ask your wife about your "color combination" or how a tie looks. She may be able to help you with color, pattern, material, and help match a tie with the suit. I have found my wife's advice very helpful. (For some reason our wives seem to know more about these things than we do.) Don't be insulted when you find her sighing occasionally over the combination you have chosen. Incidentally, the length of a tie is important too. Have you ever seen a person with a tie that is not long enough and leaves a large space of shirt eight to ten inches above the belt? The tip of the tie should come to the belt-line.

When it comes to shirts, white or pastel-colored seem best for most of us. Also, make sure they fit. A shirt that is too tight and gives a "bulging look," stretched around the buttons, is hardly flattering. Tapered shirts, designed for a man in his twenties, look frightful on a fifty-year-old man. Most of us are fooling ourselves if we think we look the same as we did thirty years ago. Shoes should be polished and socks should come up over the calf. It is not flattering to see a minister cross his leg on the platform with his trousers slightly up and lots of skin showing. (I don't know any more polite way of stating this; think about it.)

I suppose the key is to dress conservatively and not draw attention to ourselves by standing out as either a ministerial "fashion plate" or with a garish, disheveled, unkempt look.

Again, let me state that I realize many pastors cannot afford to dress "well." However, here are some general rules that may help you no matter what your financial status.

> 1. Be sure that you are always clean. (This goes for hair, face and nails as well as clothes.)
> 2. Don't put dressing on your hair that makes it look slick or greasy.
> 3. Wear only jewelry that is functional.
> 4. Avoid clothes that appear feminine.
> 5. Dress conservatively when in doubt.
> 6. Don't make a habit of taking off your jacket in public. (I apply this rule especially when I am preaching, even when the room is hot and sticky.)

John T. Molloy adds:

> I recommend that every morning before you leave home, you station yourself in front of a full-length mirror for a minute or two. You don't have to do anything else. Questions about your dress will arise in your mind and after some thought, will answer themselves. When you do this, give yourself about ten extra minutes to get out of the house, because you'll find yourself changing clothes on many mornings.[8]

It is my personal conviction that a pastor should not be seen in public in shorts, jeans or work clothes. While eyebrows might rise at this one, I repeat that unless we are a part of a work party at the church, we should confine such dress to our homes. If this attitude seems somewhat extreme, I only ask that you give it some serious consideration before you disagree. Take time to read the two fine books from which we have quoted. Keep your eyes open as to the ways others dress. When you see something offensive, rather than criticize, learn from what you see. In other words, do all you can to let even your dress be a credit to the Lord you serve.

End Notes

[1] Kenneth H. Cooper, *The Aerobics Program for Total Well-Being* (New York: Bantam Books, 1982), n.p. Used by permission.

[2] Ibid., p. 13.

[3] Ibid., p. 191.

[4] William Thourlby, *You Are What You Wear* (NY: New American Library, 1978), n.p. Used by permission.

[5] John T. Molloy, *Dress for Success* (NY: Warner Books, n.d.), p. 35.Used by permission.

[6] Ibid., p. 36.

[7] Ibid., p. 75.

[8] Ibid., p. 149.

CHAPTER NINE
The Pastor and Evangelism

Charles Spurgeon, in his book entitled *The Soul Winner,* wrote:

> Our main business, brethren, is to win souls. Like the shoeing-smiths we need to know a great many things; but, just as the smith must know about horses, and how to make shoes for them, so we must know about souls and how to win them for God.[1]

This chapter, therefore, is a *must* chapter. If the pastor is an administrator and not a soul-winner, he is hardly more than any business or professional man of the world. His sermons must be preached with the needs of men in view. Although all of his messages may not be evangelistic in the sense that evangelism is the only purpose in them, every message ought to have an evangelistic note.

"Like preacher, like people" is a rather worn-out phrase, yet it adequately describes the condition of many churches. The people in the churches are not winning souls because the pastors are not doing so. Often a pastor will consider himself a teacher (the scholarly type!) with a minimal interest in evangelism. Again, what is needed is balance! Balance!

There ought to be an intense desire to be a well-balanced, all-around pastor with an intense love for the

Lord and His people and a burning, soul-winning heart for the lost and dying without Christ. Any man who feels that it is an "either/or" proposition with regard to evangelism and teaching ought to consider the twentieth chapter of Acts. It would not be amiss to read it daily until one is fully persuaded that the scholarly Paul was also a man who had a burning compassion for the lost.

One of the greatest responsibilities of the pastor is not only to be evangelistic himself, but to lead his people in an all-out ministry of evangelism.

Part One: Visitation Evangelism— Organized Obedience [2]

This is a day when everyone seems to be taken up with something new, including those in the field of theology. There is neoorthodoxy, neoevangelicalism, new morality; indeed, new "everything-ism." This is a fast-moving world. Mankind seems ever to have its head turned to the latest innovation. It is said that if history could be compressed into a twenty-four-hour period, more progress has been made in the last three seconds than the remaining twenty-three hours, fifty-nine minutes and fifty-seven seconds. There seems to be no end of new things appearing on the scene.

On the other hand, there are some things that are not new; any attempt to improve or revise them would be their ruin. The gospel, for instance, is the same old story that it was two thousand years ago when it was preached by our Lord Himself. While church buildings might be subject to architectural innovations, the church itself, comprised of baptized believers, should be the same today as it was in the New Testament. It stands to reason, therefore, that in this society, with its emphasis on development and change, the Bible-believing child of God should take a long, hard look at any program that appears to be different.

In discussing visitation, the first reaction that often comes from some well-meaning people is that this must be some newfangled program in a society caught up with the new. In this everybody's-got-a-gimmick world, it is no wonder that such an observation might be made. Therefore, it is most important to establish at the outset that visitation evangelism is not a newfangled, Johnny-come-lately program. The only thing new about it is that it is New Testament. It is not man's program but God's! Nothing is more disgusting than to observe what is taking place in the world today in religious circles. Man's attempt to revamp and improve on God's program has brought professing Christendom to an all-time low. Shame on those groups who couple Madison Avenue techniques with Hollywood glamour to replace the old-fashioned Holy Spirit power in the church!

Shame on the church which, while pretending to hold to its old-fashioned religion, is sitting on its orthodoxy and singing, "Anywhere with Jesus, I can go to sleep." Care must be taken not to equate slothfulness with spirituality, or to disguise failure to grow with the excuse of taking a stand, thus declaring that increases in attendance are almost impossible. It is difficult to tell which is worse, innovation or petrification—a watered-down program or a drying-up program!

The devil's message with divine methods. What ought to break the heart of every true Christian is the fact that the devil's crowd is using God's method (door-to-door visitation) with the devil's message—and getting results!

In fifty years the Mormon church has increased over five hundred percent. As I write these lines, one-third of their young people are out in the field from daylight to dark, five days a week, doing door-to-door evangelism. They average twenty thousand converts per year through this method. Theirs is one of the fastest growing cults in the world.

Take the so-called Jehovah's Witnesses. Many of them are lacking in grace; they are fanatical and determined! Yet this group averages over ten hours a witness per month in door-to-door evangelism. In one year they spent 132,695,540 hours going every Sunday morning spreading their erroneous doctrine. They get into one out of every seven homes. Persistence and hard work have made this cult, also, one of the fastest growing in the world.

What has happened? Too often our churches have the right message and the wrong method. These groups have the wrong message and the right method. While they are growing with their false doctrines, many of our churches are drying up. We are not doing the job as we ought to do it! May God give us the grace to face up to it!

The greatest drawback with most of our churches is the lack of old-fashioned zeal for the Lord and a passion for lost souls. Visitation evangelism *will work* in your town. There are churches all over the land that have dared to obey the Lord and stepped out in faith. These churches are moving ahead. Pastors and churches must stop rationalizing their failure to go and grow. They must face up to the real problem of indifference and a lack of faith.

Many of our churches today need to confess their neglect to the Lord and get about the business God has called them to do. They must get busy in *organized obedience.*

Growth through God's Method

Let us consider some of the major passages in the Word that show the growth of God's people when God's methods are used. These verses are not new. They have been quoted for years as a basis for visitation evangelism, but they never lose their freshness as they are applied to believers' hearts and to the program of their churches.

> And it came to pass afterward, that he went throughout every city and village, preaching and shewing the glad tidings of the kingdom of God: and the twelve were with him (Luke 8:1).

The method of our Lord was simple. It was "*every city and village.*" Christ was thorough in His outreach. It was total evangelism. The *message* was the glad tidings of the kingdom; the *method* was to go to every city and village.

This involved His personal attention to personal evangelism along with the Twelve. This was, without a doubt, a training period for these disciples. He was the master personal worker, as a reading of the Gospel of John will show. He is seen dealing with individuals more than He is preaching to crowds!

> After these things the Lord appointed other seventy also, and sent them two and two before his face into every city and place, whither he himself would come. (Luke 10:1).

The Lord appointed the seventy to go out two by two. Note carefully His method. Thirty-five teams were established, two on each team. And, consistent with His earlier plan, they were sent to *every city and place*. Then we read:

> Therefore said he unto them, The harvest truly is great, but the labourers are few: pray ye therefore the Lord of the harvest, that he would send forth labourers into his harvest. Go your ways: behold, I send you forth as lambs among wolves (Luke 10:2, 3).

Note the order: *pray ye;* then, *go ye.* A man who prays and does not go is lazy and inconsistent. Bent knees and lazy legs do not go together. Such a person's insincere prayers never get beyond the ceiling. On the other hand, a man who goes and does not pray is a presumptuous fool. It is hard to decide which is worse: a lazy lounger or a presumptuous fool. God's powerful combination is *pray;* then *go.*

What will be the result? In Luke 10:19 Jesus said, "Behold, I give unto you power." What a promise! In the events described here the power, peculiar to the age before the Bible was complete, was one of signs and miracles. The important implication for today is that of obeying God's command in praying and going. Burdened hearts in praying and blistered feet in going will terminate in powerful results.

Christ said, "All power is given unto me in heaven and in earth. Go ye therefore" (Matt. 28:18, 19a). Again, "But ye shall receive power, after that the Holy Ghost is come upon you: and ye shall be witnesses unto me both in Jerusalem, and in all Judaea, and in Samaria, and unto the uttermost part of the earth" (Acts 1:8).

Pray! Go! Power! That is the divine combination. It always works; it never fails. The disciples went two and two . . . thirty-five teams . . . door-to-door . . . in the power of the Lord. This is clearly the Lord's method. His disciples were getting invaluable training which would be used in the days to come.

> And in those days Peter stood up in the midst of the disciples . . . (the number of names together were about an hundred and twenty) (Acts 1:15).

Occasionally one comes across a person who holds to the belief that if something is big it is bad. Growth, to that person, is a sign of compromise; progress and advancement are signs of letting down the bars. He has come to believe that numbers are nonsense and that quantity and quality can never live together.

To be sure, "growth at any price" is a downright sin. On the other hand, God is interested in the growth and advance of His church. Why did God the Holy Spirit lead Dr. Luke to write that parenthetical statement, "The number of names together were about an hundred and twenty"? Because God is interested in numbers! Numbers represent people, and people are the recipients of this message of the gospel.

Generally, anything that is important to a person is numbered and counted. Ask someone "How many children do you have?" I cannot imagine him saying, "Oh, three or four." "Say, how much money do you have in the bank?" "Oh, give or take a thousand, I have. . . ." "How many hours did you report last week at your place of employment?" He would know exactly how many hours he worked and exactly how much per hour he made. Why? Wages are important to him. He has mouths to feed, bills to pay. His weekly paycheck is serious business. Yes, if it is of any value, it will be counted.

How much more important is this principle when we are dealing with the recipients of the most important message in the world. How much more important is it when we are dealing with the most valuable commodity in the world—souls. Yes, God the Spirit is interested in numbers and we should be also.

Then they that gladly received his word were baptized: and the same day there were added unto them about three thousand souls (Acts 2:41).

Added unto what? Obviously, the one hundred twenty of the first chapter. That is a total of 3,120. The number is growing!

Howbeit many of them which heard the word believed; and the number of the men was [or, more
literally, came to be] about five thousand (Acts
4:4).

Now note—there were 120, then 3,000. Between Acts
2:41 and Acts 4:4, 1,880 were added. This makes a total of
5,000. Yes, indeed, there was growth!

Thus far in this study we have not seen any compromise, any doctrinal vacillation, any theological aberra-
tion, any invertebrate theology, any "India rubber" conviction. Yet, there was healthy growth. The church advanced spiritually and numerically.

And believers were the more added to the Lord,
multitudes both of men and women (Acts 5:14).

This verse speaks for itself. Converts were still being
added.

And in those days, when the number of disciples was multiplied, there arose a murmuring
of the Grecians against the Hebrews (Acts 6:1).

Someone has pointed out that the mathematics have
changed—from adding to multiplying. The church is
growing to gargantuan proportions. The first mention
of a problem in the church is the result of growth. If problems are going to exist (and we are convinced that even
the best church has them), why not have problems resulting from growth? Growth in a church will solve more
problems than it creates. A working, active membership is less likely to find fault and quarrel with one another. One of the best remedies for a bickering, biting, acri-
monious membership is to give them a steady diet of the
Word and get them involved in some old-fashioned door-
to-door work.

And the word of God increased; and the number of the disciples multiplied in Jerusalem greatly; and a great company of the priests were obedient to the faith (Acts 6:7).

God is seen honoring His people's obedience. Some of the group, the priests, who had seemed impossible to reach, were coming to Christ. In response to obedience, the Lord began to do what seemed, at first, to be impossible.

How large was the church at Jerusalem? There have been estimates ranging from 65,000 to 250,000. One thing is sure, it was no secret that something was going on and the church was growing.

How did they do it? What was the secret? Whatever it was, do you not covet the same power and those same results? Can you be satisfied with what you are when you see in this chapter what can be done in a community?

And when they had brought them, they set them before the council: and the high priest asked them, Saying, Did not we straitly command you that ye should not teach in this name? and, behold, ye have filled Jerusalem with your doctrine, and intend to bring this man's blood upon us (Acts 5:27, 28).

This passage shows the impact of the church and its ministry. The apostles had preached the Word and caused no little concern to the magistrates.

There is no doubt about it; few churches today make such a stir. One wonders, sometimes, if people even know that the church exists in town. How many city councils in America have had to meet to decide what they were going to do with gospel-preaching churches because they were causing an upheaval in the town and filling the city with their doctrine?

How did these early believers do it? What is the answer? The next passage will help us.

> And when they had called the apostles, and beaten them, they commanded that they should not speak in the name of Jesus, and let them go. And they departed from the presence of the council, rejoicing that they were counted worthy to suffer shame for his name. And daily in the temple, and in every house, they ceased not to teach and preach Jesus Christ (Acts 5:40-42).

That is the answer! Every house! Every house! Every house! This was the text of the first message Charles Spurgeon delivered in the new Spurgeon Tabernacle in London.

Visitation evangelism is the answer, and *every house* is the way it is done. This is the Biblical basis for it! "Every house" evangelism in our cities would turn them upside down (or, should I say, right side up).

No doubt there were many excuses stating why it could not be done. If one were looking for an excuse, one of the most evident arguments would be the lacerated backs from the beating just received. It is not easy to make one's way up and down the dark streets and alleys of a city after being mistreated, hated and pummeled by religious antagonists. Why did the apostles persist? Their answer was plain: "We ought to obey God rather than men" (Acts 5:29). Yes, *House-to-house evangelism is obeying God!*

Visualize Peter and John involved in visitation evangelism, having the same spirit and feeling about it that we often have. It might go something like this:

Peter and John are making their way down Main Street. Needless to say, they are a little nervous, aware as they are of the general attitude of people toward them.

They are talking in whispers.

> *Peter:* Now, John, as we make this church canvass, we ought to get together and work out a system.
>
> *John:* That's fine with me, Peter; what do you suggest?
>
> *Peter:* Well, here's how we'll do it. As we approach this house, being that I'm a little better talker than you are, I'll talk and you do the knocking. Then, I will tell the people who we are, why we are here, give a witness for the Lord and invite them to our services. Then, when I am finished, you give them a gospel tract.
>
> *John:* Sounds good to me, Peter. Now, here is the first house. Are you ready?
>
> *Peter:* Ready; go ahead and knock.
>
> *John (hesitating):* Say, Peter—
>
> *Peter:* Go on, John, what are you waiting for? Knock!
>
> *John:* But, Peter, you don't understand; I can't. It won't really do any good.
>
> *Peter:* Now, really, John! Why?
>
> *John:* Well, I happen to know who lives here, Peter.
>
> *Peter:* Who?
>
> *John:* Well, a Jew lives here. These are Jews, orthodox Jews.
>
> *Peter:* Really? A Jew? A Son of Abraham? And orthodox?
>
> *John:* That's right! And everyone knows that Jews can't be saved; that is, it's terribly hard to reach them.
>
> *Peter:* Well, John, what should we do?
>
> *John:* Let's try the next house. The procedure will be the same; I'll knock and you do the talking.
>
> *Peter:* Here we are, John, knock. Say, John, are you thinking the same thing I am?
>
> *John:* I'm afraid so. A Jew lives here too!

Peter: Say, what town is this anyway?
John: It's Jerusalem . . . JERUSALEM!
Peter: JERUSALEM! Why, they are *all* Jews. This town is an impossible situation!

Now, of course, the story is ridiculous, and you are right if you think I have gone overboard. But what I have written is no more ridiculous than the excuses church members give today for not obeying the Lord. In my traveling and presenting the calling program to churches, I have heard almost every conceivable reason why "It won't work in our town." Sometimes it is because "The Methodists have taken over." Or it may be the Mormons or the modernists. Some have claimed their town is inhabited mostly by older people or by a disinterested, educated class of people.

Each of the above excuses has been accompanied by the words, "No, it won't work in our town. This is a hard city." There is probably no more hackneyed, worn-out, dilapidated claim than this one: This is a *hard city*. Every city is hard! Every town is difficult!

Yet you could not find a more difficult situation than this one in Acts. Christ had just been crucified! The Jews were opposed to Christians because of their religious faith and objectives. The Romans were antagonistic to Christianity because there was an allegiance to someone other than Caesar. The whole city of Jerusalem was steeped in the Jewish religion. The Jews were as narrow and insular as one group of people could get. No council of churches or opposing force has ever existed to equal the one in that day of the early church. The cost of standing for Christ often meant laying down one's life. Nevertheless, the Christians obeyed the Lord. They went house to house! Every house! Every house in Jerusalem! They filled the whole city with their doctrine!

Starting a Visitation Program

Did you know there is a pernicious punctuation mark in the Bible? That's right; there is one little "carnal comma" which, if left undisturbed, is both troublesome and damaging to the growth of the local New Testament church.

It is found in Ephesians 4. The King James Version renders it, "And he gave some, apostles; and some, prophets; and some, evangelists; and some, pastors and teachers; for the perfecting of the saints, for the work of the ministry, for the edifying of the body of Christ" (vv. 11, 12). While there are six commas in the passage, only one ruins the real sense and meaning of the passage.

Leaving the words exactly as they are and omitting one punctuation mark, the passage reads: "And he gave some some, apostles; and some, prophets; and some, evangelists; and some, pastors and teachers; For the perfecting of the saints for the work of the ministry." You will note that there is no comma after the word *saints*. Many get the idea that God has given us gifted men to (1) perfect the saints; (2) edify the body; etc.

Now, while it is true that pastors and evangelists are in the work of the ministry, one of their main duties is the *perfecting* or *equipping* of saints that they might join them in the work of the ministry. The ministry is not a one-man proposition. While it is true that a church has a pastor who is the undershepherd of God tending the flock, it is also true that the entire membership should be involved in the total work and ministry of the church. Anything less than this is falling short of God's plan for His church. The ministry is *ours*.

What is the best program for such participation? I believe it is a church and a Sunday School visitation program. It is *organized obedience*. It is putting into practice what has been learned from the New Testament example.

It has been pointed out that visitation is not just a newfangled, Johnny-come-lately program. It is God's plan. To do it is to be obedient in the work of God. The idea that "If you can't go, then send someone" preached and promoted in many churches across the country is not a Scriptural one. The Great Commission does not say, "Go, . . . and if you cannot go, then *send* into all the world to preach the gospel." The commission is GO.

You go! Go *ye!* While it is not wrong to send, to be content to send when you can go is but to rationalize away your responsibility to God. It is God, not the believer, Who asks, "Whom shall I send?" This is God's prerogative, not ours. Ours is to obey and go! Whether it is to go with the gospel to a distant part of the world (designated as foreign missions) or into the local community (home missions), it is still going. And *going is obeying.*

A. Visitation: Concrete answers to two questions.

Granting that visitation is right and proper, and that it is Scriptural, how is it to be done? There must be a program—organized, planned and prepared. First, let me state what the program is; then we will consider steps to inaugurate such a program.

1. What is a visitation program? A visitation program is an organized effort of the local church in which the total church membership participates in reaching the lost and unenlisted in the community. Specifically, the calling program should have at least four prongs.

a. Door-to-door calling. While we will be enlarging on this in another place (as to what is involved and how it is to be done), suffice it to say here that this is a concerted effort of the church to reach every family in the town or city for Christ. It is known in the business world of salesmanship as "cold turkey" calling. It is the initial contact. This was done in the New Testament in teams of two.

b. Follow-up calling. After the person or family has been contacted, if there is no favorable response in attendance, couples should be selected to go back with the express purpose of making a specific invitation to the services of the church. This follow-up call emphasizes getting into the home and visiting a few minutes, explaining the program of the church and Sunday School. Generally this will be considered a "good prospect" call and, if followed through correctly, should result in the person or family attending the church for a visit. Often there will be couples who feel that this is their specific ministry and who delight in such follow-up work.

c. The new pupil call. Now the Sunday School comes into action. When a child or adult comes to Sunday School for the first time, he should be called on by his teacher or someone else in his department on visitation evening the next week. While the "cold turkey" call and the follow-up call are designed to feed the Sunday School with new pupils, exposing them to the gospel, the new pupil call is the first step in holding them.

d. The absentee call. If a pupil is absent once, he should receive a card or a letter from the teacher. If absent twice, a personal call should be made.

The plan is rather simple. By bringing in new people Sunday after Sunday (through the first two prongs), and by keeping and holding them (as a result of the last two prongs), there is resulting growth. There are numbers of people, teeming throngs of people; and where there are people—with the power of God and the message of God—there are souls for God. It is as simple as that!

2. Why emphasize the Sunday School? While there are many areas of emphasis in calling, there ought to be one particular thrust of appeal when a contact is made. It goes without saying that there ought to be a clear witness for Christ by word and tract (or booklet) when a visit is made. However, souls are not won in every home. Often, a strong invitation is extended to the family to participate

in the growth in the Sunday School of the church. Now, why the Sunday School? There are two basic reasons:

First, it is not good business to give the people upon whom you are calling a sixty-minute rundown of the services of the church. If you emphasize everything, they will remember nothing. Talking in generalities will get a general response. By the same token, if you give the whole program and invite them to come "sometime," that is exactly what they will do—come "sometime," which means never. Therefore, one should be explicit and pointed in giving an invitation.

Years ago, when I sold shoes in a shoe store in Detroit, I was given careful training as to how it was to be done. I was told, "Don't show any more than three pairs of shoes at a time." The greenhorn who strewed the floor with five to ten pairs of shoes seldom made a sale. When a Fuller Brush man goes into the home he has one particular item that he will emphasize. When the Avon lady comes to the door with her cheerful smile, there is one cosmetic that is offered—the very latest shade which you "must have." That is good psychology, whether it is selling cosmetics, shoes or brushes. There ought to be a main emphasis.

Second, the Sunday School is a way—the best way—to reach people. There they can be saved and from there be trained to become involved in the total program of the church. This is borne out by the fact that at least eighty-five percent of church workers come up through the Sunday School.

A survey was made of the workers who have gone out from Temple Baptist Church of Tacoma, Washington, to the ministry, to colleges to teach, to mission fields and to the chaplaincy. In every case the workers came up through the ranks of the Sunday School. This is where the emphasis should be made.

B. Vision: A correct attitude of pastor and people.

Before there can be venture, there must be vision. Before there can be a program of power, there must be a program of preparation. The preparation begins with the pastor. Here is why. The greatest hindrance to a successful visitation program is usually the pastor. He can make it or break it. His attitude toward it—his possession of vision as to what God can do—is a determining factor in its success.

1. Conviction. There must be a convinced people and pastor who believe that visitation is the answer. Some people are pessimists by nature. Someone has said that a pessimist is "one who feels bad when he feels good for fear he'll feel worse when he feels better." How many times have I met "Pastor Pessimist" in my seminars on visitation evangelism. The stock answer to a message on a pastor's need to lead the program is, "But it won't work here." Should some of our leaders run out of excuses and want a complete list to aid them in avoiding and dodging their responsibility, I can furnish such a list. I have heard all the excuses. Here are some of the most recent:

> It won't work here because the town is small; the town is too big; they are all farm people and won't come to visit; they are all city folk and have to drive too far; our church is downtown—everybody knows downtown churches can't be filled; our church is out of town—we can't be seen; this town is Catholic; this town is Lutheran; this town is liberal; this town is too helter-skelter and can't be divided up into blocks; it's too dangerous to call in this town; it won't work in Canada; it won't work in the staid East; it won't work in pleasure-loving California.

Yes, there are literally thousands of reasons why it won't work. The major one is that a pastor and people lack the vision to do it! As reluctant as I am to say it, usually these excuses are first given by the pastor.

Some pastors will try anything—gimmicks of all sorts—before God's plan. But God's plan of visitation works! To the pastor who may be reading these lines: It will work in your community! It is God's program, and God has promised to bless it. Stop finding a difficulty for every solution. There are some well-meaning preachers who are born pessimists and look around for the funeral every time they smell a flower. They make their opportunities their difficulties. Often the reason the program does not work is because they are not fully convinced themselves and too often throw a wet blanket on the fires of their members' enthusiasm.

2. Participation. Not only must there be a convinced and enthusiastic pastor, there must be a participating pastor. He must participate in the program as its leader and as its example. As the leader he should lead the program himself. It is not good enough for him to find someone to carry the ball. He must carry the ball. He must be the spark. A visitation director may be good, but *the* director of the program should be the pastor. I cannot emphasize this too much. He must be totally involved in it.

Then he must set the example; that is, he must visit himself. To *send* them out and not to *go* out is unforgivable and inexcusable. It will spell the failure of the program.

C. Venture: The action of the pastor and the people.

To see the need, and do nothing about it, is a sin. *Vision* must be followed by *venture*. Many visitation programs fail because there is a lack of preparation. This is often the case of those who spark the enthusiasm about visitation and yet fail (often because of lack of time) to explain how it is to be done. The planning of the program includes the following:

1. Meeting with the boards. The pastor ought to meet with the official boards and explain the program to them, soli-

citing their help. They will often be reluctant at first. The major reason usually is, "We have tried this before and it didn't work." Assure them that it is God's plan, and if effectively planned and presented *it will work.*

2. Meeting with other leaders. Meet with the Sunday School superintendent and other officers of the church. They are key people in this program. If the pastor is the leader that he should be, they will respond to his burden. Then, meet with the teachers and spend a few (three or four) evenings with them explaining and outlining the program. They will appreciate your confidence in them and will stand with you. The pastor should be in constant prayer for wisdom and proper leadership in working with his people in this program.

3. Meeting with everyone else. Meet with the whole church and set aside a number of midweek services in which you can give messages on soul-winning, evangelism and visitation. Solid Bible presentations of New Testament examples of visitation should be made.

4. Other considerations.

a. Set a target date for the visitation program six to eight weeks ahead. Then, with that date in mind, begin your visitation classes, visitation publicity, etc.

b. Preach messages, especially on the Sunday before the target date, on soul-winning evangelism. The need of total involvement in visitation is important. Nothing takes the place of compassionate Bible preaching—proclaiming the need to obey God at any cost.

c. Select workers for the program. A superintendent over each prong of the visitation program should be appointed. This is particularly important with the cold territory and follow-up work. Generally, the Sunday School will be responsible for the pupil and absentee calls. A superintendent of the bus ministry will be needed; also a head for the kitchen crew if a supper is involved in the program, and the special youth workers for all ages. These will be considered in some detail later.

d. Pray . . . pray . . . pray. In the Sunday services, Wednesday night, during the day, pray for the blessing of God upon this project. Seek His face continually. Pastor and people need His power.

The point is, there must be preparation. If you do not plan carefully and prayerfully, then, regardless of the enthusiasm, the program is liable to fail.

Illustration: Two great preachers. Perhaps the two preachers who stand out in recent history as being most greatly used of God are Spurgeon and Moody. Both were successful in their ministries. Both built great churches. Both were evangelistic and great leaders of people. Both were intensely interested in soul winning. And both saw the need of personal witnessing and visitation.

Sometimes there is reflected a feeling among pastors that visitation is simply a modern substitute for good preaching. To them, visitation to fill the church is a rather recent idea reflecting the lack of power in the pulpit. But all great soul-winning preachers have counted on the active participation of the people in order to get results.

Charles Spurgeon is an example. What was the secret of the great crowds and souls won? To be sure he was a great preacher, but it must be remembered that at least once a year, for many years, three thousand or more of his people would come forward in a church service, pledging to give themselves to soul winning. Thousands of unsaved people were in his meetings as a result of the visitation and invitations of his people.

Conant has written in his book, *Every Member Evangelism:*

> The result was that Spurgeon never stood up to preach without looking into the faces of un-

saved people to whom his own members had been witnessing of Christ in their own homes, and who had the demand for salvation sufficiently aroused to come to the church services to have that demand satisfied. Like Peter's sermon on the day of Pentecost, Spurgeon's sermons were the climax of the witnessing to Christ that had preceded, and the private witnessing, reaching its climax in the public testimony, bore a wonderful harvest for God. . . . Who couldn't preach in power in an atmosphere created by such a passion for the lost, and who could not be a soul-winning preacher with three thousand Christians backing him with the kind of praying and personal work that such a passion produces.[3]

Yes, Spurgeon, one of the greatest of all pastor-preachers, depended on the visitation of his people for the success of his meetings.

Walter Knight wrote:

One Sunday morning, in 1856, a congregation of well-dressed people had been ushered to their rented pews in Chicago's Plymouth Congregational Church. Suddenly there was a commotion near the door. Many turned and looked. Something occurred which had never before been seen by that elite congregation. In walked a young man—a nineteen year old salesman. Following him was a motley group of tramps, slum people and alcoholics. The young man led them into four pews he had personally rented for the visitors. He continued to do this important work each Sunday until God called him into a world-wide ministry. You ask the name of that young man? Dwight L. Moody.[4]

Oh, that we would have the same compassion for the lost as Spurgeon did. Oh, that we would share the burden of Moody for people everywhere. Yes, greater than this, that we would look through the eyes of Christ and share the same compassion and burden of the Lord as He wept for the lost.

Christ said, "Go!"

Organized obedience is the answer!

"And from House to House"

"We shoot every third salesman, and the second one just left." That was the sign that stared me in the face as I approached the door in my personal door-to-door visitation. I had confronted all kinds of signs—"Beware of Dog," "No Solicitors," "Day Sleeper,"—but this was a new one. I knocked briskly and bravely (and breathed a prayer, as I recall). You can guess my first words as the door opened. They were spontaneous and certainly not out of a book I had read on visitation evangelism.

"Sir, I'm not a salesman."

He smiled and I sighed. The expected barrier was broken down and we both had a good laugh at the sign which, of course, was meant to be facetious, as well as serving as a reminder that bothersome salesmen were not welcome.

"I'm Pastor Wagner, from Temple Baptist Church of Tacoma." I had hardly gotten the words out before I was firmly assured that they were Mormons. The reaction of some would have been, "Well, as long as you are going to church somewhere . . . we are just interested in the unchurched." This would not be allowed by my conscience, and it certainly was not the truth. I was looking for *people*. If they were not going to a good, Bible-believing church where Christ was honored and preached, they were prospects as far as I was concerned and an "open field" in door-to-door evangelism.

My answer was simple and to the point.

"I am not interested in simply filling the seats in our church; we are genuinely interested in you." Then I added, "Did you know that your next-door neighbors are coming to Sunday School this next Sunday? They are Catholics." I continued, "Now, certainly, if Catholics may come, Mormons may."

"Really?" he answered. "You will let Mormons and Catholics come to your Sunday School?"

"Yes, and we would be delighted to have you with us." He told me that before long they would be moving. I asked if we could pick them up until they moved.

The next Sunday both the Catholic and Mormon families were represented on the bus and exposed to the gospel; they have been coming ever since!

As I write these words, I recall the Lord's goodness to us when I spoke to our Sunday School in a general assembly in the main auditorium of our church. There were thirty-five decisions for Christ that day; many of those responding had been contacted through door-to-door ministry. How many Catholics, how many Mormons were there, I do not know. I only know that we are responsible for getting the gospel to every family in our city.

Of course the pastor should be involved in this work, but not just the pastor. Remember that the work of the ministry is *ours*—every member of the church. We ought to be involved together in the harvest fields of the world.

A. The "who" of door-to-door visitation.

Let us assume now that a regular weekly visitation program has been inaugurated. Perhaps twenty to a hundred people have come to be involved in the work of calling on the designated night. Some will be doing door-to-door work; others, follow-up; and still others will be working on absentees in the Sunday School.

Generally, when a visitation room or center is arranged at the church, it is advisable to prepare at least three tables, representing different areas of service in the visitation program. One of these will be a table for door-to-door work. A map of the city should be hanging on the wall. The door-to-door captain should have block cards prepared and be ready to give the assignment of the streets. Prospect cards to be used when prospects are contacted and plenty of tracts and church brochures should also be distributed. A ten to fifteen minute preliminary time of challenge, instruction and prayer is helpful. Then the teams of two go out into the field to serve in the "King's Business."

1. Qualifications of the workers.

a. Each person must be saved and separated. This is the major qualification for each worker. These people are not engaged in social work, which simply demands someone with a good personal appearance and a smooth approach. They are dealing with eternity. At stake, according to how this work is done, are the souls of men. We dare not send out groups of people who are not both saved and living separated Christian lives from all manner of worldliness. Moreover, God cannot, and will not, bless the program when there are participants who have compromised their stand in the things of the Lord. One who has made "friendship with the world" is not only an "enemy of God," but an enemy of God's program (James 4:4). Unless the workers have "come out" in separation, they cannot "go out" in service.

b. Each person must be totally dependent on the Lord. This dependence needs to be emphasized constantly to the *organized obedience* crew. This is not a program where the most important feature is a gift of gab. It is not brushes or cosmetics that are being offered. Christ said, "Without me ye can do nothing" (John 15:5). It is in His might and power, and with a total abandonment of self that these workers make their way along the "highways and hedges" of door-to-door visitation. Encourage the teams to pray silently as they approach each door and to ask for wisdom in their approach and testimony.

c. Each person must realize that dress is important. Whether one likes it or not, the first impression is a lasting impression. While, to be sure, the inward heart and motives are more important than the outward man, the person answering the door sees only the outward appearance. If the church visitors are carelessly dressed, a barrier may be erected between them and the person they are hoping to reach. Not everyone can afford expensive clothes, but one can be neat and clean and modestly dressed in a manner that exhibits good taste.

B. The "how" of door-to-door visitation.

Now, as far as the inner and outer man are concerned, the callers are ready. They are prepared both in what they are and how they look. Here are a few more vital requirements and equipment that they should have as they begin.

1. A cheerful attitude. A cheerful attitude is important. I once heard of a person making a door-to-door call and the door was opened by a man who, when he saw the lugubrious face of the pessimistic caller, said, "No thanks, I have troubles of my own."

2. Necessary tools. The visitors should have their Bibles. Each one should have a supply of gospel tracts—the simpler the better—something that gets right down to cases and gets the gospel into the home. Then, there are the prospect and block cards—don't forget them.

3. Tact and contact. These are twins and go together. One of the important points in the matter of tact is that of avoiding the "knocking" of any other person's affiliation. For example, the people may have a Methodist background. Do not begin criticizing the Methodists or pass on to them

what you just heard about the Methodists. Do not go into a long diatribe about Methodists belonging to the National Council of Churches. While everything you say might be true, to handle the contact this way may alienate them right from the start.

You must not construe this tactfulness as being compromise. I am a strict separatist and have strong convictions about unholy alliances. But the time will come for them to be enlightened about such matters. What matters at this point is to get them exposed to the gospel. If you leave with a "Well, I told them" attitude, it is highly possible that you won the argument and lost the person. Your victory could be a tragedy. Win the people for Christ first. This settles the argument—*posthaste!*

While tact is important, there are some who seem to specialize in *how* visitation is to be done and yet never *do* it. Often when a zealous person accumulates a little educated "know-how," he suddenly loses his fervor.

"Two fellows, Tact and Contact, were courting the same girl. How different were their methods of approach. While Tact was engaging the girl's father and mother in conversation at the front door, Contact was at the back door proposing to the young lady. Do I need to tell you which one won the heart and hand of the fair young lady?" (T. W. B. Callaway, D.D.)

4. Two and two. While I have done a great deal of calling alone, going with another person is ideal and brings good results. This method is supported by Scripture.

The best arrangement is for two men or two women to go together. Obviously, if a man and woman go together, it should be a husband and wife team. However, when new teams are being formed or the calling program is just getting started, it is better to put an experienced caller with an inexperienced one. Discretion and care ought to be used in selecting just the right team for this vital door-to-door method. There will be some discourage-ments, and the new callers need the support of those experienced in the work. One thing is sure: if you call often enough, have the right attitude and approach and do it in the power of the Lord, you will get positive results.

One soul-winner remarked, "The average insurance agent makes forty-five weekly calls on prospects. Only fifteen listen to him. Of these fifteen, only two put their names on the dotted line. If an insurance agent calls on forty-five people and sells only two policies, should soul-winners be discouraged if they make a thousand calls, and bring only one soul to Jesus?" Never! I have found that an average of from three to six contacts can be made in an hour of solid, persistent visitation work. This means more than that the law of averages is on our side!

5. Knocking and talking. Dr. Fred Barlow insisted that the layer of fat on the lower part of a fist is a God-given cushion for the purpose of knocking on doors! Knock briskly and with confidence. When a person comes to the door, it is important that you introduce yourself and your team partner and that you tell what church you represent. This often puts the person at ease since the general public expects an approach with a gimmick and a subtle concealment of purposes from strangers. When I call, I usually have a rather large photo of the church which I immediately show. Other times I have had pictures of our Sunday School buses with boys and girls getting on them.

a. The first words are important. Something like the following might open your conversation. "Good evening! I'm Robert Brown, and this is George Smith. We are from the First Baptist Church here in town, and we are establishing a bus route in this area for boys, girls and adults. I wonder if you would like to ride our bus next Sunday? Perhaps you have seen our buses in town; we have a fleet of ten that bring in people to our growing Sunday School from all over the city."

There are many who feel that the call should be made expressly to win the soul to Christ. Let it be understood that this is our primary purpose, although the actual dealing with the soul does not always happen during the first contact. The longer view is taken with an intense desire to get the family to come and be exposed to the gospel in the Sunday School and church. The Sunday School is particularly emphasized and now, during the call, you are offering transportation. It is important to remember that you must be specific in your approach. Be brief and right to the point.

b. Close one. Often, salesman (whether they are selling books or pots and pans) have what they call "closes." Each "close" is designated to "wrap up" the sale as soon as possible. If, however, it is not done in the first "close," then continue to the second, third, etc. While we have emphasized that we are not to consider this a commercial venture or limit ourselves to the methodology of the world, there is good psychology in a great deal of its methods.

In scores of cases, with just the first words, there has been a favorable response and the family has been lined up for the next Sunday. If the response is favorable after the first "close," there is a danger of talking them out of coming by saying too much. Again, this is not a hard and fast rule but should be remembered as a general principle. It is important to observe the person with whom you are talking and to be prayerful that the Lord will lead you in handling the situation. Eternity is involved in this call! Don't forget it!

c. Close two. "Yes, we have six hundred people in our Sunday School every Sunday, and many of them have taken advantage of this free service. We will be willing to pick up your children right here at the door, take them to Sunday School and church,and return them at 12:30.

There are no streets to cross, and we will have someone meet them at the church and take them directly to their classes."

Now this is a very important point. Their first reaction to the suggestion of taking their children to Sunday School is: Will it be safe? You have answered this before they have a chance to ask about it. Then they wonder about the children getting lost. They visualize all kinds of things happening. Again, you have dealt with this problem—you have related to them in showing that you understand just how they feel.

At this point, make it clear that this service is not simply for children; remind them that adults may ride the bus and that this is the ideal. The family should be coming together. Many parents will allow their children to come, yet not come themselves; do not despair about this—a contact is being made that will have lasting results not only in the children but in the family.

d. Close three. "How many children do you have, Mrs. Green?" The response to this question will determine your next remark. Whatever the ages of the children, you can comment about them. Perhaps you have a child that age, or you have just lined up someone down the street that age who is coming this Sunday.

"You say Johnny is nine; well, then, he must know Noel Johnson down the street. He and his parents are real excited about coming this Sunday. Perhaps you could all come together."

In a normal conversation there are a number of things that could lead to a witness for the Lord. I make it a practice to talk a minute or two about the times in which we live (people are generally concerned), and how necessary it is to get the right kind of training. It is fitting that you talk favorably about the Sunday School staff and the other members of the church.

Emphasize the wonderful fellowship and warmth of the church. People are interested in people and the section of the country from which they have come. If the people are Southerners, I tell them that my father and mother are from the South (Virginia and Tennessee). I talk about the Southland and some experiences there. If they are from the East, I tell them that I pastored a church in New Jersey for a number of years. The point is simply that you must relate to the people; show them that you are human. Seek to develop some degree of friendship and rapport with them. After all, they have good reason to want to know about you and the church you represent.

You should be friendly, open and aboveboard about everything. If you cannot fully support your church and its stand and policies, you should not be involved in the programs of the church. If there is reservation and you hesitate to recommend your church heartily, then do not waste your time knocking on doors. It is hard to convince people to come when you have reservations yourself. This may seem blunt, but it is important.

In giving the suggested approach, I have emphasized a service that may not be available in every case—the buses. While a calling program can survive without a bus ministry, it cannot be successful without offering some kind of transportation. "Ye have not chosen me, but I have chosen you, and ordained you, that ye should *go and bring* forth fruit (John 15:16). As one pastor has often said: "Go is visitation—bring is transportation." These cannot be separated.

e. Close four. This is always the final step and is never to be omitted. When it is indicated that there is a willingness to come to the Sunday School, immediately take your prospect card and fill it out in their presence. Ask for the full name, address and telephone number of the party. Get the names and ages of the children. Then say (while you are writing), "Will you folks be ready at nine o'clock this Sunday morning?" Circle the time as you speak—or underline it. I generally write, in the presence of the mother or father, "Pick up at 9 A.M. sharp."

As the first four or five bus routes for our church were established, I told the prospects I would be on the bus to greet their children personally. Again, it is important to give assurance to the parents regarding this service. You should be sure a brochure or church paper and a gospel tract are left. After you get home, you should write a letter or card (this may be done by the church secretary) reminding the family of the call. Assure them that you will be at their house at the stipulated time.

Visitation and transportation go together. This will be emphasized again in a later section. You should have observed that in making a contact call we were brief and to the point, yet the job was done. Each visitor must design an approach that fits his personality; however, the above points have proven to be successful. These can serve as guidelines and should be considered.

How vividly I remember calling in one particular home. I knocked on the door and heard a masculine voice saying, "Come on in out of the rain." I folded my umbrella and, drenched to the skin, willingly complied with his request.

"Thank you, sir! My, what a rainy day. I appreciate your kindness. I'm Pastor Wagner from Temple Baptist Church of Tacoma. We're just starting our bus route in this area, and we'd like very much to offer our services to you and your family.

"Baptist," he said. "I'm not interested in the Baptist church."

I could tell by the tone of his voice that he was willing to let me make my way out into the rain again.

"Yes, we're Baptists, and we are interested in this community. You see, we aren't just trying to fill pews.

We're interested in sharing a wonderful message with you about Christ. Now, take this boy of yours; how we would like to have him with us in our Junior High Department!"

"Sorry, we aren't interested in the Baptist church."

He was definite, unmovable; the boy seemed interested—Dad wasn't!

Somehow the rain seemed to be more aggravating as I stepped out the door. Up went the umbrella as the door closed behind me.

"Please, Dad, I'd like to go," I could hear the boy saying. If I stand here for a minute, maybe he'll change his mind, I thought. It didn't work that way.

Trying to ignore the liquid sunshine, I started out again door-to-door—to the next house, then the next, then another. The block was finished, and another was started. A few more prospects were contacted and with a brief, "Thank You, Lord," I made my way to the car.

"Hello there," someone called from a car. "Are you the man I talked with about an hour ago?" I was puzzled for a minute. Walking closer to the car, I recognized him. He was the father who had expressed no interest in the Baptist church.

"Yes, sir, I am." What did he want, I thought. Did I leave my Bible there?

"I've been thinking over what you said, and besides, my son insists he wants to come to your Sunday School. Could you pick him up this Sunday?"

"Yes, sir, we would love to have him." I went back to the house and made the arrangements. As I left I breathed another prayer: "Thank You, Lord, for the opportunity of reaching another young person for Christ." I didn't even notice that it was still raining.

Keeping Up on Follow-Up

Someone has written: "I hate the guys who criticize and minimize the other guys whose enterprise has made them rise above the guys who criticize and minimize." For every man or church that has seized upon the "sanctified enterprise" of going out and getting involved in organized obedience, there are ten who will tell you why it won't work, will disagree with your methods or will explain your motives for doing it. But as stewards of the Lord, it is required that we be found faithful. Our accountability is to Him. If we fail to serve with all our hearts, then the blood of others will be on our hands.

The apostle Paul himself said to the elders from Ephesus: "Wherefore I take you to record this day, that I am pure from the blood of all men. For I have not shunned to declare unto you all the counsel of God" (Acts 20:26, 27). Earlier he had said, "I kept back nothing that was profitable unto you, but have shewed you, and have taught you publickly, and from house to house, testifying both to the Jews, and also to the Greeks, repentance toward God, and faith toward our Lord Jesus Christ" (Acts 20:20, 21). Later he continued, "I ceased not to warn everyone night and day with tears" (v. 31). Yes, Paul was criticized (cf. Phil. 1:15, 16). But this did not thwart his enterprise; zealously he worked, called and preached because it was the order of his Captain Who had said, "Go!" To evangelize was his enterprise, while looking to the prize. He died with the satisfaction that this had been done (2 Tim. 4).

It is important that we get on with the work of organized obedience with firmness of purpose and a resolve to please the Lord at any price!

A. The system of follow-up.

We have pointed out that the visitation program has four prongs. First, there is the "cold turkey" or house-to-house contact. Then comes the follow-up program. This includes calling on families whose names were acquired from the cold territory contacts, as well as other prospects given by members and friends of the church.

In both cases it is assumed that the people have never been to the church. Therefore we call this a prospect call.

Again, it must be remembered that a prospect is one who has shown interest in the things of the Lord and the church and is not attending a Bible-believing church at the present time. This could be an unsaved person who shows some interest, or a person who is backslidden but knows he should be in church and back with the Lord. It may be a person who has just moved into the community and is looking for a place where he can hear the Word preached and get involved. Some of these may well have come as a result of the initial call. This vital follow-up may be the one to bring someone to the church or to the Lord.

Now, let us assume that twenty-five couples were out last Monday night for the calling program and, as a result of their work, there are thirty prospects. The cards for these thirty prospects are given to couples whose work will be to visit the families in their homes. Whereas each door-to-door team may have knocked on thirty or forty doors, the follow-up corps will concentrate on one or two calls for the evening.

1. Heading up the follow-up. In organizing a follow-up department, there should be a captain who will be responsible for heading the program. When prospect cards are turned in to the door-to-door captain, he will direct them to the follow-up department. Then the follow-up captain, or an appointed secretary, should arrange the cards according to geographic location, and according to the age and interest of the prospects as nearly as possible.

The follow-up captain should be a Spirit-filled, dedicated, faithful servant of the Lord with a good attitude and exercising one of the most luscious fruits of the Spirit—longsuffering! He will be sending out various couples to individual homes and will be directing the callers in the weeks and months to come—in many cases to the same homes. A stable, dependable man is needed, one who works well with people and has a good degree of wisdom.

The captain should instruct the callers to fill out in detail the results of their call. He should insist that the report be turned back to his department promptly after the call is made. He should also have a duplicate record of the assignment and follow through with immediate attention if the cards are not returned. In other words, he should be a leader and have his heart in each particular call. He should work closely with the pastor and share with him any unique case or difficult problem. If the family that is contacted already attends, then the call is handled by another department—the Sunday School. Because he is dealing constantly with those who are promising, yet not coming, he should be one that does not discourage easily.

2. Teaming up for follow-up. In the follow-up program an attempt should be made to send couples to homes where some interest is shared. For example, if the prospects are young people, it would be reasonable to send young people there. If they are professional people (doctors, lawyers, dentists, etc.), you should send someone with professional training and interest, if possible. If a prospect has a special interest or hobby, it would be good to send someone who shares these interests. This does not mean that the subject of conversation will mainly relate to the occupation or hobby—we are on business for the Lord—but it can help establish a rapport in reaching them for Christ. Certainly the Lord must have used Luke, the physician, in some very special cases of witness. Peter's occupation must have been useful in dealing with the common man, and Paul's ability to reason with the best of the kings was certainly used of the Holy Spirit.

3. Looking up in follow-up. Although we now assume that we have the right captain and the right workers to follow up the prospects, it is vital that we never feel that our natural acumen will be sufficient to do the job. *There must be persistent prayer!* This should be emphasized in any calling program and in every phase of the program. Every team ought to pause in prayer before they enter the home, asking for the wisdom of the Lord in the contact. Even while one member of the team is talking, the other member can be in silent prayer. This praying should not be obvious to those in the home, however.

4. Speaking up in follow-up. Now with the callers matched, sent out and aware of their dependence on the Lord, it is important to make the right approach. The following suggestions will serve as guidelines.

a. Introduce yourselves and tell the family the name of the church you represent. The following is a sample approach:

"Good evening, I am James Jones and this is Paul White. We are from the Temple Baptist Church of Tacoma. Last week two of our people were here and mentioned the fine reception you gave them. We want to add our invitation to theirs. May we come in?"

Now the words do not have to be exactly as I have given them; however, it is important that you are a kind, courteous visitor, and that you speak up. The words, "May we come in," may seem to be a little forward, but such initiative usually has been blessed of the Lord. We have tried and tested it many times. While it is not proper to barge in and put a "foot in the door," thus cramming our way into people's lives, there is a holy aggressiveness that is not impertinent.

If you expect to get into the home and have prayed about it, you will, in most cases, get into the home. Often an invitation to enter is extended without having to ask. Remember, these are prospects; they are people with some interest or you would not be there. Occasionally, especially when you first begin the program, you may find that the first team which made the contact mistook courtesy for interest. That is, because the family was friendly to them, they assumed they were prospects. This is not always the case, and the sooner you can divide the prospects from those who are just friendly people, the sooner your program will be successful. It takes wisdom and discernment to know the difference.

b. Visits should be short and to the point. Ten or fifteen minutes could do it. On the other hand, this is often a time of soul-winning. The team should have Bibles ready and be able to witness as the Lord leads and directs, pointing the person to the Lord. If there are evident signs of conviction, do not wait until a future time to deal with the person. This may be God's time! Therefore, it is important that you have the mind of the Lord in these matters, for cases vary. Many souls are won to Christ in the home by those who are doing follow-up work.

More often than not, they will respond favorably to the call. These usually assure you that they are pleased that you have this much interest in them and will make an effort to be in church or Sunday School the next week. After a few minutes of witnessing and telling them of your interest in their coming to a place where the Bible is preached and taught, you should thank them for their time and leave. Results should be recorded immediately when you return to the car. The record should be given to the captain upon your return to the church.

This friendly visit at first may seem to be unproductive; but if it has been committed to the Lord, it may be the beginning of an eternal relationship between the family and the Lord.

B. The secret of follow-up.

1. Prayerful persistence. Up to this point we have been involved mostly with mechanics. These are tested, tried

suggestions which should help you in your follow-up call. But there is a secret ingredient in this kind of call that is most important. Without it, this phase of the visitation program will be lost and the whole program will be damaged. The secret ingredient is prayerful persistence, or call it prayerful stick-to-itiveness if you wish.

When William Carey was told the many reasons why he would not be successful in his desire to go to India and why it would not work if he did go, he answered, "I can plod." Great things have been wrought by God through His persistent plodders, those who continue to press on in spite of obstacles. Most successful programs have this element of persistent, prayerful and plodding effort.

What A. T. Pierson said about successful men can also be said for successful churches and visitation programs: "Where there is found a *patience* that can wait slowly to gather, a *perseverance* that can hold fast an end yet unreached, a *method* that can store up results in an available form, an *industry* that does not shirk effort, there is all that is essential to a man thoroughly furnished for his work; give him time and health, and the wealth of success is his."[5]

Again, said Sir Fowell Buxton: "The longer I live the more I am certain that the great difference between the feeble and the powerful, the great and the insignificant—is energy, invincible determination, a purpose once fixed, and then death or victory."[6]

This is also true of visitation programs. There must be a willingness to go, and go, and go again. Then, go some more!

2. The Biblical example. Is not this the teaching of the parable of the great supper? We read in Luke 14:16 and 17: "Then said he unto him, A certain man made a great supper, and bade many: and sent his servant at supper time to say to them that were bidden, Come; for all things are now ready."

First, note that the invitation was preceded by preparation. All things were ready. What a pity that, having the most wonderful story to tell, and often the finest in facilities, we have so few present in our churches with whom to share it. All is in readiness but the invitation to come has not been given out.

"And they all with one consent began to make excuse. The first said unto him, I have bought a piece of ground, and I must needs go and see it: I pray thee have me excused." The word "excuse" means to "beg off." The first man's excuse was because of possessions, particularly real estate.

"And another said, I have bought five yoke of oxen, and I go to prove them: I pray thee have me excused." His excuse was in the area of commerce.

The third is almost pitiful. "And another said, I have married a wife, and therefore I cannot come." His excuse was in the area of affection.

These are typical of all excuses. Most reasons for refusal are because of possessions, commerce or personal affections. While they are not legitimate excuses, they are typical excuses even in our day. One pastor has named the three men in the parable "Real Estate Ralph, Farmer Fred and Henpecked Henry" with some justification.

Thus far in the going, there was not much to show for the work. "So that servant came, and shewed his lord these things. Then the master of the house being angry said to his servant, 'Go out quickly. . . .'"

The servant might well have responded, "You can't be serious! After all our effort, and the ingratitude shown us, and humiliation of being refused, are we to go again?"

The answer was obvious! "Go out quickly into the streets and lanes of the city, and bring hither the poor, and the maimed, and the halt, and the blind." The word was go—go again!

Once in a while people berate a visitation ministry, especially if it appears that it is mostly children who are responding. They claim that it is not paying for itself. Right now it is important to set the record straight. If the concern is monetary, it is right to say it does not pay for itself. But are we in the business to make it pay financially? Indeed not! If we are after souls, then let us be consistent in our programs and let that be the criteria for our service.

In the passage in Luke it was the lower class to whom the appeal was made. While there is no need to deal with this group exclusively, neither is it right to exclude them.

Notice the next part of the parable: "And the servant said, Lord, it is done as thou hast commanded, and yet there is room. And the Lord said unto the servant, Go. . . ." Do you get the impression that there is one very vital word in the vocabulary of the Lord? Go! Go! Go! Go! But we *have* gone! Go again! "Go out into the highways and hedges, and compel them to come in, that my house may be filled" (Luke 14:16-23).

Applying this to our contemporary scene, at least one lesson learned is that there must be persistence. Not only must we persistently call in different homes, but we must also persistently follow-up—sometimes going back again and again with a holy interest in one family.

What trophies of grace we will see through the years as a result of persistent, prayerful effort. It all begins with the faithful week-by-week visitation ministry of the Lord's people in the local church—going, going, going and going again because they care about those precious souls. Only God knows how many lives will be affected through the ministry of a faithful group of Christians who refuse to give up in their visitation ministry.

In the Tacoma area there is a young pastor doing a fine piece of work for the Lord. He was reached through constant contacts. Looking back on his life he said, "I just went because they invited me so many times I wanted to be courteous." Actually, it was a result of constant prayer and persistence that he was reached for Christ. The feeling among the church people was, "Let's visit him one more time." Then, one Sunday morning he attended, and the Holy Spirit spoke so strongly to his heart that he stepped out and made the greatest decision of his life.

I think of a businessman in the area who had little time for church. His children came but he had no interest. For about fifteen years, many calls were made in the home but with no encouragement from the head of the house. Then, after some misfortune and a brief stay in the hospital, this man was called on again and he promised to come. He kept his promise and three weeks later he walked the aisle with tears in his eyes, trusting Christ as Savior. There were tears in the eyes of others too! A calling program that had lasted fifteen years had paid off!

Let me urge every reader who is born again to remember that we are responsible to the Lord. We dare not turn from God's plan in disregard or indifference. Our response to the need should be willing hearts and ready feet in God's program of organized obedience.

Conserving the Results of a Visitation Program

"What in the world are we going to do with these buses sitting in our Sunday School yard? They are just costing us money and they have not been used for months."

Often this kind of reasoning precipitates a move on the part of the trustees to make a motion that the buses be sold. They conclude it is just good business to sell them and use the money for something else; and, what is more, they will dispose of an eyesore. Such reasoning is right! This may seem to be strange language coming from one who is sold on a bus ministry, but if the buses are not going to be used, then they are a waste of money. If a bus could talk and defend its case, it might say something like this:

> While it is true that I'm of little value now, you must understand that when I was purchased the pastor and people had some very worth-while plans for me. As a matter of fact, they had been to a Sunday School conference and were absolutely carried away with enthusiasm when they saw what some Sunday Schools were doing in a bus ministry. Evidently they didn't get the whole story as to how it was done, because I was used for only a few weeks. A visitation program was started in the church and a goodly number of boys and girls and adults were enlisted. I would say that there must have been close to fifty of them enrolled.
> Then it happened! In three weeks the number dropped to about thirty, then twenty. Then to justify my use, I was re-routed to pick up a few who had already been coming by automobile before the route started. Finally, even the last group of new contacts stopped coming. It was eventually reasoned that I wasn't of much value because the folk on the bus have always been coming and could get there by car again.
> Yes, I was an embarrassment to the pastor and the Sunday School superintendent. And I am a mute testimony of a Sunday School failure. While my battery is dead, so is the enthusiasm the people once had for a growing, thriving Sunday School. When the pastor passed by a few days ago, he just shook his head and remarked that a bus ministry just wouldn't work in our area.

This may seem to be a juvenile illustration of the problem, but this is the way it is in hundreds of situations.

It is not our intent to give a full article on the bus ministry, but it is important to discover why so many visitation programs and bus ministries fail. In an earlier chapter we mentioned that the lack of enthusiasm and vision was reason for failure. Yet it is possible, as in the above case, for a pastor and people to have those vital ingredients and still fail. What causes the failure? It is the lack of a plan in the Sunday School and church designed to keep the pupils once they start coming.

Along with vision and enthusiasm there must be planning and follow-up calling on all absentees. Specifically, there are three vital steps to a successful visitation program that will last indefinitely.

Total teacher involvement in a visitation program. We want to remind our readers that the emphasis in the visitation program is the Sunday School. Earlier we stated that there are four prongs in a calling program. First, there is the door-to-door program seeking to enlist new scholars. Second, as we saw in our last section, there is the follow-up. This involves persistent calling and follow-through. The last two prongs deal specifically with Sunday School teachers themselves, who are the key to holding the pupils. These prongs are the absentee call and the new scholar call.

Let it be explained that the reason the bus ministry failed in our illustration was that, while the first two prongs may have been in full operation in the program, the last two were not used. Door-to-door visitation will bring them in, but to keep them there involves the enlistment of the teachers and officers of the Sunday School to call on all new scholars and absentees. Otherwise you have a mission situation: a flowing through of people in the Sunday School. The Sunday School becomes transient, lacking stability. Continuity is lost and the over-all plan of seeing the pupil come to know Christ, follow the

Lord in baptism, then advance through many years of maturing is defeated.

When we first started our visitation ministry in Temple Baptist Church, literally hundreds of families were contacted and busloads of boys and girls were enlisted. I personally went door-to-door and contacted hundreds of homes for the Sunday School. From the standpoint of an outsider, this is the dramatic, impressive part of visitation. But unless the teachers follow through on these pupils, the church parking lot could well develop into a graveyard for buses.

Total teacher vision in a visitation program. Every Sunday School teacher ought to be impressed that he is not doing his job properly unless he is out on visitation night, calling on his pupils. He may be talented and gifted, but he is certainly less than what he should be if he is not involved in the visitation program weekly.

Of course, pastor and superintendent run into cases where the teacher refuses to visit. What can be done? First, there ought to be prayer that the Lord will open the eyes of the staff as to the need of weekly visitation. Secondly, there ought to be a decision that, if the teacher does not see the importance of this ministry, he will eventually be replaced with another teacher. This does not mean that someone in authority should go around "chopping off heads." Tact is needed in every situation; but if the teacher knows that this is a vital part of the program, with proper leadership and prayer he will step down from his position.

It ought to be resolutely determined that no new teacher will be enlisted who does not agree to call on his pupils. I say without fear of contradiction that if you do not have the teachers calling on the pupils you cannot maintain a successful, growing Sunday School. New contacts will mean very little if there is not the cooperation of every teacher in visitation maintenance. This involves more than visitation compulsion; it involves visitation vision. Teachers must be made to see that this is the only way to hold the pupils, and this is part of the total staff responsibility.

When the program is set up, the teachers should be instructed about the plans of the Sunday School and well informed regarding each method and detail.

Total teacher venture in a visitation program. God is not the author of confusion. Yet there are many churches defeating the work of the Lord through their confusing methods. If we are going to see the program work we must have a workable plan or method. We are interested in flesh and blood, but we are also interested in a workable method whereby the "flesh and blood" can be used properly. In explaining what we feel to be a workable method, let us follow a student from the very first time she comes into the Sunday School through the ensuing weeks.

1. New scholar contact. The door-to-door work has been done and Mary Jurnigan comes to Sunday School for the first time. She is in the Primary Department where Mrs. Meyers is the departmental superintendent. Mrs. Jones is the teacher of the class to which Mary has been assigned.

Sunday morning the red carpet is rolled out for Mary Jurnigan. She is brought to the welcome table of the Sunday School and a new scholar slip is made out in triplicate for her. Then she is given a welcome tag with her name on it, and a Scripture pencil is presented to her as a gift. One copy of the new scholar slip is retained at the table and the other two copies are taken along with Mary by a good-natured, friendly helper to the correct department. She is enrolled in the department for the first time. It is important that Mary is enrolled as a regular scholar the very first Sunday. While she is new and will be called upon the next visitation night, she should be considered a part of the Sunday School from the very first Sunday. The idea that a pupil must come three Sundays before being enrolled as a regular pupil ought to be relegated to the wastebasket. Whoever came up with the idea made a grave mistake. We lose many young people this way. The only advantage it has is to keep the class enrollment and the class attendance about the same.

If I hear of a Sunday School with an attendance of 300 and an enrollment of 295, I conclude that the work of follow-up visitation is not being done and new scholars are not enrolled when they attend for the first time. On the other hand, when the pupil is enrolled the first Sunday as a regular class member, that person automatically becomes the responsibility of the teacher to hold through visitation. While it might not look good to have attendance considerably lower than the enrollment, it does indicate that the church is facing up to its responsibility to new scholars. They are recognized as regular members and not as outsiders for several weeks—thus encouraging them not to drift away.

Returning to Mary Jurnigan: she is enrolled and welcomed into the class. On the first visitation night, her teacher, Mrs. Jones, should receive a follow-up card from the primary department. Mrs. Jones should call on Mary and tell her that she was happy to have her in the class. It is important that the teacher does not ask whether or not Mary enjoyed Sunday School. This is inviting a "yes" answer which is likely to be given whether it is true or not. When Mary has been welcomed to the class, Mrs. Jones can make the first important contact with Mr. and Mrs. Jurnigan, inviting them to the Sunday School and church as well.

2. The regular absentee call. Four weeks pass and Mrs. Jones's class is doing fine. Others like little Mary have joined the class and the teacher has called on them. However, the next week Mary is absent. Now it is important that the teacher look at the record system.

As in most Sunday Schools, each class has a roll book. When the roll is taken and Mary Jurnigan is not there, her name, along with the other absentees, is listed as absent. This book is given to the departmental superintendent. A special mimeographed sheet has been prepared for each class. The names of the pupils are listed on the left-hand side. Mary's name has been added at the bottom of the sheet. The departmental secretary uses the roll book and lists the results on the sheet. She checks all one-time absentees in the first column and all who have been absent two or more times in the second column. Mary Jurnigan is marked in column one. This means that on visitation night her teacher, Mrs. Jones, will pick up a card from the card rack and send it to Mary, reminding her that she was missed in Sunday School. If she is absent the second time, the departmental secretary will list this on the sheet in the second column.

These sheets are distributed to each teacher on visitation night. The teacher picks up the cards to send to those marked in column one. Personal calls are made on those marked in column two. After the cards are sent and the calls are made, the results are recorded in the third column. The sheets are returned to the department (generally a box is prepared for this) by a designated time. The only time a call will not be made is if it is marked "C.O.D." This means that the home is being called on by another department. When a family of six or seven is absent and it represents four departments, it would be unwise to make four calls there in one night! The teacher notes those marked "C.O.D.," therefore, when she picks up her sheet on visitation night. Although a call is not made, it is advisable that the teacher will still send a card to the pupil in her class.

Another very important part in the filing system of the Sunday School visitation is the "master file card." This file is to be kept in the Sunday School office and is to remain there. There is a card for every member of the Sunday School. On the front of the card is general information about the student. On the back of the card there is space to record the results of the call, transcribing it from the visitation sheet. This should be done weekly by a Sunday School secretary and kept up-to-date. It will be necessary for the superintendents of the various departments to see that the sheets are passed out, returned and properly submitted to the Sunday School secretary.

Some Sunday Schools record the information on the master file card in two steps: first, on the day prior to the visit which simply records the fact that the pupil was absent; second, on a day during the week after the visit has been made, which gives the result of the call. This helps in keeping the record straight if the teacher fails to call or does not record the call. The secretary will know that there was an absence and the teacher can then be contacted as to why the regular procedure was not followed.

This record-keeping system is extremely important. The superintendent can at any time evaluate the class and its progress by observing the attendance of the class and the faithfulness of the teacher in calling. A comparison of calls and the results of previous years may help to explain problems and the reason some are not returning.

Remember, we are dealing with souls! We are responsible for them and dare not be slipshod in our record-keeping. It is important that the pastor and superintendent know at all times the direction the Sunday School is going, the degree of cooperation on the part of the teachers and the effectiveness of the visitation program. It is not as simple as going out and rounding up a few children to fill the Sunday School. We want to know if the pupil is saved, baptized, a member of the church, and to what degree he is growing in the Lord. When one is absent chronically, it is important to know why.

I feel that the lack of record-keeping and follow-up is the reason a great many visitation programs fail. Records are important! The system suggested can be enlarged upon; basically, it is a workable system which has proved helpful over the years in churches where I have been pleased to minister.

Persistence pays off! How many times should the Sunday School teacher go back and call? There is no set amount; suffice it to say we should not give up! After the teacher calls a number of times it might be helpful for the departmental superintendent to call. Often the pastor and the Sunday School superintendent serve as "troubleshooters" and call on the "hopeless" cases. More often than not, they are not hopeless at all!

Teachers need to consider the business of teaching a full-time business. It is more than an hour or two a week. It is preparing, teaching, calling, saturating every child in prayer daily and bringing him to a saving knowledge of Christ. Hard work in visitation will result in a growing, thriving Sunday School, but never is the pupil to be lost in the masses. He is an individual for whom Christ died; he is to be loved and cared for as a very precious jewel in the eyes of the Lord.

The answer to a successful Sunday School is teachers who will be totally involved in the program of organized obedience.

"Go and Bring"

For every optimist there are usually a half-dozen pessimists who will throw a wet blanket to dampen the fires of your enthusiasm. I learned this quickly when I spoke to a number of pastors and friends about building a Sunday School in our church, located in downtown Tacoma. Our church, surrounded with business establishments, is not a community church. I had been reminded

of this fact too often to be able to forget it. But encouragement did come from reading the Word of God. The secret
of a growing, going, glowing Sunday School was found
written in clear, bold letters in the Gospel of John. What is
more, it was from the Lord's own words.

Visitation and transportation. "Ye have not chosen me,
but I have chosen you, and ordained you, that ye should go
and bring forth fruit, and that your fruit should remain;
that whatsoever ye shall ask of the Father in my name, he
may give it you" (John 15:16). There it is! In the commission of the Lord there is the note of transportation: "Go
and bring!" I can remember my pastor, David D. Allen of
the Calvary Baptist Church, Hazel Park, Michigan, emphasizing those two words: "Go"—that is visitation;
"bring"—that is transportation.

Yes, visitation and transportation go together.
There was only one answer if our church was to build an
effective Sunday School: *Visitation coupled with transportation.*

First, we began to organize for visitation. A great
deal of what we did to organize has been covered in the preceding pages. However, without adequate transportation, I am convinced the program could not have succeeded.

Our next problem was *what kind* of transportation.
I approached the church about renting a bus from the
Baptist day school in our area. The church agreed and arrangements were made with the school for a bus to be
used beginning Sunday, September 15. The bus was
scheduled; however, as yet we had no one to ride it. An exciting week of preparation was before us.

Perspiration and transportation. Some of our people
were quite reluctant to believe me when I suggested that
we would have a bus of young people the following Sunday. The plan was simple: I would personally canvass an
area the week before, and our visitation would begin fol-

low-up on the prospects the day following our first Sunday. Thus we started our door-to-door program.

I picked an area known as Highland Hills. It was a middle-class housing area, encompassing six blocks square. There were several churches in the area, none of which was evangelistically concerned about the souls in their area. Day after day I contacted homes, told them of our bus service, and assured them that eventually hundreds of young people would be taking advantage of this available transportation. I knew after the first home was contacted and signed up that we had committed ourselves to the area; there was no turning back now!

The first Sunday we had thirty-four passengers. I personally went with the driver. My son, Mark, and I were the two "hoppers"; we made our way to every door and assisted the youngest on the bus. The first Sunday was a real victory! The next Sunday we had forty-eight passengers, and on the third, fifty-eight. By now the visitation program in our church was well under way and proper follow-up was being made. Those absent were called on and in the weeks following we contacted new scholars.

Three weeks later, October 6, we started our second route. Again we sought the will and mind of the Lord as to where we should go. He seemed to direct us to another middle-class housing area in a section of the city (south end) known as Lincoln Heights. Once again I called house to house daily, making the initial contacts. The first Sunday thirty came from this new route. The second Sunday fifty-seven passengers were on their way to the church to be exposed to the most precious message in the world.

The second week in Lincoln Heights brought much delight and a few surprises. After we had picked up one little girl on the route, we noticed a car trailing behind.

Thinking that they were trying to pass us and were unable to do so because of our constant stops, I asked the driver to stop, stepped out of the bus and apologized to the family in the car, telling them that they could pass. Their response was almost humorous: "But, sir, you don't seem to understand. You see, our little daughter is in the bus. We would like to go to Sunday School also, but since we don't know where the church is, we decided to follow the bus. But our little girl won't go with us. She's in love with that bus."

We learned right there that there was something very special about a big yellow bus to many youngsters. That whole family was enrolled in our Sunday School.

Everyone was enthused by what was happening. We had already increased our Sunday School attendance by 50 percent, and less than a month had gone by. Again, we prayed about another bus route. Several suggestions were submitted but we had no real peace about them. Then we considered the area called Salishan, a large, low-class housing project. "You'll never get anyone from there," was the response from a number of "prophets." Again, the answer was work—door-to-door visitation. We pounded the pavement in organized obedience and once again the hand of the Lord was manifested.

I told our secretary that I was going to Salishan, and if I got any prospects I would know it was the will of the Lord in this difficult area. It was a rainy afternoon (something not too unusual in the Northwest at that time of year), but we found twenty-six prospects. What a happy day it was! Twenty-six souls for whom Christ died had been contacted and signed up for Sunday School. At this writing, we have four buses in that one area.

We felt we had just begun! God's direction and leading were evident; His seal of approval was clearly upon the program. December found us at it again through the rain and snow. We launched out into the deep in another area. Up to this time we had been renting school buses, but we had come to the end of available buses. We began to pray that the Lord would supply buses of our own.

The way the Lord directed us to the exact buses is as much a miracle as was filling them. One school gave us two for the price of one. They cost us the total sum of five hundred dollars. While there was a great deal of work to be done on them, it was a good investment. The generous people of the church began to give liberally toward the bus ministry. We bought two more from a Roman Catholic school—even buses can be converted for a more sanctified use!

One evening I answered the doorbell and a man handed me an envelope, telling me he had been instructed to deliver it from an anonymous source. The envelope contained seven hundred dollars for a bus. We were constantly alert to the possibilities of starting new bus routes.

Organization and transportation. While I have outlined the historical development of the bus ministry in our own church, it goes without saying that there must be some organization as it grows. Much of our experience was gained through trial and error. While such a method is better than no method, we learned some things through it, including the number of workers needed in order to avoid pitfalls. In establishing a visitation program, the following should be considered:

1. Bus superintendent. The bus superintendent is a person appointed by the pastor or board to give general oversight to the entire bus ministry. He should know something about the operation of buses; therefore, it will help if he is a mechanic or is mechanically inclined. He should also be a leader with the ability to work with people.

In our situation, we had a man who was the superintendent of a large fleet of trucks in the area. This was his work for years, and with his background he did a commendable job with the buses. He also was a spiritual man with leadership ability. This was the perfect combination.

The bus superintendent has the same responsibility as a departmental superintendent. He is in charge of the drivers, hoppers and bus pastors. It is advisable that the bus superintendent meet with the pastor or Christian education director at least twice a month to seek solutions to problems and to consider future plans.

2. Bus drivers. The bus driver is in charge of his route. He is to be given full responsibility for the bus route to which he is assigned.

3. Bus pastors and wives. It is an ideal situation to have a bus pastor for each bus, and his wife to assist him as hostess. They will act in the same capacity for their bus route as a pastor does for a church. They will visit the pupils, get acquainted with them, ride with them and look after their interests.

4. Hoppers. By far the most strenuous job is that of the hopper. One must be in good physical condition. When the bus stops in front of the house, the hopper will go to the front door, knock firmly, inquire as to the pupil's readiness and assist him onto the bus. We require this to be done at each house on the route. Often young people of high school age make good hoppers. They must be well dressed, friendly and dependable. They are taught to observe all safety precautions, to lead little ones to the bus by hand and to be general helpers on the bus route.

5. Registration crew. Generally the one in charge of the registration crew is also in charge of making up the routes. He (or she) works closely with the bus superintendent, noting any changes in the route and adding new names as they are secured in the visitation program. These updated routes are given to the drivers and hoppers each Sunday morning.

6. Welcome staff. This group works in connection with the registration crew. They help the children off the buses (with the hoppers) and assist by directing them to the registration desk. The children are registered there and taken by other members of the crew to the various departments. This group must be warm, friendly and endowed with plenty of patience.

7. A typical schedule. Following is a typical Sunday schedule for the bus ministry. While the times at various Sunday Schools will differ, the general order can be used.

8:30 A.M. Bus drivers and all workers check in for prayer and preliminary instructions. They receive route assignments, check buses, etc.

8:45 A.M. All buses ready for departure, depending on the length of the route. The bus is checked for cleanliness and is now ready with a driver, bus pastor and at least one hopper.

9:00 A.M. The bus stops at the first home and the hopper assists the children. As the children get on the bus, the bus pastor and his wife stamp the number and name of the bus on the child's hand.

9:45 A.M. Arrival at the church with load. It is important that the route be compact enough to get the job done and get the bus load to the church on time. For this reason we suggest small buses and short routes that do not cover a large area. New pupils are taken to the registration desk and given a dose of T.L.C. (tender loving care). They are welcomed, registered and given a pencil with the church name on it. A "hello" tag with the name and number of the bus written on it is given to each child. The new scholar is then taken by a worker to the department to which he or she belongs.

8. After the morning service. Bus drivers are back at the buses ready to receive the children following the morn-

ing service. This helps the children identify their buses. One pupil was heard to say, "Lady, can you tell me where the yellow bus driver is?" Not very flattering, to say the least, but the yellow tag helped to identify the bus.

Books and pamphlets have been written on the bus ministry which include material not mentioned here (we have found Beebe Publications has excellent materials to use). Methods vary according to the needs of the church. Most of the suggestions in this book have come from personal experience of starting with one bus and seeing the ministry grow.

Realization from transportation. When we talk in terms of realizing genuine results, we naturally think of the precious souls involved. If we could see as God sees, and look into eternity, we would agree that the investment of time and work in each child was well worth it. True, there will be problems—and many of them will be discipline problems, to say nothing of a stubborn bus that just will not start. But when you see the Lord work, even these things seem minor.

Once I heard a person make a remark something like this about a bus rider: "That boy is a potential criminal; he is the type that will kill a dozen people by the time he is sixteen." Yes, he already seemed to be a misfit in society. He kicked and threw himself on the floor and was rebellious and defiant. But after a few weeks of help and exposure to the Word of God, he was a different boy. Some cared enough to show a little love, all the way from the hopper that met him at the door to the Sunday School teacher who told him how to be saved.

These little "heart warmers" jump into your heart when you work with them long enough. Their enthusiasm in getting others to come is a delight to one's soul. Their participation in contests between bus routes shows that they are also potential Christian workers.

Yes, visitation and transportation go together. "Go and bring" is the command. Organized obedience includes both. The prospect of exposing many hearts and lives to the Lord makes this business worthwhile. Whether it is knocking on doors, following up or shifting into high gear on a bus full of precious lives, it is an exciting business. It is doing business for God.

Outline of a Typical Weekly Visitation Night

6:00 P.M. Supper for those who desire to participate. These are good, balanced meals. The fellowship is excellent and a good "warm-up" for the visitation to follow.

6:45 P.M. Visitation assignments and children's programs.

> 1. Workers who are going visiting meet together for encouragement and assignments, with the pastor in charge.
>
> a. Reports from previous week or preceding Sunday given.
>
> b. Encouragement given by pastor.
>
> c. Prayer and assignments.
>
> 2. Children's programs begin. These can take varied forms for various ages: children's choirs, nursery for babies, toddlers' hour, craft times, etc.

7:00 P.M. Visitors are on their own for organized obedience, going two by two.

8:15 P.M. Visitors return to make reports, and to pick up their children.

9:00 P.M. Items for praise and prayer burdens noted.

Is the Church Visitation Program Outdated?

Added to the many other reasons why the visitation program will not work, is the most recent idea that it is outdated in today's culture. It is interesting that we keep compiling more updated reasons for failure. It becomes necessary, therefore, to respond to this rationale, which is articulated in different ways.

Lifestyle evangelism is more
workable in today's society.

I have no problem with lifestyle evangelism if it simply means a constant heart for souls and an attempt to incorporate a practice of talking about the Lord into one's general lifestyle. Developing close friendships for the pur-pose of witnessing is commendable, but it need not be an "either/or" proposition. If some contend that church visitation is a means of "getting you off the hook" in your witnessing responsibilities, they are not only judging motives but have the wrong idea about the program and those involved in it. Actually, a regular visitation program ought to stimulate lifestyle evangelism. Moreover, lifestyle evangelism can be, and should be, an extension of the church program, not a replacement for it.

At this point, I must state that there is one aspect of lifestyle evangelism that I feel is dangerous, and that is the idea that this type of approach (often called "friendship evangelism") is less offensive. Sin does not become an issue, and confrontation is decidedly forbidden and is replaced with a "win-them-to-yourself" approach. Although no one would recommend an impolite, unrefined approach, it must be realized that sin *is* an issue in the matter of salvation. A classic case of one-to-one soul winning is seen in the Lord's ministry to the Samaritan woman. His technique is a prime example of contact, tact and yet Spirit-led confrontation.

The cults are involved in house-to-house work, which
makes visitation less acceptable today.

The fact is, the cults have always used this method successfully. It is interesting that while evangelicals are putting less emphasis on this method, the Roman Catholics, having observed the success of "false religions," have adopted this method. If the devil can use the divine method to promote his diabolic doctrine, should we abandon the method? The answer should be obvious.

Visitation evangelism no longer gets results.

We need only say that this has always been said. Probably it would be more suitable—and believable—if one said, "It no longer gets results *here.*" If I had a dollar for every time I have heard that statement I could finance several young men's seminary training for several years. It is disturbing that frequently the people of a church are more willing to implement such a program than the pastor. It has been my experience that the greatest hindrance to a visitation program is the leader of the flock. People want to be led and encouraged, and they are looking for men who will give them direction *in* the work, not diversions *from* the work.

Emphasis on the Sunday School is from a bygone period and is no longer needed.

I am constantly asked why our Sunday Schools are not growing. One reason is that "tails are wagging dogs" these days, and we are letting the church's ministries be replaced by other ministries. As much as I believe in the Christian school movement, I have seen many a church become an appendage to the school, with the latter becoming the main force in the church life. This is unhealthy and can be the demise of the institution that God has promised to bless—the church! When we think in terms of the church facilities existing primarily for the Christian school, and fail to emphasize the importance of the church and its other ministries (including the Sunday School), we are hindering rather than helping the church. After all, while education, and development of the children are important aspects of the church life, we run the risk of being isolated from the world and think in terms of personal aggrandizement rather than personal evangelism. The Sunday School should continue to be a means of reaching the lost for Jesus Christ and helping them grow in grace and knowledge. But the Sunday School needs the outreach capabilities of the visitation program to keep it fresh and growing and to reach those who might not otherwise be reached. Yes, let's continue our Christian education approach in schools, colleges and seminaries, but let's not abandon tried and true ways of reaching the lost. As a pastor, your leadership in this area is vital .

THE LAST BOY OFF

We waited as the bus pulled up,
Such life, and such variety.
The teeming tiny tots who squirm,
The young adults' propriety.

Some smiled, they'd been to Sunday School
Before, these young enthusiasts
Now felt the place belonged to them,
And hustled off to class.

Still others, quite reluctant yet,
The maiden voyage on the bus,
The buildings new, the faces strange,
All seemed still quite mysterious.

Off jumps a happy little girl
Holding a Bible in her hand,
Mischievous John follows behind
Dressed like a little gentleman.

Then, pushing, teasing little Paul,
And prim and proper Jane,
Some dressed in fancy clothes,
Others, still sweet, just clean and plain.

The last boy off, a little guy,
Came to the door, expressed alarm,
The steps were long, his legs were short,
He closed his eyes—jumped in my arms.

That little fellow touched my heart,
So young, so sweet, so free
From the distracting world
Had leaped and trusted me.

Reflecting on that incident
I realized that my Lord too—
Had now, this hour, entrusted me
To give that child the message true.

So little—now—so ready to
Receive the Word, I knew that he
Would face a day, a month, a life,
And then, through death—eternity.

"Dear Lord, the value of this soul
Make each of us keenly aware;
Our bus brings him to Sunday School,
Now, may he find salvation there."

C.U.W.

Part Two: Evangelistic Campaigns

While the church should have an evangelistic emphasis the year-round, there is a very important place for the evangelistic campaign. It is a specified effort made by the church to bring in the unsaved and expose their hearts to the gospel. It is certainly revealing to hear a pastor state that he feels no need of evangelistic campaigns. The one who makes such a statement is one who really needs them. Such a series of services with an evangelistic emphasis should be conducted at least once a year.

The Choosing of an Evangelist

Choose an evangelist. It should be understood that we are not simply talking about "special meetings." Other kinds of meetings might be included under this heading, such as prophetic Bible conferences, or conferences with a Bible teaching or missionary emphasis. These are all excellent, but they should not be called evangelistic meetings. If the primary emphasis is to draw the unsaved, a conference on the "Ten Toes of Daniel Two" is not what one wants. Certainly an evangelistic application can be made from such a passage, but a Bible or prophetic conference is not the same as one where preaching the gospel is the major emphasis. In selecting an evangelist, be sure you invite a man gifted of God to do work that is primarily directed to the unsaved.

Choose an evangelist who will not be embarrassing to the church. If you select a man who does not have the same stand as the church and who is not in sympathy with what the church is doing, you are inviting trouble. If you invite an evangelist who is not ethical in his practices and consistent in his spiritual life, you will reap a harvest of barren results.

A few evangelists resort to gimmicks and high pressure salesmanship. These make you wonder if you are not promoting the cause of the evangelist rather than the cause of the Lord. Most evangelists that I know personally are men of high standards. When they come to minister in a church they have but one goal—that of seeing people saved. However, the one exception often leaves a bad name for the others. This is, of course, as unfair as it would be to judge all pastors in a fellowship by a few who are misfits.

We are not suggesting that the evangelist ought not to strike hard—where it hurts—or ought not to "step on toes." This is certainly vital if the "hammer" of the Word is going to do its convicting work. This is not embarrassing to the church but the very thing for which the church has prayed. Certainly a true revival is desired, a true ingathering of souls, not simply a week of meetings.

Choose an evangelist who is recommended by people whom you trust and respect. A man should be chosen who has a good "track record." I am not simply talking about the number of decisions. I am referring to a man who has been faithful to the Word, preaches with power and has had real fruit in his meetings with blessings continuing after he has left. There are many who fit in this category from which to prayerfully choose.

Preparing for the Evangelistic Campaign

Preparation in prayer. The prospective campaign ought to be the object of much prayer as to the choosing of the evangelist as well as the time and over-all planning of the meeting. Cottage prayer meetings could be organized, involving the whole membership of the church.

Preparation in finances. One of the most sensitive areas in planning a campaign is the matter of finances. There are those who feel that a financial outlay for evangelistic meetings is not necessary and is, in fact, a waste of the Lord's money. The problem here is not simply one of finances; it is a spiritual problem. As a pastor, it is your responsibility to seek to correct such an attitude.

The yearly evangelistic emphasis should be a part of the church budget. Months ahead of time, much thought should be given to the expenses of the meetings in order to avoid having to make strong appeals to the congregation during the meetings. While it is true that a church will often use the offerings of the first few evenings to help defray the expenses, we feel that a better route would be to prepare for the expenses beforehand so that more emphasis can be placed on the message itself. Included in these expenses will be not only the housing of the evangelist but his travel and other campaign expenses, such as publicity, utilities, etc.

There should be an understanding between the church and the evangelist regarding the love offering. Misunderstandings are not only unfortunate but sometimes ruin the spirit of the meetings. The pastor should do all he can to help the evangelist in this respect. It should be remembered that the evangelist does not generally receive a regular salary and is dependent on the offerings taken in these meetings. What may seem to be a "great" offering is not generally that great when you consider an evangelist might have only twenty meetings per year.

This offering is generally taken the last few nights of the campaign. Often love offering envelopes are given to the whole membership. It is always appreciated when the pastor understands the evangelist's need and leads his people in the matter of supporting the evangelist's ministry.

Preparation for the evangelist. Remember, the man you choose is the man of God for the hour. Everything possible should be done to get the maximum benefit of the Lord's ministry through him. He should be provided a place to stay which will be conducive to prayer and study as he prepares for the nightly meetings. A clean, comfortable motel room is recommended. The expenses for this are insignificant considering the benefits derived by both the evangelist and the church. While some meals will be with the people, it is my judgment that this be no more than once a day. Eating in the homes of the people two or three times a day is time-consuming and difficult physically. It is hard to watch one's diet when being served "Sunday dinner" twice a day, seven times a week. Be reasonable here.

Preparation for the meetings.

Publicize the meetings

a. Through word of mouth. Nothing takes the place of personal contact. This should be done by the friends and members of the church in their places of employment, schools, neighborhoods, etc.

b. Through the visitation program. Instead of making regular absentee calls or follow-up calls in the visitation program, it would be advisable for each caller to emphasize the evangelistic campaign and cover the area with invitations to the meetings.

c. Through newspaper advertising. This can be done with paid ads and news releases.

d. Through the mail. If the church has a weekly or monthly paper, this should be used to broadcast the meetings. Cards and letters should be mailed to those on the church mailing lists.

e. Through fellow pastors. While in some cases the meetings might conflict with the programs of other churches, generally some nights are free for people of sister churches to attend and to bring in their unsaved friends.

f. Through other contacts. Radio, television and other media can be used in getting out the message concerning the meetings. Sometimes a radio or television interview can be arranged.

It goes without saying that if you expect to see conversions, the unsaved must be there to hear the gospel. Too often the evangelist preaches to a congregation of saved people, many of whom will end up complaining that the decisions were sparse. Employ every available means of getting the unsaved to the meetings.

Follow-Up

Follow-up is done after the evangelist is gone. The complaint that there were no permanent results is often the fault of the pastor and the church for not properly taking care of the follow-up on each one who made a decision. A planned program should be arranged whereby each convert is coupled with a mature Christian who will help him in the early stages of spiritual infancy. Instruction should be given through the steps of obedience in baptism and church membership. Enrollment in a new converts class will assist the converts in their spiritual growth. A good booklet to help them find answers in the Bible for themselves is *Basic Bible Truths for New Converts* (published by Regular Baptist Press, Schaumburg, IL). Another good book is the Moody paperback, *The Abundant Life.*

End Notes

[1] Charles H. Spurgeon, *The Soul Winner,* condensed and abridged by David Otis Fuller (Grand Rapids: Zondervan Publishing House, 1948), p. 26. Used by permission.

[2] Charles U. Wagner, messages on "Visitation Evangelism" first published in *The Biblical Evangelist* (Brownsburg, IN: June-November 1970), vol. 5, issues 2–7.

[3] J. E. Conant, *Every Member Evangelism* (NY: Harper and Brothers, 1922), p. 112.

[4] Walter B. Knight, *Knight's Treasury of Illustrations* (Grand Rapids: Wm. B. Eerdmans Publishing Co., 1963), p. 380. Used by permission.

[5] A. T. Pierson, *Life-Power or Character, Culture and Conduct* (Old Tappan, NJ: Fleming H. Revell Co., 1895), p. 112.

[6] Ibid., p. 129.

CHAPTER TEN
Pastoral Visitation

In the preceding chapter we studied the importance of getting the people to join the pastor in organized obedience, i.e., serving the Lord in a church visitation program. In this chapter we will consider the pastor's personal visitation program. We will consider the types of calls and the proper handling of them by the pastor.

Types of Calls

House-to-house calling. If a pastor is going to lead a church and help build it, it will often become necessary for him to involve himself in house-to-house visitation. This leadership will inspire his people to join him. He should be the "expert" in this and be able to teach others to do it. I have personally knocked on thousands of doors in each community where I have been a pastor. It is certainly a rewarding work.

When one examines the great successful churches and Sunday Schools that are on the constant increase, it will not be surprising to learn that the pastor himself is doing what he is asking his people to do—calling.

1. The best time to call. I suggest that the pastor set aside at least one afternoon a week for house-to-house calling. Thursday or Friday afternoon may be the best time. The most productive hours are probably between two and five o'clock. One advantage of these hours is that children come home from school then and calling when they are home often helps in the response to the invitation. Evening calls can be made, but the later hours present some

definite difficulties with family plans.

2. Where should the calls be made? A logical starting point is for the pastor to begin near the church and then branch out. Five or six square blocks can be covered in a few days. It is much easier to refer to the church when you are in an area where people are familiar with it. Of course, as the months go by, if this door-to-door calling is done consistently, the perimeter of outreach will expand more and more.

3. What is the major emphasis of the call? The ultimate objective is to bring people to Christ. However, each call is made with the realization that this may not be consummated there on the doorstep. Nevertheless, a witness should always be left. The first step toward the goal may be that of inviting the family to church. Seek to assure them that you are not simply trying to fill pews but that you have an earnest desire to meet their spiritual needs.

The opening for future contact may be made when the pastor expresses that he is anxious to meet some of the people in the community. He can then tell them something about the church activities and assure them that he would like to be at their disposal to help at any time. While many of them will not react immediately, when there is a spiritual need they will remember the pastor who called in their home and showed a genuine concern for them. If the door-to-door contact can be made on the basis of getting better acquainted with the people, and to better acquaint them with the church, many of them in time will be reached for Christ. I have found it helpful to approach people from the vantage point of inviting them to Sunday School, applying the rules that are mentioned in the foregoing chapter.

4. What are the areas of soul-winning calls? Every pastor ought to be a soul-winner! There are those, however, who find it easier to preach about it than to do it. Tragically,

some who are the best-trained in the techniques of soul-winning are the most inactive. Do not fail in this aspect of the high calling of God to reach men with the gospel. The various areas of soul-winning from the vantage point of the pastor are many. A few are listed here:

a. Community calls. This has been touched upon in relation to church calling under the heading of house-to-house calling. But the pastor as well as members need to be constantly mindful that the major objective in any calling upon the unsaved is to bring them to a saving knowledge of Christ. Often the Spirit of God uses the pastor to lead someone to the Lord in the initial contact in the house-to-house calling in his community.

b. Follow-up calls. Frequently the pastor will follow up a call on someone whom he or a member in his congregation has initially visited. The ground having been prepared by the initial contact, the pastor is in a position to lead that one to Christ as the Spirit directs.

c. Referral calls. Members of the congregation may fill out a card or call the church office, giving the name of someone who has a particular need or who is interested in spiritual things. The pastor can approach that home on the basis of having a mutual friend. With this opening he may gain entrance to home and heart and find the people ready to respond to the gospel.

d. Special calls. Some of the best opportunities for the pastor to witness are presented when calls are made on the bereaved, or when counseling with people who have special pressures and problems.

Another important occasion for giving the plan of salvation is when the pastor counsels a young couple about to be married. His initial meeting with them should always deal with whether or not they know Christ as Savior; if not, he can then give them the gospel.

Hospital calling. One of the outstanding areas of pastoral ministry and service is hospital calling.

1. General suggestions for hospital calling.

a. Hospitals across the country differ in procedure. When calling in a hospital for the first time, go to the receptionist at the information desk. Introduce yourself to her and tell her the name of the patient you would like to visit; also ask about the hospital's policies regarding ministers calling on patients.

b. Many hospitals have a special file for pastors which can be checked to see who else from your church may be in the hospital. Those patients who have indicated Baptist preference but who are not affiliated with a local church will also be listed. This file ought to be checked as you enter the hospital, for there may be two or three of your people on one particular floor. If you find others listed under "Baptist" who do not have a pastor or a church, permission can be secured to call on them. In some instances you may want to check with the chaplain in the hospital and discuss the case with him.

c. When you arrive at the correct floor of the hospital, go to the nursing station. Introduce yourself and give the name of the patient upon whom you would like to call. The nurse will probably check the room to make sure that everything is all clear. Never go into a room when the door is closed without checking with the nurse. The patient may not be prepared for visitors or the doctor may be in the room.

d. Avoid calling during visitors' hours. If you are going to talk to the patient about spiritual matters, you will find it difficult with other visitors present. The best time is probably just before visiting hours. Late hours should be avoided, as often the patient is tired.

In his unpublished writings on the *Pastor's Approach to the Sick Room,* Dr. Robert L. Powell has observed:

A wise pastor would try to work in close cooperation with the doctors and nurses. There can be wonderful helpfulness in this field of mutual understanding. A nurse who feels that the pastor is an intruder is a serious hindrance to the spiritual well-being of the patient, regardless of the malady. I have had the finest attitude shown me in this matter, and on the other hand, some few who have been very rude, resulting in a discordant and unhappy situation. At the same time I am fully aware of the fact that some preachers have been just plain pugnacious and temperamental, and that is the worst form of discord to introduce in a sickroom. There ought to be an understanding attitude on the part of the doctors and the nurses, and in all cases where there is consecrated common sense, there will be such an attitude.

2. Specific suggestions for hospital calling.

a. Be yourself. An air of professionalism is not becoming to a minister of the gospel. There is no need to be pompous and overbearing in your approach.

Again, Powell says:

I know of no field where more wisdom is needed than in a sickroom, especially where a bit of lack of wisdom may bring disastrous results to the patient. One does not have to precipitate a brawl in order to create tension in the mind of the patient. A sickroom patient is psychic in his or her feelings, and will register discord without a word being said. If there is a feeling of serious opposition on the part of either the visiting pastor or the attending nurses and doctors, the patient will sense it. For this reason I am very careful of my approach to the patient, and if the doctor is available, I will always defer to him first.

b. Do not stay too long. Five or ten minutes is ample. While you do not want to give the impression that you are in a hurry, many pastors make the mistake of staying too long. Brief visits which do not seem hurried will be greatly appreciated.

c. Do not talk about yourself or an illness you have had that is similar to that of the patient. It is enough for the patient to have his own burden. Do not expect him to bear your burden as well.

d. Do not sit on the bed. It is bad manners and against hospital rules. Do not lay your hat or coat on the bed. If possible, these should be checked in the hall. If this cannot be done, wear the coat or fold it across your arms or lap.

e. Do not talk against the physician or agree with the patient if he feels that the care is not good or the physician is not doing the right thing.

f. Listen to the patient but do not discuss the illness. Certainly do not give any information concerning the diagnosis of the case. Do not ask what is wrong with the patient; do not encourage lengthy explanations.

g. Read some appropriate Scripture, make a few comments regarding it and pray. Do not preach; be careful that you are not loud or rude. There will be some cases where you will not read Scripture but will simply pray. In other rare cases the Lord may even lead you not to pray but only to say a few words and leave.

h. Do not be a "joker" or facetious. While you should have a happy spirit, reference to parts of the patient's anatomy or the equipment in the room in crude attempts at humor is unforgivable. Remember the dignity of your office as a pastor.

i. Be willing to listen to the patient. There is much therapy in just having an ear ready to hear and sympathize with the needs of the person. This will give you ideas in selecting Scripture portions to read that will help the patient cope with his problems.

Again quoting Powell:

Medicine is not all that a patient needs. Nor is

physical care all the needed help. There is no case where spiritual help may not be the greatest help, if it can be used wisely.

3. Special types of calls.
a. Calls on those to undergo surgery. It may be better for the pastor to call the night before. Sometimes the pastor can see the patient in the morning just before the surgery. However, he must get there at least two hours before the surgery is scheduled because the patient will be given his preoperative medicine early.
b. Calls on those who are dying. If the patient brings up the subject of death or eternity, do not avoid it by assuring him that everything is all right. Do not give him false hope! If he is in need, he often knows it and wants help. Help him! At the same time, you can assure him that you will be praying for him, and even in your prayer you can thank the Lord for what He is pleased to do on the patient's behalf. If he wants to discuss the subject of death, be a good listener. You must remember that God gives special grace to those of His own who are dying. Many Christians are willing and even want to talk about Heaven and the Lord during those last hours. Appropriate verses on the subject will be helpful.

If the patient is unsaved, do not take advantage of him and force a decision. Be gentle and understanding, and do all you can to bring that person to a saving knowledge of Christ without making him do something against his will.

In all hospital calls be cheerful and optimistic. Pray that God will direct and lead you in the exact Scripture and words to be used.
4. Verses to use in hospital visitation. The following series of passages comes from a book entitled *Scripture Portions for the Afflicted,* especially for the sick. It was put out by the Presbyterian Board of Publications in 1840. While

each portion of Scripture has an accompanying reflection from various authors, space does not permit including them here.

Old Testament

Genesis 42:36; 47:9
Deuteronomy 8:5
1 Samuel 3:18; 2 Samuel 24:14
2 Kings 1:2; 2 Chronicles 16:12; 32:24, 25
Job 1:22; 2:3, 10; 5:6, 17; 7:3, 17, 18, 20; 10:2;
13:15; 14:1; 23:10; 34:23, 31, 33; 35:10
Psalm 6:1, 2, 5; 9:10; 16:4; 23:1-6; 25:18; 30:2, 5;
31:15; 32:4; 34:7, 19; 38:1, 6-8; 39:4, 7, 9-11, 13;
41:3; 42:4; 46:1, 10; 50:15; 51:4; 55:22; 66:10;
73:26; 77:7, 8; 78:34, 38, 39; 86:7; 88:7; 89:30-33;
90:12; 91:5, 9, 10; 94:12; 103:2-5; 107:17-21;
112:4; 116:3, 5, 8, 9; 119:50, 67, 71, 72, 75, 83, 92;
126:5
Proverbs 3:11, 12; 11:31; 13:1; 17:17; 18:10; 29:10
Ecclesiastes 7:13, 14; 9:1
Isaiah 1:5; 12:1; 26:16; 32:24; 38:9, 12, 14, 16,
19, 22; 43:2; 48:10; 57:16; 63:9
Jeremiah 5:3; 9:7; 10:24; 12:1; 22:21
Lamentations 3:1, 19, 20, 22, 39
Daniel 4:37
Hosea 2:6; 5:15
Amos 3:6
Micah 6:9; 7:9
Zephaniah 3:12
Zechariah 13:9

New Testament

Mark 5:5; Luke 22:42
John 5:14; 11:3, 4; 18:11

Acts 14:22
Romans 5:3-5; 8:18, 28; 12:12
1 Corinthians 3:21-23
2 Corinthians 1:3, 4; 4:16, 17; 5:1, 4; 7:6
Philippians 1:21
Hebrews 4:15; 6:19; 12:5, 6-11
James 1:2, 4, 12; 5:7, 13
1 Peter 1:6, 7; 5:6, 10
Revelation 3:19; 21:4

Every member calling. In smaller churches it may be expected and it is advisable to call on every member once a year. With the pastor's many pressures and responsibilities, this is difficult, if not impossible, today unless the congregation is confined to the local community. However, if you state you are going to do it, then be sure that you follow through. Do not make promises you cannot keep; many have done this to their own detriment. Every member calling can be done in alphabetical order, or by calling on the members on a given street or in a given area. The latter is preferable, reducing the time to complete the work.

New visitor calling. This area of calling has been touched on in an earlier paragraph under soul winning. However, there will be a great many people attending the church who are Christians looking for a church home. Many of these calls can be referred to the deacons; some of them should be called upon in your regular calling program. While it is good to send your deacons to visit those who attend your church for the first time, nothing takes the place of the pastor himself going. It is better to phone first and let the party know you are coming. Otherwise they may be embarrassed because the house is not in order. This call can be just a friendly call with the purpose of becoming acquainted. Take information relating to the church to leave in the home. This will give opportunity for the family to get to know you and to ask questions about the church you represent.

Keeping the Records

A system must be established for recording the calls and contacts made. There are various record books on the market designed for this purpose, some of them particularly for the pastor. I personally have found that the *Seven Star Diary* (may be purchased from Global Sales Corp., 1021 S. Linwood Ave., Santa Ana, CA 92705) is handy and lends itself well to keeping a record of all personal contacts, calls and engagements. With this system I am able to refer back to the last several years and find out where I called on a particular day, how many calls were made, and what verses were used in the call. It is very important to keep an accurate, up-to-date record of this kind of information.

The Benefits of Pastoral Calling

E. D. Dolloff gives the following benefits and fruits of visitation:

1. The pastor comes to know his people.
2. The people come to know their pastor.
3. It furnishes vital homiletic material.
4. It strengthens the financial life of the church.
5. It affords the finest of evangelistic opportunities.[1]

End Note
[1] Eugene Dinsmore Dolloff, *The Romance of Doorbells* (Valley Forge, PA: Judson Press, 1951), pp. 26-48. Used by permission.

CHAPTER ELEVEN

The Pastor as a Counselor

Dr. Gary R. Collins poses the question, "When you have a personal problem and need help, where do you turn?" Then he continues:

> Several years ago, a question similar to this was included as part of the national survey. Of the respondents who had actually gone for help, about ten percent had consulted community clinics, eighteen percent had visited psychologists or psychiatrists, twenty-nine percent had talked with a physician, and an amazing forty-two percent had taken their problems to a pastor.[1]

The Pastor-Counselor and the Dangers He Faces

The danger of considering himself a psychologist. This is not to suggest that only the psychologist can counsel adequately. Conversely, it is felt by a number of qualified people that the most adequate person for counseling is the pastor who can meet the spiritual need of his parishioners. This view seems to be held by Jay E. Adams. He states that as a young minister he sought to improve his counseling acumen by reading various books on the subject. However,

> I soon became disillusioned with the standard books and was tempted to fall in the common

practice of referring nearly all counselees with serious problems to psychiatrists or state mental institutions. After all, that was what the mental health propaganda advised. As a matter of fact, stern warnings against counseling anyone with difficulties more serious than a psychic scratch studded the pages of books and pamphlets published by the Mental Health Association. Pastors were threatened with the possibility of doing serious harm to people if they did not refer. One trouble with this otherwise convenient solution, however, was that people who were referred frequently returned worse off or no better. And, then, there was the problem of the non-Christian counsel given by unconverted psychiatrists. How could that be justified?[2]

The point I am making is that although you are competent to counsel and you will be doing a great deal of it, you are first and foremost a pastor-teacher. It might be ego-inflating to have a line of people at your door waiting for your professional advice, but you must remember that it is possible to be so involved in this area that the major work of ministering the Word is neglected. I therefore advise:

1. Do not advertise your services.
2. Be careful to confine most of your counsel
   ing to your own people.
3. Watch your schedule and do not let counseling rob you of study time and other vital aspects of your ministry.
4. Maintain a balanced ministry. Pray for it!
   Insist on it! Do not let the tail wag the dog!

The danger of being poorly equipped to do serious counseling. One of the chief assets of the well-rounded, balanced pastor is his ability to see himself and his limitations. He should keep himself well-read in the field of counseling. It is my opinion that three of the finest books written on this subject are: *Competent to Counsel* by Jay E. Adams (Presbyterian and Reformed Publishing Co., Nutley, NJ, 1974); and his advanced book, *The Christian Counselor's Manual* (Baker Book House, Grand Rapids, MI, 1973); Clyde Narramore's helpful book, *The Psychology of Counseling* (Zondervan Publishing House, Grand Rapids, MI, 1960; available at Christian bookstores or from the Narramore Christian Foundation, Rosemead, CA).

The Pastor-Counselor and His Family

Know thyself! This is rule number one for helping others. If the pastor has serious emotional or spiritual problems, it is difficult for him to help others. Paul said to Timothy, "Take heed unto thyself, and unto the doctrine" (1 Tim. 4:16).

A right relationship with his own family will help in counseling others. A good family life and right relationship between the pastor and his wife and between the pastor and his children are important.

Few things leave a counselor more vulnerable to possible sexual complications growing out of the counseling relationship than the lack of a satisfactory home life. If a minister cannot enjoy a family outing without feeling guilty that he ought to be doing something at the church; if, out of anxiety or ambition, he feels compelled to maintain a facade of outward perfection which never allows him nor any member of his household the normal human prerogative of mistakes; if his wife insists on placing him upon a pedestal so that he cannot relax and be human even at home, he has potentially explosive problems that require immediate attention.[3]

The Pastor-Counselor and His People

C. E. Colton lists a number of prerequisites for pastoral counseling. They are:

1. He must manifest a love for and interest in his people.
2. The minister must know and understand his people.
3. The minister must have some knowledge of the principles of psychology and psychiatry.
4. The minister must give evidence in his own life of having conquered problems in the power and leadership of Christ.[4]

Gary R. Collins lists the skills and abilities in counseling as follows:

Helping Others
1. Learn to listen.
2. Don't be afraid of silence.
3. Be a careful observer.
4. Learn to make appropriate responses.
5. Be knowledgeable.
6. Keep quiet.
7. Be yourself.[5]

In his excellent book, *The Christian Counselor's Manual*, Jay E. Adams lists fifty failure factors regarding counseling. With permission from the editors we have taken the liberty of listing them here.

Fifty Failure Factors
For a quick check on what may be behind counseling failure, consider the following factors:

1. Is the counselee truly a Christian?
2. Has there been genuine repentance?
3. Is there a vital commitment to the Biblical change?
4. Are your agendas in harmony?
5. Do you have *all* of the necessary data?
6. Are you trying to achieve change in the abstract or concretely?
7. Have you been intellectualizing?
8. Would a medical examination be in order?
9. Are you sure that you know the problem(s)? Is more data-gathering necessary?
10. Are there other problems that must be settled first?
11. Have you been trying to deal with the *issue* while ignoring the *relationship*?
12. Did you give adequate Scriptural hope?
13. Did you minimize?
14. Have you accepted speculative data as true?
15. Are you regularly assigning concrete homework?
16. Would using a D. P. P. (Discovering Problem Patterns) form help?
17. If this is a life-dominating problem, are you counseling for total restructuring?
18. Are you empathizing with self-pity?
19. Are you talking about problems only or also about God's solutions?
20. Have you carefully analyzed the counselee's attitudes expressed in his language?
21. Have you allowed the counselee to talk about others behind their backs?
22. Has a new problem entered the picture, or has the situation changed since the counseling sessions began?
23. Have you been focusing on the wrong problem?
24. Is the problem not so complex, after all, but simply a case of open rebellion?

25. Have you failed to move forward rapidly enough in the giving of homework assignments?
26. Have you as a counselor fallen into some of the same problems as the counselee?
27. Does doctrinal error lie at the base of the problem?
28. Do drugs (tranquilizers, etc.) present a complicating problem?
29. Have you stressed the put-off to the exclusion of the put-on?
30. Have you prayed about the problem?
31. Have you personally turned off the counselee in some way?
32. Is he willing to settle for something less than the Scriptural solution?
33. Have you been less aggressive and demanding than the Scriptures?
34. Have you failed to give hope by calling sin *sin*?
35. Is the counselee convinced that personality change is impossible?
36. Has your counseling been feeling-oriented rather than commandment-oriented?
37. Have you failed to use the full resources ofChrist (e.g., the help of the Christian community)?
38. Is church discipline in order?
39. Have you set poor patterns in previous sessions (e.g., accepting partially fulfilled homework assignments)?
40. Do you really know the Biblical solution(s) to his problem? (Can you write it out in thematic form?)
41. Do you really believe there is hope?
42. Has the counselee been praying, reading the Scriptures, fellowshiping with God's people and witnessing regularly?
43. Could you call in another Christian counselor for help (with the counselee's knowledge, of course)?

44. Would a full rereading of your Weekly Counseling Records disclose any patterns? Trends? Unexplored areas?
45. Have you questioned only intensively? Extensively?
46. Have you been assuming (wrongly) that this case is similar to a previous case?
47. Has the counselee been concealing or twisting data?
48. Would someone else involved in the problem (husband, wife, parent, child) be able to supply needed data?
49. Are you simply incompetent to handle this sort of problem?
50. Are you reasonably sure that there is no organic base to the problem?[6]

In another listing Adams sets down "Some Don'ts in Counseling" and suggests that it would be useful to reread these before each period of counseling. They are as follows:

Don't allow counselees to:
1. Act on feeling.
2. Avoid problems.
3. Blame others.
4. Lose hope.
5. Remain undisciplined and disorganized.
6. Harbor grudges.
7. Simply talk about problems.
8. Stop with forgiveness.
9. Talk about another behind his back.
10. Shut off communication.
11. Give up when they fail.
12. Goof off on homework.
13. Settle for solutions to immediate problems when wrong underlying patterns remain.
14. Neglect regular prayer, Bible study and church

attendance.
15. Leave without hearing the gospel.
16. Generalize rather than specify.
17. Use any other basis than the Bible for belief or action.
18. Make major decisions when depressed or greatly pressured.
19. Use inaccurate language to describe their problems.
20. Call sin sickness.
21. Hurt others in solving their own problems.
22. Wallow in self-pity, envy or resentment.
23. Become dependent upon the counseling session.
24. Set unbiblical agendas for counseling.
25. Continue counseling in an uncommitted manner.[7]

The Pastor-Counselor and His Use of Scripture

The following verses have been compiled by Clyde Narramore, a Christian psychologist, in his book, *The Psychology of Counseling*. I suggest that you refer to these when dealing with the situations listed.

Selected Scriptures for Use in Counseling

Anxiety and worry: Ps. 43:5; Matt 6:31, 32; Phil. 4:6, 7, 19; 1 Pet. 5:7.

Bereavement and loss: Deut. 31:8; Ps. 27:10; 119:50, 92; 2 Cor. 6:10; Phil. 3:8.

Comfort: Ps. 23:4; Lam. 3:22, 23; Matt. 5:4; 11:28; John 14:16, 18; Rom. 15:4; 2 Cor. 1:3, 4; 2 Thess. 2:16, 17.

Death: Ps. 23:4; 116:15; Lam. 3:32, 33; Rom. 14:8; 2 Cor. 5:1; Phil. 1:21; 1 Thess. 5:9, 10; 2 Tim. 4:7, 8; Heb. 9:27; Rev. 21:4.

Developing confidence: Ps. 27:3; Prov. 3:26; 14:26; Isa. 30:15; Gal. 6:9; Eph. 3:11, 12; Phil. 1:6; 4:13; Heb. 10:35; 1 Pet. 2:9.

Discipline through difficulties: Rom. 8:28; 2 Cor. 4:17; Heb. 5:8; 12:7, 11; Rev. 3:19.

Disappointments: Ps. 43:5; 55:22; 126:6; John 14:27; 2 Cor. 4:8, 9.

Discouragement: Josh. 1:9; Ps. 27:14; 43:5; John 14:1, 27; 16:33; Heb. 4:16; 1 John 5:14.

Faith: Rom. 4:3; 10:17; Eph. 2:8,9; Heb. 11:1,6; 12:2; James 1:3, 5, 6; 1 Pet. 1:7.

Fear: Ps. 27:1; 56:11; Prov. 3:25; Isa. 51:12; John 14:27; Rom. 8:31; 2 Tim. 1:7; 1 John 4:18.

Forgiveness of sin: Ps. 32:5; 51:1-19; 103:3; Prov. 28:13; Isa. 1:18; 55:17; 1 John 1:9; James 5:15, 16.

Forgiving others: Matt. 5:44-47; 6:12; Mark 11:25; Eph. 4:32; Col. 3:13.

Friends and friendliness: Prov. 18:24; Matt. 22:39; John 13:35; 15:13, 14; Gal. 6:1, 10.

Growing spiritually: Eph. 3:17-19; Col. 1:9-11; 3:16; 1 Tim. 4:15; 2 Tim. 2:15; 1 Pet. 2:2; 2 Pet. 1:5-8; 3:18.

Guidance: Ps. 30:21; 32:8; Isa. 58:11; Luke 1:79; John 16:13.

Help and care: 2 Chron. 16:9; Ps. 34:7; 37:5, 24; 55:22; 91:4; Isa. 50:9; 54:17; Heb. 4:16; 13:5, 6; 1 Pet. 5:7.

Loneliness: Ps. 23; 27:10; Isa. 41:10; Matt. 28:20; Heb. 13:5.

Love (God's): John 3:16; 15:9; Rom. 5:8; 8:38, 39; 1 John 3:1.

Obedience: 1 Sam. 15:22; Ps. 111:10; 119:2; Matt. 6:24; John 14:15, 21; James 2:10; 1 John 3:22.

Peace of mind: Isa. 26:3; John 14:27; 16:33; Rom. 5:1; Phil. 4:7; Col. 3:15.

Persecution: Matt. 5:10, 11; 10:22; Acts 5:41; 9:16; Rom. 8:17; 2 Tim. 3:12; Heb. 11:25; 1 Pet. 2:20.

Praise and gratitude: 1 Sam. 12:24; Ps. 34:1; 50:23; 51:15; 69:30; 107:8; 139:14; Eph. 5:20; Heb. 13:6, 15.

Protection from danger: Ps. 23:4; 32:7; 34:7, 17, 19; 91:1, 11; 121:8; Isa 43:2; Rom. 14:8.

Provision: Ps. 34:10; 37:3, 4; 84:11; Isa. 58:11; Matt. 6:33; 2 Cor. 9:8; Phil. 4:19.

Return of Christ: Luke 21:36; Acts 1:11; 1 Thess. 4:16-18; Titus 2:13; 1 John 3:2, 3.

Sickness: Ps. 41:3; 103:3; Matt. 4:23; John 11:4; James 5:15, 16.

Sin: Isa. 53:5, 6; 59:1, 2; John 8:34; Rom. 3:23; 6:23; Gal. 6:7, 8.

Sorrow: Prov. 10:22; Isa. 53:4; John 16:22; 2 Cor. 6:10; 1 Thess. 4:13; Rev. 21:4.

Strength: Deut. 33:25; Ps. 27:14; 28:7; Isa. 40:29, 31; 41:10; 2 Cor. 12:9; Phil. 4:13.

Suffering: Rom. 8:18; 2 Cor. 1:5; Phil. 1:29; 3:10; 2 Tim. 2:12; 1 Pet. 2:19; 4:12, 13, 16; 5:10.

Temptation: 1 Cor. 10:12, 13; Heb. 2:18; James 1:2, 3, 12, 14; 1 Pet. 1:6; 2 Pet. 2:9; Jude 24.

Trusting: Ps. 5:11; 18:2; 37:5; Prov. 3:5, 6; Isa. 12:2.

Victory: 2 Chron. 32:8; Rom. 8:37; 1 Cor. 15:57; 2 Cor. 2:14; 2 Tim. 2:19; 1 John 5:4; Rev. 3:5; 21:7.

Selected Scriptures for Use in Soul Winning

Man's need of salvation: Isa. 64:6; Rom. 3:10, 23; 5:12; 6:23; Heb. 9:27; 1 John 1:10.

Jesus Christ is the Savior of the world: Matt. 1:21; Luke 19:10; John 3:16; 14:6; Acts 4:12; Rom. 5:8; Eph. 1:7; 1 John 5:12.

God's Word gives the plan of salvation: Isa. 55:7; John 1:12; 3:3; 5:24; Rom. 10:9; Eph. 2:8, 9; Titus 3:5; 1 John 1:9; Rev. 3:20.

Assurance of salvation: Matt. 24:35; John 5:24; 6:37; 10:28; 20:31; Rom. 8:16; 1 John 5:13.

Overcoming temptation: Isa. 41:10; Matt. 26:41; 1 Cor. 10:13; Phil. 1:6; 2 Thess. 3:3; 2 Pet. 2:9.

Living the Christian life: Ps. 119:11; John 15:7; 2 Cor. 5:17; Col. 2:6; 1 Pet. 2:2; 1 John 1:7.

Christian fellowship: Matt. 18:20; John 13:34; Acts 2:42; Heb. 10:25; 1 John 1:3.

Witnessing for Jesus Christ: Ps. 66:16; Mark 5:19; Luke 24:48; Acts 1:8.[8]

The Pastor-Counselor and Personal Observations

1. Counseling should be confined to the pastor's office or study. When counseling women, a secretary should be near at hand and instructed to respond to a call if needed. Pure intentions can be misunderstood. Be not ignorant of the devil's devices.

2. A good counselor must be sympathetic but never get personally involved.

3. The pastor should make it clear that he is not simply a counselor and that he expects the person who asks for help to be in church on Sunday. This should be a requirement for counseling.

4. Verses related to the need should be assigned to be read for the week following the counseling session. This must be done before the next appointment.

5. A book, or chapters of a book, to be read may be assigned.

6. A person must be willing to discuss his or her personal salvation. The plan of salvation should be given in each case even if the person claims to be a Christian. This is especially important with those whom the counselor has not met prior to this time. Some really mean they are "not heathen."

7. Always keep the conversation in strictest confidence.

8. Do not take sides in marital counseling. Be honest. Do not be afraid to tell the truth; do not water down advice. Sincerity, sympathy and honesty will go a long way in helping others.

End Notes

[1] William Kerr, ed., *Minister's Research Service* (Wheaton, IL: Tyndale House Publishers, 1970), p. 131. Used by permission.

[2] Jay E. Adams, *Competent to Counsel* (Nutley, NJ: Presbyterian and Reformed Publishing Co., 1974), p. xii, introduction. Used by permission.

[3] Ralph G. Turnbull, ed., *Baker's Dictionary of Practical Theology* (Grand Rapids: Baker Book House, 1967), p. 196. Used by permission.

[4] C. E. Colton, *The Minister's Mission* (Grand Rapids: Zondervan Publishing House, 1951), pp. 115-116. Used by permission.

[5] Gary R. Collins, assistant ed., *Minister's Research Service* (Wheaton, IL: Tyndale House Publishers, 1970), pp. 133-134. Used by permission.

[6] Jay E. Adams. *The Christian Counselor's Manual* (Grand Rapids: Baker Book House, 1973), pp. 459-461. Used by permission.

[7] Ibid., p. 462.

[8] Clyde M. Narramore, *The Psychology of Counseling* (Grand Rapids: Zondervan Publishing House, 1960), pp. 258-273. Used by permission.

CHAPTER TWELVE
Baptism

Paul Jackson in his book, *The Doctrine and Administration of the Church,* speaks of the ordinance of baptism and its importance:

> The Lord established baptism and the Lord's Supper as the two rites, or ceremonies, to be observed by His church. He knew the practical value of such repeated enactments of truth. Each time we witness a baptism we are reminded tangibly of our union with Christ as we are identified with Him in His death, burial and resurrection. Each time we participate in the Lord's Supper we are reminded of our communion with Him. These practical reminders should produce renewed devotion to our blessed Lord. The Lord did not suggest these ceremonies, He commanded them! He said: "This do . . ." (1 Cor. 11:24); "Go . . . teach . . . baptizing . . ." (Matt. 28:19). These ordinances are His orders, and we should observe them as sacred, God-given responsibilities.[1]

Eligibility of the Candidate for Baptism

First and foremost, a person must be saved to qualify for believer's baptism (Matt. 28:18-20). Some believe there should be a long waiting period between a person's salvation and his baptism. Others feel that it should be immediate, even the same day the person is converted, although he may not understand the meaning of the ordinance. Both of these positions seem to be extreme. I

have no objection to a person being baptized the same day
if he is not forced into it, and as long as there is sufficient
instruction for him to understand the meaning of it.
However, there is a benefit to a short waiting period. I
suggest the following reasons:

1. The person being baptized should have the advantage of at least one full session where baptism
is explained in detail. The Bible not only com-
mands baptism, but it *explains* its significance.
Should not the candidate be taught this truth?

2. Baptism is a church ordinance and it is proper
that the church make the decision on it.

3. The person being baptized can use the occasion
as an opportunity of testimony and invite his
friends. Certainly baptism is a public identification with Christ. It can be used effectively and
Scripturally as the unsaved witness the fact that
one has died to the old life and has a desire to live in
"newness of life."

On the other hand, to wait for long periods is to go beyond the Word. There is no Scriptural precedent for long
waiting periods.

A person should not be baptized who is not coming into the membership of the local church. While the eunuch
in Acts 8 might seem to be an exception to this, exceptions
simply prove the rule. Well does Paul Jackson say:

The New Testament certainly teaches that if
there is a Bible-believing church, the new convert should be baptized and come into the fellowship of that church. Under every ordinary circumstance, failure to do so robs the convert of
the Biblical responsibilities that are his in attendance, administration, tithing, etc., and
frees him from proper restraint of Biblical discipline. This policy in practice actually devel-

ops many "church tramps" who are little or no good to the cause of Christ, but who "flit here and there" whenever another pasture looks green-er.[2]

To allow a person to be baptized without joining the church simply encourages his not joining; the pastor, in a sense, is catering to his disobedience. If the person prefers to join another church, then it is proper and fitting that he be baptized there.

Instructing the Candidate in Preparation for Baptism

The major basis for baptism is obedience to the Lord. And if we did not know the meaning of baptism we would still baptize because the Lord commanded it. The fact of the matter is, however, we do know what it means, and it is right for the candidate to be informed as to its significance. Generally there is an indication that the candidate desires baptism. Sometimes this desire is in response to a call during the invitation for those who want to be baptized. At other times the desire is expressed as a result of personal counseling. In either case the deacons should be sure to meet with the candidate, although various Baptist churches do differ as to the procedure here. Sometimes a committee meets with the candidate and his name is presented to the deacons. In other churches he will meet with the full board for questioning regarding his salvation and desire for baptism and church membership. In any event there ought to be proper instruction of a candidate in at least one or two sessions.

The purpose of the instruction is twofold: doctrinal and practical.

Doctrinal instructions. Teach the candidate the *meaning* of baptism. The following outline can be used:

1. It is the command of the Lord (Matt. 28:18-20).

2. It is an expression of love for the Lord and willingness to obey (John 14:15, 21, 23).

3. It was practiced in the New Testament by believers only (Acts 2:40, 41; 8:26; 9:18, 19; 10:44, 48).

4. It was done immediately after salvation.

5. It signifies the death, burial and resurrection of the Lord and our identification with Him (Rom. 6:1-3).

It is helpful to illustrate the meaning of identification through baptism in the following comparison: While putting on a badge does not guarantee that a person is an officer, it identifies him as one.

The illustration of a uniform can be used in the same way. The uniform is worn, indicating that a person is in the army. It is possible (although against the law) to wear a uniform and not be a bona fide soldier; as the uniform does not make the soldier, it identifies him as one. So baptism identifies the believer with the death, burial and resurrection of Christ.

6. Questions concerning baptism. The doctrinal section of the instruction should include answers to the following questions:

a. Does baptism have anything to do with salvation?

b. What does baptism mean?

c. Who can be baptized?

d. What effect should this have on a person's life?

Practical instructions. For baptism to have its proper significance, nothing should detract from its beauty and reverence. The dignity is lost, however, if the baptizing is done poorly. If not carefully planned and executed, the service almost becomes entertainment. Here are some suggestions to help avoid this potential problem.

Set the candidate's mind at ease with regard to possible

mishaps. Show him or her the baptismal pool. Explain that the water will be about thirty-two inches deep and that it will be warm. It should be explained that mishaps and accidents are rare, and there is no reason to be frightened. Also emphasize that this is a reverent and holy hour, and one must not be so occupied with the mechanics of the baptism as to miss the maximum blessing from the beautiful symbolism.

If the candidate is unusually large, he or she ought to be assured that one is buoyant in the water, and that this presents no problem. Do not make light of the candidate's apprehensions. Answer each question with the quiet assurance of a mature spiritual leader.

Show the candidate how to stand and what to do. Pastors vary in regard to the position in which they want the candidate to stand. Choose that with which you are most confident and comfortable. It also makes a difference whether the pastor is right-handed or left-handed. I have always felt that the following is the safest method to pursue:

1. The candidate will hold his own right wrist with the left hand, with the arm projected slightly in front of the body. The arms should be fairly rigid.

2. The pastor will place one hand on the candidate's back, the other on the candidate's left wrist. The arms of the one being baptized should be rigid enough to make it possible for the pastor to pull him up with the left hand as he supports the back with the right hand.

3. Instruct the candidate not to throw his head back or to fold in a limp manner. If a person is tall, the pastor and the candidate should stand so as to make sure that there is plenty of clearance for the head. The person who is being baptized should be directly in front of the pastor. If, however, the person is exceptionally heavy, it would be better for the pastor to be slightly to the right of the candi-

date, giving more leverage with the right hand.

4. All candidates should be instructed to arrive twenty minutes early. Explain that someone will be on hand to help them. Often the deacons help the men and the deacon's wives help the ladies. It is also important that they be told exactly what to bring: a change of clothing (coat and shoes not necessary); towel and personal effects; socks to be worn in the baptistry. If the baptismal service is to be held early in the program, the clothes in which the candidate will be baptized may be worn to the church. Regular dress clothes can be put on after the baptismal service.

Presenting the Candidate to the Church

I would suggest that the candidates be presented before the baptism takes place. Remember that baptism is a church ordinance; it is to be done on the authority of the church. An excellent time is after a hymn is sung and just before the baptismal service begins.

It will be helpful to explain briefly to the congregation the meaning of baptism. This can be done from the baptistry. Emphasize that baptism is not a sacrament; it is not a means of grace; it is not a way whereby we are saved. The order may be for the chairman of the board of deacons, or a representative of the board, to present the candidates to the church while the pastor is in the baptistry. If the location of the baptistry makes this an awkward situation, the pastor may present them before he and the candidates are dismissed to prepare for the baptism.

Baptizing the Candidate

Once the preliminary remarks are made, the pastor will offer his hand to the candidate as he or she comes into the baptistry. Generally the men come from one side and the women from the other. There will be a tendency on the part of the candidate to be nervous. The pastor, however, can put the person at ease with a smile or a word of encouragement. He can whisper any instructions necessary to the person.

The pastor will ask the candidate to testify of his faith in Jesus Christ as his personal Savior. Sometimes the candidate will give a testimony concerning what the Lord has done for him. More often, however, he will give an affirmation of the fact that he is trusting the Lord as his Savior.

When the candidate has finished speaking, the pastor will state, "John Jones, upon the profession of your faith, I baptize you in the name of the Father, and the Son, and the Holy Spirit."

Having taken the proper position as instructed, the pastor will place his right hand on the back of the candidate and will gently, slowly immerse him. While the candidate is being immersed, it is appropriate to say, "Buried in the likeness of His death"; then, bringing him up out of the water, "and raised in the likeness of His resurrection."

The songleader should be prepared to lead the congregation in a stanza of a song, or a few measures from the organ or piano may be played, while one candidate leaves and another enters the baptistry.

Personnel Needed in Preparing for Baptismal Service

A number of helpers will be needed to assist those being baptized.

1. The deacons will examine candidates as to their testimony and eligibility to be baptized and become members of the church.

2. The secretary will prepare baptismal certificates.

3. It will be helpful if name tags are placed on the clothing of those to be baptized so that the pastor can immediately call them by name. Generally he will know them but if

there are a number of candidates being baptized, a momentary lapse of memory can be embarrassing.

4. It is important that someone be appointed to clean and fill the baptismal pool, to see that enough water is in the tank, and to be sure the water is heated to the desired temperature.

5. Someone must be responsible for having the robes ready for the baptismal service. They must be clean and neatly ironed.

6. A committee of women and a committee of men should be appointed to help the candidates for baptism. The men will also help the pastor put on the boots and baptismal robe if these are used.

7. A clean-up crew will be needed to empty the tank, mop the floors, care for the robes, etc.

Post-Baptism Activities

After the candidates are baptized they should change into their dry clothes and return to the auditorium. It is important that the pastor remember to give them sufficient time to prepare themselves. They will then be called to the pulpit and extended the right hand of fellowship by the pastor. A baptismal certificate is presented to them. A Bible verse can be quoted or read at this juncture and then a brief prayer offered.

Helpful Hints on Installing a Baptistry in a Church

It is rather surprising, since so much emphasis is placed upon immersion in a Baptist church, that generally very little consideration is given to the baptistry and its size when a church is being built. The following suggestions should be helpful:

Locate the baptistry so that the pulpit will not have to be moved every time a baptismal service is held. This will necessitate the baptistry being higher than the platform level, or to one side. Either of these locations can be designed in a manner which is pleasing architecturally.

Build the baptistry with a glass in front, if possible. The area should be well-lighted.

Be sure that the baptistry is large enough for two or three people to stand in at one time. Depth and width are equally as important as the length. It should be at least four feet wide, seven and one-half feet long (not including the steps) and deep enough to fill with water to the depth of thirty-two inches.

End Notes
[1] Paul R. Jackson, *The Doctrine and Administration of the Church,* rev. ed. (Schaumburg, IL: Regular Baptist Press, 1980), p. 58. Used by permission.
[2] Ibid., p. 61.

CHAPTER THIRTEEN
The Lord's Supper

The Significance of the Lord's Supper

The observance of the Lord's Supper is symbolic. It speaks of the Lord's death for us (Matt. 26:17-30; 1 Cor. 11:22-34). In the same way that the ordinance of baptism speaks of *union* with Christ, so the Lord's Table speaks of *communion*.

Dr. Paul Jackson says:

> Baptism, scripturally administered, is a single act, just as the union with Christ is an already accomplished, never-to-be repeated act. The Lord's Supper is regularly repeated, just as our communion with Him is a constantly enjoyed experience in the normal Christian life.[1]

Union precedes communion. Therefore, it seems proper for a person to be obedient in baptism before he partakes of the communion table. Each pastor must decide the extent of applying this principle. Because every saved person in the New Testament was baptized immediately following salvation, the issue of whether or not one should take communion before baptism never arose. However, the significance of the Lord's Table is more clearly seen and understood when it is kept in this perspective.

The Administration of the Elements of the Lord's Supper

The ordinance of communion, because it is a church ordinance, should be administered in the church, not

285

privately. While some practice a private administration to individuals who are away from the church, I feel this is unwise because it often results in confusion as to its true meaning. It gives support to the impression that communion is a sacrament or means of grace. The pastor should emphasize clearly that it is the *Lord's* Table; it is practiced by the church. Scripture says, "Wherefore, my brethren, *when ye come together* [italics mine] to eat, tarry one for another. And if any man hunger, let him eat at home" (1 Cor. 11:33, 34a). The implication here is that it was practiced in the church, not at home. (Of course, sometimes the New Testament church met in homes, having no church buildings, in which case it was proper.) If a pastor is asked to administer the Lord's Supper privately, he should use this as an opportunity to explain the true meaning of the Table, pointing out there is nothing in the elements which will bring favorable physical effects. The pastor must ever be on guard that his people understand the difference between the Lord's Supper as a symbolic picture of the death of Christ and the error of transubstantiation (the belief that the wafer is blessed and becomes the literal body of Christ) or consubstantiation (the belief that it is both the literal bread and literal body of Christ). The Romanists hold the first view; the Lutherans hold the second view. It should be emphasized in every service that when Christ said, "This is my body, which is broken for you," He was speaking figuratively.

The Procedure in Administering the Lord's Supper

The deacons will come together to the front of the church in an orderly fashion and be seated. They may sit either facing the congregation or with their backs to the congregation. I prefer the second method, although it is not practiced as much as the first method. In the second arrangement the pastor and deacons are taking their places with the congregation as they worship the Lord. The emphasis, then, is not on the men before the congregation but on the Lord Whose work is being commemorated.

Scripture will be read, either from the Gospels or 1 Corinthians 11.

Some explanation should be given as to the meaning of the elements and who is to partake of them. The pastor should be kind but frank as he mentions that it is for believers who are walking in obedience to the Lord. The dangers of deviating from the Word of God should be briefly explained. However, in warning the congregation with regard to the elements, one should be careful not to lose that warm, devotional spirit that is needed as the elements are considered. That is, let not the communion table be simply a place of polemics but rather a place of deep spiritual meditation on the work of Christ.

At this point the pastor will ask one of the deacons to pray, remembering the meaning of the bread, the symbol of Christ's broken body.

When this is done, the pastor will stand at the communion table and pass the bread trays to the deacons who will distribute them to the worshipers.

During this time, organ music can be playing softly. Occasionally an appropriate hymn can be sung spontaneously, led by the pastor, or even a special number on the subject of the body or blood of Christ can be rendered. However, the pastor should be careful here lest the emphasis be on entertainment rather than on remembering the Lord and worshiping Him.

The deacons return to the front, place the trays on the table and are seated. The pastor will serve the elements to them, then to himself. Sometimes the chairman of the board of deacons or the assistant pastor will serve the pastor before he passes the elements to them. After a quiet moment of meditation (do not rush) the pastor will say, "Take and eat."

The same procedure is followed in administering the grape juice. After this is done, the cups are either collected or left in the pew stands designed for such.

Scripture says, "When they had sung an hymn, they went out" (Matt. 26:30). Often, then, a hymn will be sung with no benediction, or sometimes a verse (like John 3:16) might be quoted or the Doxology sung.

End Note
[1] Jackson, *The Doctrine and Administration of the Church,* p. 63.

CHAPTER FOURTEEN
The Wedding

It brings delight to a pastor's heart to see a Christian man and woman united in holy matrimony. It is an especially joyous occasion when the pastor has observed the young man and woman grow up in the church and give themselves in service to the Lord, and then observed how the Lord has brought them together.

The Initial Approach

It is regrettable that one of the most vulnerable areas in the ministry of the pastor is in the matter of weddings. If he is not careful, he may be misled into situations that will prove embarrassing for both him and the congregation. Therefore, he should have firm and settled convictions about what is required of those whom he will marry. His position should be made clear to the church. Some of the situations which will arise in the normal course of a pastor's ministry are considered here.

Requests from couples raised in the church and known to the pastor.

1. Settling primary questions. When the couple approaches the pastor to request marriage, there are some initial questions which must be asked even though he may be sure he knows the answers. They are as follows:

a. Are both saved? This is the most important of all questions. It is my conviction that to marry a saved party with an unsaved party is contrary to the Word of God. An unequal yoke is *never* justified. In the case of young people who have been raised in the church, the pastor will generally know by their testimony and witness the answer to this question. However, he should take nothing for granted. The couple should be asked to state their relationship to the Lord.

b. Has either one of them been married before? When the pastor knows the couple, this question may bring a smile to their faces; but once again it is best to let them make the affirmation. The pastor might explain in good humor the importance of asking this question.

c. How long has the couple known each other? One should be careful and try to avoid marriages where the couples have been dating for only a few weeks, or engaged after knowing each other for only a short time.

d. How do the parents feel about this marriage? This is important. Both sets of parents should consent to the wedding and, if possible, be happy about it. Objections on either side will present serious problems later. This must be faced and thoroughly discussed by the couple and with the pastor's counsel.

e. In the case where one party is a member of your church and the other party is a member of another evangelical church, you might make it clear that the general procedure is for the couple to be married in the church where the bride is a member. Be very kind and gentle in suggesting this to them, trying not to offend them.

f. Is this a forced marriage? This might cause embarrassment to ask, but it will be more embarrassing if you find out later that it was, and that while others knew it, you did not.

g. What type of wedding is being planned? Will it be a large or small wedding? What facilities of the church will be needed?

2. Setting a time for counseling. The pastor should meet with the couple for counseling at least once, and probably two or three times. Dates should be set for both the coun-

seling sessions and the wedding. The office calendar should be checked immediately as to the availability of the church for the date desired.

Requests from nonmembers outside the church.

It is a common occurrence for people outside the church to call the office and ask the pastor if he will marry them. If the church has a secretary, she might ask some preliminary questions to avoid bothering the pastor in his busy schedule.

1. If either party has been divorced, it has been my practice not to marry them. Each pastor, of course, must come to his own personal conviction on this matter. One problem involved in marrying divorced people is the very difficult one of determining who is truly "the innocent party." Once such a pattern is established the pastor will be on the defensive, having to assert why he married some and not others. In some cases he may have to show reasons why the cases are different, involving some unpleasant revelations. This will be totally unnecessary if a pastor takes a stand early in his ministry and does not get embroiled in such marital situations. The pastor can make clear to those who are divorced and seek remarriage that, based on his convictions, he does not involve himself in either mixed marriages or in marriages where divorce is involved.

2. If either one of the couple is not saved, marriage would be improper. In some cases the parties can be led to Christ. However, the pastor has to be very careful that the individuals are not simply going "through the motions" in order to meet the prerequisites for the marriage. On the other hand, I have dealt with a number of cases where the unsaved one has been led to the Lord. The couples are married and very happy, grateful that not only are they married in the Lord, but they are also members of the Bride of Christ.

3. Another problem the pastor will face is whether or not to marry two unsaved people. While I feel that it is right and proper for unsaved people to be married, complications can arise from this situation. For example, if one of them decides to trust Christ as Savior during the interview, according to his convictions the pastor cannot marry them. There will be some cases where two unsaved people will be married by the pastor, but this should be the exception and not the rule.

4. Finally, avoid "quickie" marriages. People often call the church office and want to be married immediately. If the couple is informed that two or three counseling sessions are necessary before marriage, the problem is often solved.

Requests from couples involved in forced marriages.

It is proper for a couple to be married in the unfortunate circumstance in which the woman is expecting, as a result of a premarital relationship. This is one of the sad but very real patterns in the church today. The pastor should be clear and definite regarding his attitude toward premarital sex; he should do everything he can in his general preaching and personal counseling to make it clear that such is sin. It is a disgrace to both the individuals involved and their families, and it is dishonoring to the Lord and the church. When the couple expresses that they are compelled to be married, it should be very clear to them that they have sinned against the Lord. However, the sternness should be tempered with love. There should be a genuine desire to help them. While it is proper for them to be married, it should also be understood that such a marriage is not mandatory. Two wrongs do not make a right! If the couple is not in love, it is better not to insist on marriage, for the relationship could well end in divorce. Both counseling and prayer are needed.

The Counseling Sessions

At least one counseling session should be held with the couple in addition to the preliminary meeting. Three areas of instruction should be pursued.

The first is the couple's own relationship with the Lord. Emphasize that Christ should be the Head of the home. He should be the object of their affection and their marriage should be built around Him. Positive suggestions should be made with regard to their devotions, both together as a couple and individually. There also should be discussion as to their relationship to their church and responsibility to the Lord. It can be emphasized that marriage is like a wheel with spokes; the closer the spokes get to the hub, the closer they get to each other. Christ is the hub, and a right relationship with Him will result in a finer and closer relationship with each other. Books on family devotions and personal devotions can be recommended. A strong emphasis should be made of the fact that the husband should be the head of the home, that he should not consider himself "The Department of Labor" and his wife "The Department of Religion."

The last half of the first session, or the second session (if there is more than one) should deal with the man and woman's relationship to each other. I have found Cecil G. Osborne's book, *The Art of Understanding Your Mate,* very helpful in this regard. Mr. Osborne gives the "Ten Commandments for Wives" as follows:

1. Learn the real meaning of love.
2. Give up your dreams of a "perfect marriage" and work toward a "good marriage."
3. Discover your husband's personal, unique needs and try to meet them.
4. Abandon all dependency upon your parents and all criticism of his relatives.
5. Give praise and appreciation instead of seeking it.

6. Surrender possessiveness and jealousy.
7. Greet your husband with affection instead of complaints or demands.
8. Abandon all hope of changing your husband through criticism or attack.
9. Outgrow the princess syndrome.
10. Pray for patience.[1]

I would suggest that the pastor-counselor purchase this excellent book; it will be greatly beneficial.

Mr. Osborne also gives the "Ten Commandments for Husbands" as follows:

1. Treat your wife with strength and gentleness.
2. Give ample praise and reassurance.
3. Define the areas of responsibility.
4. Avoid criticism.
5. Remember the importance of "little things."
6. Recognize her need for togetherness.
7. Give her a sense of security.
8. Recognize the validity of her moods.
9. Cooperate with her in every effort to improve your marriage.
10. Discover her particular, individual needs and try to meet them.[2]

It should be emphasized in the second session of marriage counseling that the "second party" is always a danger. This is true whether we are dealing with the proverbial mother-in-law or some good friend who may be in the home on a regular basis.

A great many young people who are newly married have problems in the area of sex. While the pastor must be discreet in handling this subject, he must realize that it can be an area of fear and frustration to the couple. It would be wise to give them some good reading material on this subject and be willing to discuss it with them. It is important to emphasize that sex within the bounds of marriage is not sin, and that guilt feelings on the part of each of them are unwarranted.

There are a number of excellent volumes written on the subject of marriage. The following are recommended:

Evans, Louis. *Your Marriage—Duel or Duet?* Westwood, NJ: Fleming H. Revell, 1962.

Granberg, Lars I. *Marriage Is for Adults Only.* Grand Rapids: Zondervan Publishing House, 1971.

LaHaye, Tim. *How to Be Happy Though Married.* Wheaton: Tyndale House, 1968.

Miles, Hebert J. *Sexual Happiness in Marriage.* Grand Rapids: Zondervan Publishing House, 1967.

Osborne, Cecil G. *The Art of Understanding Your Mate.* Grand Rapids: Zondervan Publishing House, 1970.

Peterson, J. Allan, ed. *The Marriage Affair.* Wheaton: Tyndale House, 1971.

Read a number of these books; much of the material can be used in this second session of counseling.

The third session should deal with the wedding ceremony, the significance of it and some of the details of it.

The Wedding Rehearsal

Following are some important principles to be considered regarding the wedding rehearsal.

It is important that every person participating in the wedding attend the rehearsal. This total participation should be a definite requirement; otherwise there may be awkward and embarrassing incidents and an uneasiness throughout the ceremony.

After the group has been called together and there has been prayer, an outline of the general procedure should be given. The place and part of each person should be explained.

It is wise to rehearse the entire service at least twice, answering any questions and making any necessary adjustments.

Should the bride (or other members of the party) have suggestions for change as to the procedure and order of the ceremony, the pastor should be amenable and willing to make adjustments accordingly.

Occasionally there will be a person appointed to manage and oversee the wedding. Sometimes this tends to conflict with the pastor's general instructions. Patience, however, is the order of the day. Keep a sweet spirit and be willing to cooperate at all times. Regarding the ceremony itself, the pastor's convictions about the necessity of keeping the wedding on a high plane should be respected.

Be sure that every detail is covered. Sometimes it will be necessary to instruct the ushers how to usher, even to the extent of a brief demonstration.

The Wedding Procedures

A. Every usher should be at the church at least forty-five minutes to one hour early.

B. Meet the best man and the groom about twenty to thirty minutes early and briefly go over the ceremony again.

C. Have prayer with the groom just before the wedding, asking for the Lord's blessing on the service and praying for "perfect ease" during the ceremony.

D. At a prearranged time (worked out with the organist) the pastor will make his entrance, followed by the groom, the best man and as many ushers as are in the party.

The order of march is as follows:

1. Entrance of minister, groom, best man and ushers.
2. Entrance of bridesmaids, maid or matron of honor, ring bearer and flower girl.
3. Entrance of bride and father.

E. There are various options as to the procedure after the wedding party has reached the front of the church. Songs, words used in giving away the bride, and various parts of the ceremony can be changed.

F. The wedding ceremony.

G. The recessional.

H. The ushers and their post-ceremony responsibility.

The Wedding Ceremony

While there are a number of wedding ceremonies available, the following is one that I have developed and used. It is a combination of some of the accepted wedding ceremonies with the addition of original material. Some of the parts in this ceremony may be deleted for shorter weddings. I suggest that the pastor write his own ceremony or, preferably, a number of them, some short and some longer.

It is important that the ceremony be planned and neatly typed. Throughout the ceremony and any additional message, dignity and reverence should be maintained.

In his book, *Pastoral Problems,* W. B. Riley writes:

Books along this line are a multitude and can be easily purchased by a young pastor, and at least one such should be in his possession before he is ever called to perform a wedding ceremony. He should have studied the ceremonies there suggested and decided upon one or the other of them to be committed to memory; or following the suggestions, prepare what is to him a satisfactory service.

My successor at Carrolton, Kentucky, was caught napping in this matter. He had just accepted the call when a young couple across the river on the Indiana side called him to come over and speak the mystic words that would make them one. On the way across the river, he wrote down some meditations and read them to his bride-wife. She answered, "Well, Charlie, that is pretty good; but before you have another wedding you should study up on the subject."

When the moment of the mystic words was on, the Reverend Charles said to the groom, "Do you take this woman to be your true and wedded wife? Do you promise to love . . . her . . . cherish her . . . while life shall last?" He promised.

Then turning to the bride he said, "And do you promise to take this man as your true and wedded husband, and . . . and . . . and . . ." (in the meantime, trying to think of some different phraseology he finally blurted out) "and to stick to him the rest of your days?" She blushed, but promised.

It was a lesson to Charlie, and he went home a bit humiliated, to give himself to the preparation of a fit wedding ceremony. A word to the wise is sufficient. Get ready![3]

After the couple is married, it will be appropriate for the pastor to call in the new home and encourage them in the things of the Lord. Some pastors send cards or letters on anniversaries. A letter ought to be sent shortly after the couple is married, expressing joy in having part in the ceremony. Take the opportunity to encourage them to remember the principles given in the counseling sessions and during the wedding regarding their relationship to the Lord and to each other.

A Suggested Wedding Ceremony

Dearly beloved, we are gathered together here in the presence of God and this company to join together this man and this woman in the holy bonds of matrimony. Almighty God Himself is the Author. By His Word this holy relationship between man and woman was instituted in the Garden of Eden.

"And the Lord God said, It is not good that man should be alone; I will make him a helpmeet for him" (Gen. 2:18).

After having made the woman for the man God said, "Therefore shall a man leave his father and his mother, and shall cleave unto his wife: and they shall be one flesh" (Gen. 2:24).

Moses, the lawgiver of Israel, first gave it legal sanction, and our Lord gave it spiritual sanction when He adorned and beautified the holy estate of matrimony with His presence at the first miracle that He wrought in Cana of Galilee.

The Bible is far from silent on the subject of marriage. It tells us that "Whoso findeth a wife findeth a good thing, and obtaineth favour of the Lord" (Prov. 18:22). "Marriage is honourable in all, and the bed undefiled: but whoremongers and adulterers God will judge" (Heb. 13:4).

Rightly regarded, marriage is the highest and happiest of human relationships—the preserver of true love, the foundation of the home, and the bulwark of society. This is one of the most outstanding events in this couple's lives. The decisions they are making are of cardinal importance.

This is not the most outstanding event, however. The most memorable event of their lives was the day they each, as individuals, accepted Christ as Savior. The most important decision was the one they made in trusting Christ as their Savior and thus becoming a part of the Bride of Christ.

If you are here today and cannot say that you have made this most important decision, you cannot know the happiness and joy of these two until you have received Christ as Savior.

Because they have both acknowledged and accepted Him as Savior, I can wish them both happiness and spiritual prosperity in their married life together. Although this state brings many joys, it is also attended by many grave responsibilities. The Bible makes clear these responsibilities and duties to both husband and wife.

Addressing the woman by name, say: God's Word tells us that "A virtuous woman is a crown to her husband" (Prov. 12:4).

Again, we read: "Wives, submit yourselves unto your own husbands, as unto the Lord. For the husband is the head of the wife, even as Christ is the head of the church: and he is the saviour of the body. Therefore as the church is subject unto Christ, so let the wives be to their own husbands in every thing" (Eph. 5:22-24).

Addressing the man by name, say: Your part in this holy relationship is no less grave. It is a responsible one. "Husbands, love your wives, even as Christ also loved the church, and gave himself for it; That he might sanctify and cleanse it with the washing of water by the word" (Eph. 5:25, 26). "Likewise, ye husbands, dwell with them according to knowledge, giving honour unto the wife, as unto the weaker vessel, and as being heirs together of the grace of life; that your prayers be not hindered" (1 Pet. 3:7).

Addressing the bride's father, ask: Who

giveth this woman to this man?

Father answers: I do. (The bride leaves her father's side to stand beside the groom. The father is then seated with his wife.)

Man's name, wilt thou have this woman to be thy wedded wife, to live together after God's ordinance in the holy estate of matrimony? Wilt thou love her, comfort her, honor her, and keep her in sickness and in health and, forsaking all others, keep thee only unto her, so long as you both shall live?

Answer: I will.

Woman's name, wilt thou have this man to be thy wedded husband, to live together after God's ordinance in the holy estate of matrimony? Wilt thou love him, comfort him, honor him, and keep him in sickness and in health, and forsaking all others, keep thee only unto him, so long as you both shall live?

Answer: I will.

Addressing the couple, say: Will you join your right hands, and repeat after me:

I, *(man's name),* take thee, *(woman's name),* to be my wedded wife, to have and to hold, from this day forward, for better or for worse, for richer, for poorer, in sickness and in health, to love and to cherish, till death us do part, according to God's holy ordinance; and thereto I give my troth.

I, *(woman's name),* take thee, *(man's name),* to be my wedded husband, to have and to hold, from this day forward, for better or for worse, for richer, for poorer, in sickness and in health, to love and to cherish, till death us do part, according to God's holy ordinance; and thereto I give my troth.

Addressing both by name, ask: Would you have these vows sealed by the further gift of a ring?

Answer: Yes.

For a single ring ceremony the man shall place the ring upon the woman's finger and repeat after the pastor: With this ring I thee wed, with all my worldly goods, and heart's affections, I thee endow.

For a double ring ceremony the above procedure shall be followed by each in turn—the man first, then the woman.

Forasmuch as *(man's name)* and *(woman's name)* have consented together in holy wedlock, and have witnessed the same before God in this company, I pronounce that they are husband and wife. In the name of the Father, and of the Son, and of the Holy Spirit. What God hath joined together, let no man put asunder.

Let me remind you, Mr. and Mrs. _____, that you are henceforth one; one in interest, one in reputation and one in affection. May you also be one in service to the Lord, giving Him always first place in your married life together.

Let us pray.

End Notes

[1] Cecil G. Osborne, *The Art of Understanding Your Mate* (Grand Rapids: Zondervan Publishing House, 1970), p. 116. Used by permission.

[2] Osborne, p. 127.

[3] W. B. Riley, *Pastoral Problems* (Old Tappan, NJ: Fleming H. Revell Co., 1936), pp. 81, 82. Used by permission.

CHAPTER FIFTEEN
The Funeral

Andrew H. Blackwood writes:

> Among all the problems of the parish minister few are more baffling than those that concern funerals. Not every occasion proves difficult, but in the course of the year any pastor is likely to face perplexing problems. This is especially true of the first few years. If a man learns as he goes along he will gradually become accustomed to meeting each situation as it arises. Meantime, the difficulties connected with funerals should help to make a man humble. They should also send him to his knees.[1]

The First Expression of Sympathy

No one would doubt that to the average church member the pastor is very important, but never is he more important and in greater demand than when there is a death in the family. Every godly pastor will be a shepherd who genuinely cares for his sheep, and who sympathizes with them and commiserates with them in their need. The funeral is also an opportunity to serve the Lord and to meet some very special heart-needs in the lives of his people.

When the pastor is called upon by the family for help at this time of sorrow, it should take precedence over all other considerations and engagements; he should respond immediately.

Generally the pastor will call in the home twice. The

first call will usually include:

    1. Expressions of sympathy

    2. Reading of appropriate Scripture.

    3. Offering to be of help. It is important that the pastor does not leave the impression that he expects to preside at the funeral. It may be that the family will have someone else in mind; at any rate, the pastor will generally know the situation. The primary interest at this point should be the comfort of the bereaved family. Never is it more important for the pastor to forget himself.

    4. Preliminary arrangements might be made at this time, but generally this is not done until later because the mortuary has not yet been consulted.

The second call is discussed below.

The Pastor and the Funeral Director

Generally the funeral director will call the pastor while the bereaved family is in his office or shortly after they leave. The call will verify that the pastor is to conduct the funeral and will also establish the time. The facts as given by the funeral director should be repeated and written down so that there is no misunderstanding.

While there may be exceptions, the funeral director will usually work with the pastor and the relationship will be a good one. If the pastor has pressing engagements and he cannot conduct the funeral at the suggested time, other arrangements can be made. However, again we emphasize that the pastor should defer to the family in need and make all adjustments necessary to aid and comfort them in their bereavement.

The Call on the Family

The pastor should make his second call preferably the day before the funeral. By this time other relatives will have arrived. He will want to meet them, express his sympathy and comfort them in their need. Additional information will be acquired at this time as to the order and details of the funeral; also any information to be used at the funeral concerning the deceased should be noted at this time. The reading of selected Scripture and prayer can be helpful and comforting at the conclusion of the call.

Suggested verses for use in the home of the bereaved.
    1. For non-Christian families: Ps. 39:4-7; 90:1-12; 107:8, 9; Isa. 40:28-31; John 3:3, 14-16; Rom. 5:8; Heb. 9:27, 28.
    2. For Christian families: Ps. 23; 103:13, 14; John 14:1-6; 16:27; Rom. 8:28-39; 2 Cor. 5:1-8; 1 Thess. 4:13-18; Phil. 1:21-24; 1 John 3:1-3; Rev. 22:12-20.

Have a checklist. In his fine book, *The Funeral,* Andrew W. Blackwood gives a checklist which is helpful in informing the pastor of all the pertinent facts and thus eliminating embarrassment. The list is as follows:

Where will the services be held?
On what date? At what hour? (Repeat this to verify.)
Will the services be public or private?
Is there any other minister to share in the services?
If so, which parts should be taken by the assisting pastor?
Who is to invite the other minister?
Is any fraternal order to be present? To take part?
Is there to be music? If so, of what kind?
Who is to secure the musicians?
Is there a favorite hymn to be sung or read?
Is there a favorite text or passage of Scripture?
Is there to be a formal obituary?
If so, who will prepare it?
If the minister prepares it, what are the facts?

> Where will the interment take place? Is it to be
> public or private?
> Should the deacons arrange for extra automo-
> biles?
> Is there anything else the church can do?
> Are there any suggestions about the services?
> Do the friends have the minister's telephone
> number?
> Is there any special request now before we
> pray?[2]

It is advisable to get various facts about the deceased person which will be helpful during the service. This ought to be done, not mechanically, but tactfully and with genuine sympathy. It will prove helpful in mentioning the deceased at the funeral. Be accurate.

Some questions the pastor might ask are:

Was the deceased a Christian? (Often the pastor will know this already.)

What were his or her involvements in the Lord's work, the church, etc.?

What other interests and hobbies did the deceased have?

What do friends or acquaintances say about the influence of the deceased upon them or others?

Inquire whether the Bible of the deceased is handy; if it is well-marked, request may be made to use it during the funeral service. This is often effective.

The Funeral Service

General considerations. Following are some general considerations to be kept in mind and checked prior to the service:

> 1. Be sure to arrive at least fifteen minutes before the service starts. This will eliminate unnecessary worry on the part of the family.

2. Meet with the family just before the service. This is not always done, but it is often appreciated, especially when some members of the family have just arrived from out of town.

3. Make the last-minute check with the mortician, giving him some signal whereby he will know when the services are completed.

4. Check with the organist and singers as to the order of service. This list should be typed and a copy given to each of them.

5. Check your appearance to see that grooming is proper and hair combed. Also check the obituary, Bible references, proper pronunciation of names, etc.

The funeral service itself.

1. Suggested orders of service:

a. Song/Scripture/Obituary/Message/Song/ Benediction

b. Scripture/Obituary/Prayer/Song/Message/ Song

c. Scripture (Old Test.)/Song/Scripture (New Test.)/Song/Message/Music

2. Suggested Bible verses to use at the funeral:

a. Funeral for a child: Gen. 43:14; 2 Sam. 12:16-23; 2 Kings 4:18-26; Job 1:21; Jer. 31:15-17; Matt. 18:1-6, 10, 14; Mark 10:13-16; 2 Cor. 1:3, 4; 4:17; Rev. 21:1-4; 22:1, 2, 5.

b. Funeral for a young person: Job 9:25, 26; Ps. 90:12-17; 103:15, 16; Eccles. 9:10; 11:6, 10; 12:1; Ezek. 16:60.

c. Funeral for a girl: Mark 5:22, 23, 35-42; Rev. 21:1-4.

d. Funeral for a boy or young man: Job 14:1, 2; Eccles. 11:6-10; Luke 7:11-15; John 11:25, 26; 1 Pet. 1:24.

e. Funeral for a young woman: Matt. 25:1-13; John 14:1-3, 18, 19, 27.

f. Funeral for a person in middle life: Job 14; Ps. 39:4, 5, 6, 12, 13; 49:6-20; 103:15, 16; Eccles. 9:10; James 4:13-15.

g. Funeral for an aged person: Job 19:25-27; Ps. 90 (appropriate to open any funeral service); Ps. 23:1-4; 73:25, 26; Eccles. 12:1-7, 13; Rom. 8:35-39; 1 Cor. 15:55-57; 2 Cor. 5:1-10; 2 Tim. 4:7, 8.

h. Comfort for the bereaved: Ps. 23:1-4; Matt. 5:4; John 14:1-3, 15-19, 25-27; 2 Cor. 1:3, 4; 4:7-14, 16, 17; Heb. 12:5-11.

i. Immortality: Job 1:21; 14:1-12, 14, 19, 20; 19:25-27; 2 Cor. 5:1-9; 1 Thess. 4:13-18; 1 Tim. 6:7.

j. Resurrection: John 5:25, 28, 29; 6:40, 51; 11:25, 26; 14:1-3, 19; 1 Cor. 15:12-20, 35-38, 42-44, 47-58; 1 Thess. 4:13-17; Heb. 13:20, 21; Rev. 1:17, 18; 14:13.

k. Judgment: Ps. 50:1-6; Matt. 25:31-46; Rev. 20:11-15; 21:1-3.

l. Heaven: Ps. 16:11; Isa. 33:17; 35:9, 10; 1 Cor. 2:9; Heb. 11:16; 1 Pet. 1:3, 4; Rev. 7:13-17; 21:1-4, 10-12, 14, 18, 22-25; 22:1-5.

3. After the service. When the prearranged signal to the funeral director is made, the mortician will generally open the casket and give directions for the guests to file by the casket and out of the sanctuary. At this point the pastor should stand, preferably at the head of the casket, while the people are filing by.

After the guests have left, the family will come out of the family room to view the body. The pastor should be near and have a verse or two ready to quote if necessary. He should be sympathetic, comforting and show himself to be a real pastor-friend.

After the family leaves, the pastor will stay in the room or sanctuary until the casket is closed and the flowers are taken to the hearse. He will then lead the procession from the sanctuary to the hearse. The pastor will stand at the door of the hearse while the casket is placed there. Generally he will ride with the undertaker in the hearse, leading the procession to the grave.

4. The interment. At the graveside the pastor will make brief remarks, read Scripture and pray. This is usually a short service, about five or ten minutes long. It is important that the pastor stand at the head of the casket. Following the prayer the pastor will go directly to the bereaved, assure them of his prayers and leave a word of comfort. It is good for him to linger for a few minutes after the service before he leaves the cemetery. In some cases he will be with the family after the interment. Well does Colton say:

The minister's interest in the bereaved must not cease with the benediction at the grave. There will be many lonely hours for the bereaved family in the days and weeks ahead. Perhaps at no time would a visit from the pastor mean more than on the day following the funeral. By that time the other friends and relatives will have gone and there will be a very keen sense of loneliness. Usually it is not best for the minister to go to the home of the bereaved immediately following the funeral, but on the following day or on some day within the week a visit from the pastor would be timely and helpful.[3]

Problems Regarding the Funeral

The problem of another pastor participating in the funeral service. Under no circumstances should a pastor take

a funeral in a former pastorate without first consulting
with the present pastor.

Often a family will ask for a former pastor, especially
if he has not been away from the field very long. If the former pastor agrees to come, the part that each pastor is to
take must be clearly defined. This can be done in consul-
tation with the family or presented for their approval.
Each pastor must be careful that he is completely ethical.

The problem of fraternal organizations. It has been my
policy to frown upon the involvement of fraternal organizations in the service. If the family insists on their participating in the ceremony, it should be made clear that this
should be done after the pastor's part in the funeral service is concluded. Many of the rites of fraternal organizations have heathen roots and add nothing to a service but
confusion. The pastor has the right to refuse to participate in a funeral if he feels the fraternal organization will
be taking over the service. While this is the exception
rather than the rule, such a service could be most embarrassing for the pastor.

The place of the service. It is the accepted custom to hold
the funeral services in the mortuary. There are advantages in this in view of the fact that the church auditorium
is often too large and is not conducive to having funerals.
Funerals of unsaved people are very seldom held in the
church. On the other hand, if the deceased was very active in the church and requested before death that the funeral be held there, his wishes should be obeyed. In such
cases, the order of the funeral can be different; it might be
conducted similar to a regular service.

The consideration of a fee. At no time is the pastor ever to
state or ask for a fee at funerals. Each pastor must make
up his mind as to whether or not he will accept a fee. Sometimes when a fee is offered or given, he will give it back;
other times he might sense that the family will be embar-

rassed or insulted if he offers to return it. The only rule here is not to insist on it; ask for wisdom of the Lord as to what to do.

End Notes

[1] Andrew W. Blackwood, *The Funeral* (Philadelphia: Westminster Press, 1942), p. 13. Used by permission.

[2] Ibid., pp. 59, 60.

[3] Colton, *The Minister's Mission*, p. 94.

CHAPTER SIXTEEN

The Pastor and the Sunday School

The Importance of the Sunday School

Pastors and Christian workers will agree that a well-administered Sunday School can be one of the greatest boons to the church. Clarence Benson, in his fine book *The Sunday School in Action,* quotes an 1876 commission, sent by the French government to study the educational agencies in America. In its reference to the Sunday School and its importance, the commission said:

> The Sunday School is not an accessory agency in the normal economy of American education; it does not add a superfluity; it is an absolute necessity for the complete instruction of the child. Its aim is to fill by itself the complex mission which elsewhere is in large measure assigned to the family, the school, and the church. All things unite to assign to this institution a grand part in the American life.[1]

Benson points out that it is significant that the French commission considered the Sunday School "an absolute necessity for the complete instruction of the child." Because we believe this is true, it is vitally important that the pastor take the leadership in the Sunday School administration. He should see that adults and children get the maximum benefit from the Sunday School. When the number of hours a youngster receives in training in the evangelical Protestant church is compared to that of other religious groups, the results are alarming. In the Jewish faith there is a maximum of 325 hours a year; the Catholics provide 200 hours; Protestants around 17 hours. Benson further explains:

> When we speak of the Protestant child receiving fifty-two hours of instruction a year through the agency of the Sunday School, it must be remembered that two-thirds of the Protestant constituency are not in Sunday School, and that the remaining third do not receive the full equivalency of fifty-two hours' work. Untrained teachers, ungraded lessons, and irregular attendance reduce these fifty-two hours a year to an average of not more than seventeen.[2]

According to statistics, a child enters the Sunday School at about the age of four and drops out at the age of fourteen. In these ten years, receiving approximately seventeen hours a year of instruction, the total amounts to 170 hours. Compare this to the 12,000 hours he will receive in the public school. The need of proper administration in the Sunday School is obvious!

When a man enters a church for the first time as the new pastor, he may find a variety of reactions to the Sunday School. Frequently the attitude will be that the Sunday School is an appendage to the church; that it is primarily for boys and girls; that its growth is not one of the primary objectives of the church. Because most of our missionaries and pastors come up through the Sunday School, it is important that the pastor stress at the outset his concern for the Sunday School and its rightful place in the church.

Organization of the Sunday School

Basically, there are three divisions in the Sunday School organization: the preschool division, birth to age five; the children's division, ages six to eleven; the youth and adult division, ages twelve to twenty-five and up. There are usually ten departments :

Cradle Roll: birth to two years
Nursery: two- and three-year-olds
Kindergarten: four- and five-year-olds
Primary: six-, seven- and eight-year-olds
    (grades one to three)
Junior: nine-, ten- and eleven-year-olds
    (grades four to six)
Junior High (Intermediate): twelve-, thirteen-
    and fourteen-year-olds
High School: ages fifteen to eighteen
Youth or College Age: ages nineteen to twenty-
    four
Adult: age twenty-five and up
Home Department: aged and shut-ins

First Baptist Church of Hammond, Indiana, suggests a geographical division of classes. This could be considered if the Sunday School is large, and if the church is located in a downtown area with pupils coming from several different sections of the city. This would make it possible for pupils in a given area to be in the same class with those with whom they are acquainted. An advantage in teacher visitation would be that more visits could be made within less amount of time. One disadvantage, however, would be the tendency to segregate the classes racially and economically, which could present problems.

Dr. Jack Hyles also suggests the Sunday School relax the visitor's grade level in order to give the pupils the opportunity of inviting to their class someone who may be either one grade level up or one grade level below. The advantage of this is in eliminating the problem of separating friends. Other problems, however, are formed when the pupil is to be classified as a permanent member of a class, and at promotion time.

Class Organization

Organization of the young people's and adult classes can be an advantage in promoting the Sunday School and in making it more effective in its service to the pupils.

The organization may include a *president* who can function as the leader in the opening exercises. Extreme care should be exercised in the nomination and election of this person. It should be someone who is burdened for the Sunday School and willing to make sacrifices. The president should have a good appearance and a pleasing personality. Most important, one holding this office must be saved and living a separated Christian life as an example to other members of the class.

A *secretary* may be elected who, among other responsibilities, will keep the attendance records. In some large adult classes this may involve a number of secretaries. In youth classes the secretary may work primarily in class meetings.

Other officers may include:

Group captains. These officers are primarily for large Sunday Schools. In the adult class the group captain will be responsible for ten to twenty members of the class, i.e., for keeping a record of the attendance, noting especially the absentees. The group captain should also be aware of the needs of the individual members of the group; he or she may also be responsible for seeing that birthday greetings are sent, sick calls are made, etc.

Sunshine chairman. Some Sunday Schools recommend having a sunshine chairman. The purpose of this officer is to arrange for the provision of food in times of need. This person may also be responsible for keeping the classroom attractive, and for sending cards and flowers to members of the class.

Mission chairman. The Sunday School program should be coordinated with the missionary program of the church. Contacts with the missionaries should be made, and letters from the mission field read to the class.

Social chairman. The Sunday School should be a place where the social needs are met in activities outside the classroom. This can include periodic social functions.

Songleader and pianist. These are very important officers in the Sunday School class. They should be individuals who not only have musical ability but are living separated lives and are interested in the Sunday School.

All officers should be members of the church.

Degree of Emphasis on the Sunday School

It was noted in the section on visitation evangelism that a great deal of the visitation program centers on the Sunday School. Again it should be emphasized that 85 percent of our workers come up through the Sunday School. It should also be stressed that the pastor is the pastor of the Sunday School as well as of the church. When he is not considered as such, it is often his own fault; he has shown a passive indifference to the Sunday School.

One of the major goals emphasized from the platform should be the growth and progress of the Sunday School. The pastor, as the leader in this enterprise, should meet with the Sunday School superintendent at least once a week to keep in close touch with the progress of the school.

Because the pastor is one of the most adequately equipped servants of the church, it is advisable that he teach a class, preferably one of the adult classes. The pastor should keep the work and goals of the Sunday School before the people constantly and show, both in his message and practice, his interest in it.

As mentioned in an earlier chapter, balance is important. It is regrettable that many churches have been given a "black eye" because of an imbalanced proportion of children. I am not suggesting by this that the Sunday School should not reach as many boys and girls as possible; but when a church has as many as twelve or thirteen hundred in Sunday School, with only 5 percent of that number being adults, it is out of balance. This calls for an examination of goals and direction of effort. While growth is important, care must be taken not to place more emphasis on making records than on reaching the people in the community.

It is imperative that both adults and children be sought and brought into the Sunday School. All efforts should be given to attaining a healthy balance in this respect. A Sunday School which grows steadily and maintains its growth through vigorous visitation and compassionate concern will be more stable than one which relies upon "Madison Avenue" gimmicks.

End Notes
[1] Clarence H. Benson, *The Sunday School in Action* (Chicago: Moody Press, 1944), p. 26. Used by permission.
[2] Benson, pp. 32, 33.

CHAPTER SEVENTEEN

Missions in the Local Church

The Importance of Missions

The Great Commission as outlined by the Lord in Matthew 28 is the program for missions. When the Lord said, "Go ye . . . and teach all nations," He was giving the missionary call. In one sense of the word, the establishment of churches is a missionary enterprise. This means, therefore, that you cannot disassociate any church or Christian enterprise from missions. For one to say, "I do not believe in missions," is commensurate to saying, "I do not believe in the church," or "I do not believe in evangelism." The church which is not missionary-minded is a dying church.

Reginald Matthews, in the introduction to his book, *Missionary Administration in the Local Church,* states something of the challenge which lies before the church today.

> According to the Population Reference Bureau, the world's population will more than double by the end of the twentieth century if current trends continue. This means there will be as many as 7,000,000,000 persons on the earth by the year 2000.
>
> The challenge facing New Testament believers and New Testament churches is clear, both in fact and implication. It has been estimated that two-thirds of the world is yet unevan-

gelized. Only about four percent are saved. At the current rate, by the year 2000 only two percent will be saved. If you were to draw a graph, you would see that a line signifying world population would show a very rapid rise while a line for evangelism would indicate a definite decline.[1]

The Missionary Policy in the Local Church

The policy of the Southern Baptist Church in missionary giving is a "Cooperative Program." This means that each church gives to missions through the general missionary fund of the Southern Baptist Convention. The money is allocated by a central office which determines exactly where the money goes. Obviously this directs missionary giving away from individuals or personalities and distributes the funds according to the needs on various fields. While this may seem to be practical, one serious disadvantage of such a procedure is that the local church does not know where its money is going. Therefore it is hard to be personally involved in missions.

The policy of most Regular Baptist churches and other independent churches is to support missionaries who have personally presented their needs before the church. This support is done in a number of ways.

"Faith Promise" system. The Faith Promise system is similar to a pledge. However, it is a desirable euphemism and, in all fairness to the system, is different from a pledge in that a person who does not pay a given amount is not billed by the church. A pledge is a way of saying, "I will give so much; I am accountable for paying the stated amount." Faith Promise is a way of saying, "As the Lord supplies my need, I will give a stipulated amount. However, if I am unable to give it, I understand that there will be no accountability to the local church." The Faith Promise system has many good features and involves in-

dividuals within the church in giving.

Many of the larger and more missionary-minded churches have a Faith Promise program. It is usually inaugurated during a missionary conference.

"Faith Promise Designated" system. This system permits the individuals in the church not only to promise a certain amount, but to specify exactly where it is to go. This enables the person to become personally involved in missionary giving and to make an investment in the lives of certain missionaries. One disadvantage of this system is that it limits the church as a whole from developing a missionary program. That is, if the money is designated, then the church, as the local body, is not able to vote as God leads in the support of certain missionaries. Another disadvantage is the result of fragmenting missionary giving to many different missionaries and projects. Often these are independent or interdenominational.

The better system of the two is the Faith Promise program whereby the membership promises a stipulated amount and then joins the aggregate body of people in deciding which missionaries and agencies are to be supported. This is more Scriptural than the designated program.

"General Fund" system. This is simply stipulating a percentage of the General Fund to be used for the missionary program. In one church where I pastored, the offerings were given to missions one Sunday a month. This, however, is quite unsatisfactory in that it fluctuates too much according to the week. For instance, if it were the fourth week of the month, it would not be the same amount of offering as it would the first week. Many of the people were paid monthly salaries and gave their complete tithes once a month.

Special offerings. Some churches take a special offering for missions at a specific time of the year. Temple Baptist

Church, Tacoma, for instance, takes a Christmas missionary offering. This goes into a missionary fund and is used to supplement the support of the missionaries. Sometimes these special offerings are given as Christmas gifts. In some churches these monies are reserved for any emergency needs of the missionaries during the year.

The Support of Individual Missionaries

Members of the church. A number of churches have the policy of not supporting any full-time missionaries unless they are members of their church. One disadvantage to this system is that most small churches cannot provide the full support of more than one or two missionary families. Generally the missionary must receive support from a number of churches. If all churches held this view, such support would be impossible.

Full or partial support. Some churches choose to support a number of missionaries with a small amount. For example, a church might send fifty missionaries five dollars a month. This makes an impressive number on the church report. However, although it is an advantage to the church to have an interest in that many missionaries, it is a disadvantage to the missionaries, especially if a number of churches give to them on this basis. Some balance should be maintained so that even though a church supports fewer missionaries, an appreciable part of a missionary's support is supplied.

The Question of Who Should Be Supported

Each pastor and each church faces the question of which missionary and mission agencies are to be supported. Should they all be Baptist missionaries? Should they be missionaries working with agencies approved by the General Association of Regular Baptist Churches? Should interdenominational missionaries be included?

In all fairness to the churches that are supporting interdenominational missionaries, it should be understood that some missionaries out on the field were there before our various mission agencies were established. There was no choice with regard to sound Baptist missions. However, if there are ample reasons for us to belong to the Regular Baptist Fellowship because of its stand, its fellowship and its strong baptistic doctrine, it seems, therefore, unreasonable not to support only such missionaries and to establish only churches of like faith in other areas.

One disadvantage of interdenominational missions is that while one missionary may be faithful and free to proclaim the truth of the Word of God and baptistic principles, there is no assurance that these principles will be carried through by missionaries who follow. God holds us responsible in our planning for the future in missionary work just as we are responsible for planning the future of our church affiliation here at home. In other words, we should be building a foundation and setting precedents that will be perpetuated in years to come. We feel that as true as some interdenominational missions are, because of the wideness and broadness of their concept with regard to many Baptist principles, it would be more consistent to maintain and support Baptist missions.

At the same time, it seems important that we do not label some good missions as being apostate or in deep error, even though they may not be our preference in support.

The Scope of Missions

Concerning the scope of missions, Reginald Matthews says:

There are three areas of missionary interest which are presented to our churches for which members should be greatly burdened. One area we call "foreign" missions, the second area we call "home" missions, and the third area includes our schools, social agencies and national and local fellowships.[2]

Dr. Matthews rightly points out that the three steps in fulfilling the Great Commission are evangelize, baptize and instruct. Often, the area of foreign missions is considered more missionary than home missions or the ministries of the schools. This is an error that needs to be corrected. Some would claim that the schools are out of the realm of missions, but if training men in Bible colleges and seminaries on the foreign fields is missions, certainly it should be considered so in the states.

Dr. Matthews concurs with this in saying:

It is equally without foundation to think that a school eight thousand miles away training nationals to preach is more of a missionary enterprise than the school in a neighboring state which trains men to preach. *The field is the world.* The geographic location is not an essential factor in determining the missionary nature of a project. Instead it is need and obedience to the Great Commission which determines the worthiness of support.[3]

The Administration of the Missionary Program

The pastor. The pastor's part in missions is a vital one. While missionary committees and organizations may be established in the church, it cannot be doubted that the pastor should be the key administrator in missions. It is essential that he be burdened for missions and interested in the program if the church is to have a vigorous missionary outreach.

The missionary committee. The church ought to have a

missionary committee. Usually the constitution and by-laws spell out exactly who will serve upon it. It is important that it include members who represent the various boards and departments. This will help in reaching the entire church as the missionary burdens are carried back to the groups.

The ladies' missionary fellowship. The ladies' missionary group is an important arm of the church. While comments have been made in jest about the "Ladies' Raid," the missionary emphasis of a great many ladies' meetings and their practical services are vital to the missionary life of the church.

The missionary secretary. Many churches have a missionary secretary. The purpose of this office is to report missionary information to the church, to read missionary letters in congregational meetings and to assist in an advisory capacity with the missionary committee and the board of deacons.

The official board. You cannot and must not disassociate missionary enterprises from the official boards. The deacons and trustees should be represented on the missionary committee. All of the members of both boards should be intensely interested in missions.

The Promotion of the Missionary Program

The missionary enterprises of a church can be promoted in a number of ways.

The pulpit ministry of the pastor. Nothing can take the place of the strong preaching of the Word of God as it applies to missions. The pastor should preach on missions regularly, and share his burden with the congregation.

Missionary conferences. Many churches have a missionary conference at least once a year. Often the missionary conference is the time when the Faith Promise plan is put into effect. The conference ought to be planned by the missionary committee and should have the cooperation of the official boards and the congregation of the church. It needs to be publicized.

Some conferences take the round-robin type of approach with a number of churches in an area cooperating. Several missionaries from different fields are involved. These rotate among the churches, speaking in a different church each night. This is especially helpful for small churches.

Some conferences are sponsored by a single church. The missionaries participate in a variety of programs during the week. They may speak at ladies' meetings or luncheons, or they may present symposiums, panels, etc. This type of conference allows the people more opportunity to spend time with the missionaries and to receive more than a brief pulpit ministry.

Missionary Sundays. Missionaries should be invited to speak on several Sundays during the year. When the missionaries come home, the church where their membership is located ought to have a reception for them. When it is time to return to the field, the church should gather to honor them and to take a special offering. These occasions ought to be highlights of the church life.

Special missionary offerings. In times of emergency or special need for projects, the church can receive a special offering to help the missionary.

Missionary letters. Letters should be written periodically to church members announcing faith offerings, Faith Promise plans, special missionary offerings, special needs of missionaries or general missionary information.

Prayer emphasis. Churches that have days of prayer ought to have lists of the missionaries and their particular needs posted and distributed. In the midweek prayer service a great deal of emphasis should be place on praying for missions and missionaries.

Missionary map. Most churches have a missionary map in the foyer or at the front of the church with lights or other means of designating where the missionaries are serving. This is an excellent way to visualize the missionary outreach of the church. It also serves as a testimony to visitors.

Church library. The church library should have a good selection of missionary books, including histories, biographies and novels. These should be publicized by posters and announcements in the church bulletin and by word of mouth.

End Notes

[1] Reginald Matthews, *Missionary Administration in the Local Church* (Schaumburg, IL: Regular Baptist Press, 1972), p. 11. Used by permission.

[2] Ibid., p. 87.

[3] Ibid., p. 88.

CHAPTER EIGHTEEN
The Pastor and His Family

The Pastor and His Children

One of the most unfortunate conditions of the pastorate is that the pastor and his family often live in a "fishbowl"; that is, they have little or no privacy, and they are being observed constantly. Often people in the community will be on constant watch to see what the pastor is doing. I have found that there are always a few in the congregation who can tell when the pastor is away, when he leaves for work in the morning, and generally what he does or does or not do. Some people are just naturally "pastor-watchers." There is very little that can be done about this; it must be accepted as one of the less pleasant aspects of the ministry. However, there are steps which can be taken to make it less obvious and to discourage such a practice.

One problem is often the location of the parsonage. When it is too close to the church it is in danger of developing into an annex of the church. As an annex it is often open to everyone. It is not uncommon to have Sunday School classes, ladies' missionary meetings or extra bathrooms "handy" to the church. I strongly discourage the parsonage being that close to the church. If at all possible, the pastor ought to suggest that the parsonage be away from the church or that he purchase his own house. The latter is being done more and more frequently today.

The pastor should have a home where he can have some type of private life. His children should not be the children of every member of the church. This will spoil them and make them feel privileged. It can also damage their whole outlook on life and do irreparable hurt to their personalities. The pastor's wife and children should be allowed to lead as normal a life as possible.

On the other hand, while there is a danger of the congregation spoiling a child, there is the opposite possibility of making the child feel like a second-class citizen. The pastor should provide for his children; they should not have to wear clothes from the "missionary barrel" (neither should the missionary or his children!) Having to scrimp continually can make them bitter. If the church cannot afford to pay a pastor a living wage, then he should not be afraid to work in a secular field until the church is able to fulfill its responsibility for his care. A man who provides not for his own house is called "worse than an infidel" (1 Tim. 5:8).

The pastor and his wife should not discuss problems of the church in the presence of their children. To talk about the unfairness of members of the church, including board members, is to invite trouble, affecting the child's outlook and attitude toward the ministry in later years.

The pastor should be a father to his children. He must play with them, spend time with them and let them live a normal childhood. They will enjoy being "preacher's kids" and not feel left out because Dad had more time for the congregation than he did for them.

The Pastor and His Wife

People have often asked me, "What is the best college course a woman can take in preparing to be a minister's wife?" The answer is quite simple: *homemaking*. The

pastor's wife should understand that she is just that—
the wife of the pastor, a mother to their children, a co-
laborer in the work. It is most important that the pastor's
wife understand that she is not in any way an assistant
pastor. Her first responsibility is to be a wife and mother.
Her activity in the church should be comparable to that of
other dedicated women in the congregation. She should
be available for counseling women but certainly not the
only counselor. In many cases she should refer the problem to her husband and suggest that he is better equipped
to handle it.

It is not necessary for the pastor to share every
church problem and difficulty with his wife. There will
be some cases he will want to share, and she will join him
in prayer. She should never insist that she be as informed
as he is. This can lead to problems and leave the wife in an
embarrassing position when inquiries are made as to
whether or not she knows about certain situations. It is
proper for the pastor's wife to say, "I have not been informed about that problem, and I would suggest that if
you want to know more about it you contact my husband."

The pastor's wife should be modest in her dress and
yet neat, observing the general styles of the day. She
should not stand out as being either shabby or ultra-
modern. Common sense based on the principles of God's
Word should be the rule.

She should seek to maintain the privacy of her home,
to meet the needs of her husband and children and to lead
a normal Christian life. Should she neglect her home
while doing the business and participating in the activities of the church, she is a failure.

She should be careful not to criticize her husband's
sermons in public, nor in any way to undermine him or
speak derogatorily of him. She should be careful not to tell
the congregation how much better her lot was in the pre-

ceding pastorate. She should not be excessively talkative. Her conversation and deportment should be an example to every member of the church.

It is advisable that the pastor's wife not be employed by the church in any capacity; i.e., secretary, clerk, etc.

The pastor's wife should be careful not to take over the choir or music of the church, nor to insist on playing the piano, even though she may be most talented. In this respect she should take a place in the background and be used occasionally when called upon.

She should have the work of the Lord at heart and encourage her husband in it. Under her prayerful care the parsonage can be a place where there is a happy atmosphere, a place where the children are raised in the admonition of the Lord and have a healthy attitude toward the things of the Lord.

It is indeed a shame for a pastor to be involved in instructing other families when his own family is not in subjection. This often ends in tragic bitterness. Both husband and wife must pray fervently for wisdom and direction of the Lord in this respect.

CHAPTER NINETEEN
Perils and Problems in the Pastor's Personal Life

The Peril of Laziness

A Lutheran professor once stated that the three main perils in the ministry were "shine, whine and recline." How true! Here we consider the propensity to recline. First, we need to realize that *we are all lazy by nature*. Remember this! To know it is the first step in doing something about it.

The easiest place in the world to be lazy is in the ministry. The reason for this is obvious. The pastor is his own boss. He can be easy on himself and still give the impression of being very busy about the Lord's work. The pastor must be honest with himself at all times with regard to this tendency. He must diligently plan his work and work his plan. The tactful wife of a minister can be of great help and encouragement in this regard.

Lazy pastors will develop into superficial pastors. Eventually the lazy pastor will be found out, although he may be judged as a person who lacks ability instead of one who actually has failed to apply himself. Browning speaks of the "unlit lamp and the ungirt loin." Let it not be true of you. The Bible says, "Go to the ant, thou sluggard; consider her ways, and be wise" (Prov. 6:6).

The answer for laziness.

1. Read! Read! Read! Make yourself do it. Read a

book at one sitting. This was done by James Gray, G. Campbell Morgan, Graham Scroggie, and others who are judged as great preachers. Spurgeon read Bunyan a hundred times.

2. Write as you read. Take notes; write a summary or analysis of the book.

3. Write out your messages. F. B. Meyer has written:

We are all tempted to be lazy. It is possible to spend two or three hours in the study, surrounded by books, flitting like a butterfly from one to another but girding ourselves to no great effort of thought. It is here that the pen comes in to test us. We have often found that it is possible to read listlessly one book after another, absorbing the thoughts of others, without bringing one's mind into distinct and living contact with the truths which they may be discussing. It is so easy to allow oneself to feed on milk, which is food that has passed through the digestion of another, without exerting oneself to wrestle with the angel of truth in the dark until we extort his secret. It is always better to give a little truth which we have personally discovered and hammered out in our own workshop, like the beaten work of the cherubim of old, than to give much of the results of other men's researches. Use the pen; write as you think. Even if there is no prospect of using what you write in the written form, write it.[1]

4. Learn the discipline of prayer. Turnbull writes:

To pray aright and to pray enough is to face difficulties, especially our sloth. "Oh, oh, oh," cried John Calvin, "what deep-seated malice against God is this, that I will do anything and everything, but to go to Him and remain with

Him in prayer—secret prayer!" Our danger is
that we are always "on the run," and neglect the
culture of our souls in private. This discipline is
needful in order to ward off sloth.[2]

5. Put yourself on a rigid schedule and abide by it.
One of the most prolific writers of his time was A.
C. Gaebelein. He writes:

Many times have I been asked how I managed to
write so many books, produce the Annotated
Bible, and travel from coast to coast. The answer
is very simple. I never wasted time. "Do you play
golf?" "No." "Why not?" "Not because it is
wrong, but because I can use my time in a better
way." Doing the work systematically is another
secret of my success. It is also true that for some
sixteen years I never took a vacation, but kept at
it summer and winter. But the real reason is His
mercy and His kindness in giving me the needed strength both spiritually and physically.
And so to Him be all the glory.[3]

The Peril of Pride
One preacher was said to be so proud that he had the
ability "to strut while sitting down." Of all the sins to
which the pastor is most vulnerable, pride is number
one.
Alexander Whyte wrote:

Self-love is that master passion in every heart.
Let us give self-love the first place in the inventory and catalogue of our passions, because it has
the largest place in all our hearts and lives. It is
out of self-love that all our other evil passions
spring. The fall and ruin and misery of our present human nature lies in this, that in every human being self-love has taken, in addition to its

own place, the place of the love of God and of the love of man also. We naturally love nothing and no one but ourselves. And as long as self-love is in the ascendant in our hearts, all the passions that are awakened in us by our self-love will be selfish with its selfishness, inhuman with its inhumanity, and ungodly with its ungodliness. And it is to kill and extirpate our passionate self-love that is the end and aim of all God's dealings with us in this world.[4]

Professor James Denney said:

No man can bear witness to Christ and to himself at the same time. No man can give the impression that he himself is clever and that Christ is mighty to save.[5]

Let those words be stamped upon each man's heart as he enters the ministry. God will share His glory with no man. Each pastor's motto should be, "None of self, and all of thee."

Referring to A. T. Pierson, Turnbull writes:

On November 12, 1875, he was convinced that the great obstacle to his spiritual growth and power was his ambition for literary glory. This conviction had been slowly growing, but he had almost unconsciously fought against it. Now he asked God to deal with this ambition in his own way: "I saw that my life had been full of self-seeking and idolatry, such as I had never realized. . . . From that day I was conscious of the presence of the Holy Spirit in my life and work in a way that I had before never known. I saw that all the glory was to be His, not mine. . . . From that hour I nailed my ambition for literary honors and applause to the Cross of Christ."[6]

The Peril of Substitutes and Sidetracks

If Satan can get us to "major on the minor" and "minor on the major" he has won the victory over us.

The peril of politics and social concerns. No one would doubt that the pastor should be a good citizen. But this is his responsibility as a *man* and as a *citizen*, not as a pastor. That is, he should not bring politics into the pulpit; neither should he wave the newspaper in front of the congregation every Sunday morning showing the condition of the world. They can read the newspaper themselves. Do not harp so much on the conditions that you neglect spending time on the solutions.

The peril of negativism. The pastor *should* be a separatist. I am a separatist, and I am not ashamed of it. But I do not preach it every Sunday. The pastor cannot build a church on attacks against the World Council of Churches or the National Council of Churches. As deserving as they are of any criticism they receive, even they win a point if their presence and activity distract from the main business of wielding the Word in the power of the Holy Ghost.

The peril of gimmickry. Whatever is the "latest," some preachers will be there to learn how to do it. There are seminars and workshops on everything. Some of them are good, but remember that the tried and tested "old-fashioned" methods of doing the job and the simple preaching of the Word, without fanfare, is what counts in the final analysis. Do not be a man of the fad and the newfangled. Stick to the main business of preaching the Word, exposing hearts to the Good News of salvation and shepherding the flock. Then, when gimmicks are gone, the results of faithfulness in the Word will remain.

The peril of cleverness. Cleverness can be the undoing of the pastor. His ability to do everything and have answers for everything could well be his nemesis. Clever people often become everything from public relations men to handymen with tools for every problem.

The Peril of Covetousness

Money! Money! Money! So much seems to depend on it. Well does Andrew W. Blackwood say:

> With a layman as a neighbor, the pastor may covet his house, his car, or his bank account; with a brother minister, his parish, his church equipment, or his salary. If one may judge from the sprightly talk when pastors get together for a "bull session," these things bulk large in their thinking. In a way it is natural for a minister to think much about money. He may live in the midst of neighbors whose monthly income is larger than his year's salary. His wife mingles with women who think nothing of "hopping off" to England for a respite from the social whirl. His teen-age children go to school with boys who own "hot-rod" autos and with girls able to dress like daughters of Croesus. However saintly, the head of such a household is under pressure to "keep up with the Jones." Year by year, especially in many suburbs, the pressure increases. To meet such demands the pastor feels that he must have more money.[7]

Some questions the minister should ask himself:

1. Am I willing to sacrifice after seven or eight years of study and live on less than a person who has a regular janitor's job?

2. Am I willing to work part-time, if necessary, to supplement my salary in the early years of my ministry, and to do so without whining about it?

3. Am I able to keep my eyes on the Lord and not on the affluent membership of my church, and to remain content with my lot, never having a trace of bitterness?

4. Am I willing to accept a good wage and a good home or parsonage, knowing that in the next church things may not be quite as pleasant, and yet not letting this influence my decision for the future?

I am not suggesting that the pastor be "kept down" and not be compensated for his work. "The labourer is worthy of his hire." A church ought to consider what it can do for the man in the ministry as well as what it can receive from him.

The pastor should live on a plane commensurate with the average businessman in the church. He will be required to own a number of suits, to drive an average car, to maintain a home, etc. What is important, however, is his heart motive. Many ministers are ruined because they have covetous hearts and have lost the burden for the ministry, going into more lucrative areas of employment. This raises the question as to whether these men were ever truly called to the ministry.

The Peril of Jealousy

Proverbs 6:34 warns, "Jealousy is the rage of a man: therefore he will not spare in the day of vengeance." Song of Solomon 8:6 further admonishes, "Jealousy is cruel as the grave: the coals thereof are coals of fire, which hath a most vehement flame."

Jealousy of a fellow servant. When another pastor succeeds, a man may hide his jealousy behind rationalizations to help him excuse his own failure. Consider the following possibilities:

1. "I don't compromise." While it is true that some succeed because they hold a "success at any price" philosophy, this is not always the case. Be careful not to add false accusation to the sin of jealousy.

2. "I'm sticking to the historic Baptist principles so progress is slower for us." It was never historical Baptist principle to be second-class in your vision and venture for

God. There are thriving Baptist churches; indeed, some of the world's largest are Baptist. Beware of pride in addition to jealousy.

3. "I'm not a showman." Good! Do not try to be one, but try to be everything God has ordained you to be. Blessing does not necessarily depend upon personal charisma. It will come when God has His hand upon you.

4. "I build solidly. Fast 'mushroom growth' is never good." Is not Acts 2 in your Bible? If a church's work is big, it is not necessarily bad. If its growth is fast, it is not always wrong. Work with all your heart, get your eyes off your brother, and leave the results with Him—big or small, fast or slow. "It is required of stewards that a man be found faithful" (1 Cor. 4:2).

Many outstanding men have given in to the peril of jealousy, but thankfully they were delivered from it. May it be so with all of us.

Concerning F. B. Meyer, Turnbull writes:

It is related of the late F. B. Meyer that when he first went to the Northfield Conference, he attracted the crowd. People thronged to hear his special addresses. But, later, G. Campbell Morgan came to Northfield, and the people were lured by the brilliant Bible studies to desert Meyer. Meyer confessed liability to jealousy as he ministered to a smaller group. "The only way I can conquer my feeling," he said, "is to pray for him daily, which I do." Magnanimity is the grace which can bloom if nurtured like that; in this way a Christian man triumphs.[8]

Alexander Whyte wrote:
I am a Jonah. . . . I used to say, let me die first before I am eclipsed by another in my pulpit and among my people. I fought with a Jonah-like fierceness against the remotest thought of my

reputation ever passing over, in my day at any rate, to another. I kept my eyes shut to the decay going on around my pulpit till I could shut my eyes to it no longer.[9]

Do not succumb to the sin of jealousy. The work of the ministry is bigger than that.

The Peril of Lust

A seasoned pastor stated that the three sins that are most used of Satan against those in the ministry are covetousness, pride and sex. The latter area is an increasing peril in today's moral climate. There are certain rules which, if practiced, will help you avoid being defeated by such temptation. Remember, *you* can be vulnerable to this sin. "Wherefore let him that thinketh he standeth take heed lest he fall" (1 Cor. 10:12).

If you are a married man, be a one-woman man. You should have eyes for one woman only. Love her; spend time with her. Never let that wonderful relationship and bond between you and your wife slip. For you to be everything you should be to her, and she to you, is the best guarantee against a third party.

Consider yourself vulnerable to the flesh and do not give in "even a little" in your principle regarding the opposite sex. There should be no exception. It takes two to be amorous.

Be careful about your mind—and what you feed it. This includes novels, television and magazines. Do not expose yourself to those areas which could be tools of the devil.

Be circumspect in your counseling sessions with women. Failure to be prudent and discreet can lead to downfall. Do not get emotionally involved. Be "high level" at all times. Be careful not to pry into another's background or experiences. Never counsel without your secretary or wife being available. Counsel in the study, not in the counselee's home alone. Never touch the person you are counseling, even in sympathy or concern.

Do not be a one-man army against pornography. Do not investigate or preach on this subject constantly.

Do not spend too much time on yourself; i.e., your appearance. In other words, be neat and clean, but not enamoured with yourself, seeing yourself as younger and more glamorous than you are. Vanity can get you into trouble.

These are not all the perils and problems in the ministry. Satan uses this bag of tricks most often, but he has others too. Be honest with yourself at all times. Keep humble before the Lord; never lose sight of Him. Keep in spiritual touch constantly and you can be victorious over these perils and problems. He has promised help in His Word—claim it!

End Notes

[1] F. B. Meyer, *Jottings and Hints for Lay Preachers* (London: Andrew Melrose Co., 1906), p. 117.

[2] Ralph G. Turnbull, *A Minister's Obstacles* (Old Tappan, NJ: Fleming H. Revell Co., 1965), p. 23. Used by permission.

[3] A. C. Gaebelein, *Half a Century: The Autobiography of a Servant* (Publication Office: Our Hope, 1930), pp. 97, 98.

[4] Turnbull, *A Minister's Obstacles,* quoting Alexander Whyte in chapter "The Paralysis of Pride."

[5] Turnbull, *A Minister's Obstacles,* quoting James Denney in chapter "The Paralysis of Pride." He found the words on the wall of a church vestry in Scotland.

[6] Turnbull, pp. 45, 46.

[7] Andrew Watterson Blackwood, *The Growing Minister* (Nashville: Abingdon Press, 1960), p. 107.

[8] Turnbull, pp. 37, 38.

[9] Alexander Whyte, *Bible Characters (The Old Testament),* Vol. 1. (Grand Rapids: Zondervan Publishing House, n.d.), p. 387. Out of print.

CHAPTER TWENTY
Ethics and Etiquette

Should a pastor be concerned about his image? While there is probably an excess of material on the importance of one's image, this should not deter the pastor from giving it consideration in connection with his ministry. He should not think of himself as above his people; neither should he allow his ego to swell and the concept of himself to soar. However, the pastor has a high calling, and he should always remember that he represents the Lord. The way a pastor acts will reflect on Him either favorably or unfavorably. Generally, people do have a high regard for the ministry; thus, there are some things a pastor does not do, even though it might be legitimate for others. The ministry is a holy calling. One must be careful that he does not degrade it.

Keep the High Calling Uppermost in Mind

For a pastor to boast, "I'm independent," or, "I'm a maverick," does not give him a license to kick over all the traces in the ministry. To have people state, "When they made him, they threw away the mold," is not necessarily a compliment.

A. The demands of the ministry should be weighed before a man decides this is what God wants him to do.

B. The pastor should be courteous and ethical regarding the ministry of others. While it is impossible to approve those who compromise their ministry, it is not becoming to downgrade them constantly (with different degrees of disdain). The man who does this continuous downgrading is implying that he alone is standing.

C. The pastor is a minister of the Word, not a showman. He should not imitate others; it could ruin him.

D. The pastor should make good use of his time. He should not have the reputation of always having time for everything and never being busy. He should not be a gadabout, giving the impression he is a nonworking man who preaches twice a week.

E. The minister must not let thoughts of money sway him or get him down. He should not measure his work by his salary. This can make him, as well as his family, bitter.

F. The man of God must watch the use of his name. He cannot endorse everything or let everyone use his name for a recommendation. When General Lee was asked, after the Civil War, if a company could use his name as the president of the concern, he answered, "Gentlemen, I have nothing left but my name, and that is not for sale."

G. The pastor should not become a "Mr. Fixit" or a handyman for every member of the church. He is really ahead if (like myself) he is all thumbs when it comes to repairing things. If he is a good plumber but a poor preacher, he is liable to "go down the drain" posthaste.

Fellow Pastors in the Ministry

Generally carpenters are not jealous of doctors, and plumbers are not jealous of gardeners. But carpenters are sometimes jealous of other carpenters. Jealousy is more likely within the same fields of work—thus it may be in the ministry.

The pastor should not talk about the shortcomings of his predecessor. There will always be someone who will tell the present pastor how inadequate the man before him was, implying that he saved the day. Remember, the same people may rate the present pastor equally inadequate when *he* leaves. Commend the work of the predecessor whenever possible. Keep silent about his imperfections. That is a mark of maturity.

The pastor should not be jealous and decry or minimize the work of his successor. He should praise the Lord for the success he has had, not make excuses for it.

Rejoice in the success of a fellow minister in your same state or city or fellowship. The reaction among many is to make excuses when others are succeeding and they are not. Each pastor should work as hard as he can and leave the rest to the sovereignty of God. The work is the minister's—the results are His. If He is blessing others, praise Him.

When a fellow pastor speaks in the church be sure that the church's financial responsibilities to him are taken care of immediately. To say, "We'll send a check," and fail to do so is inexcusable. Likewise, to take a "love offering" for him and fail to see that he gets it is reprehensible.

The trustees should reevaluate the system of honorariums annually and keep them in line with the current economy. Some churches are still giving the same amount for expenses and honorariums today as they did twenty years ago.

CHAPTER TWENTY–ONE
Problem Areas in the Church Life

While we must be careful not to emphasize the negatives, there is a need to consider the problem areas. To be forewarned is to be forearmed. Some of the following material (as in other parts of the book) is more related to church administration than to pastoral theology. However, because most of these areas involve the leadership and administration of the pastor, they should be discussed.

The Music Problem

Some refer to the music department as the war department of the church because of the problems that develop in this area. That music is a vital part of worship cannot be gainsaid. The Word of God makes it clear that music is not simply an appendage to the church program but an important and integral part of the Lord's work. However, if Satan can get in a wedge of disagreement he will do it, and the music department is one of his prime targets.

The kind of music. Possibly there is no area in evangelical churches in which there are more divisions than this one. The pastor and music director, along with the music committee and the deacons, ought to give priority to the kind of music used. While the music should not be only eighteenth-century in quality, neither should it be the contemporary rock of the present day. Admittedly, the style of music does change. It is the better part of wisdom, however, to scrutinize these changes and to move slowly in accepting or adopting them. In the selection of music one must be careful not to become secularized, to simply conform to the world and give a religious flavor to the fleshly appetites.

The quality of music. This is as great a problem as the kind of music because the church is faced with a serious choice. Are we using music because we want to use various individuals, however untalented they are, or will we use the best that we have in order to present the message? Some churches minimize quality. They feel that if the spirit is right and the attitude is good, a person ought to be permitted to sing or play an instrument. While this may help the person performing, and there may be sympathy and understanding on the part of the people, it can be disconcerting to someone visiting for the first time, especially the unsaved. Rather than conveying the gospel message to visitors, the singing may offend them and perhaps they will not return. On the other hand, if we give consideration only to ability, there is the danger of showmanship, and a feeling on the part of the people that the music is a performance rather than an integral part of the worship or praise service. The spiritual administrators of the church should consider both extremes and pray that balance is maintained. Strive to provide quality music and also to encourage those lesser lights who want to be used.

One answer is to use new musical groups in departmental areas of the church rather than in the worship services. In this way the novices receive training, confidence and poise. Their problems may be worked out so they can be used in the worship services at a later date.

Song leading. The songleader in the church is very important. Care should be exercised in selecting someone to fill this position. It must be understood that it is much easier to get people to accept a position than it is to remove them. Therefore, the selection of a person who will be continually in front of the church leading the singing should be made with caution. He must be a spiritual man; he should have musical ability; and he should know the basic principles in directing music. He ought to be neatly dressed and not characterized by idiosyncrasies or extremes in fashion. If someone qualified to lead the singing cannot be found in the congregation, the pastor should do it.

The instrumentalists. Several people in the church may play the piano or organ with varying degrees of ability. Therefore, it may be difficult to ascertain exactly who will be the church instrumentalists. The music committee should establish guidelines and be careful to follow them in selecting the pianist(s) or organist(s). There should be an understanding also as to who will play the instruments on occasions such as special meetings and weddings. Can someone other than those regularly assigned be allowed to play for such events?

The Clique Problem

Churches are often criticized because cliques have built up within the membership and some individuals seem to be left out. A church that is properly administered should care for this problem and do all it can to solve it. First, it should be recognized that churches may not have as many cliques as claimed. Some people are naturally introverted; wherever they go they feel that the church is not friendly. However, there are a number of areas in which most churches can improve, and this is one of them. Consider the following suggestions:

An awareness of the problem. If the pastor and the deacon board are aware of such a problem and make an effort to correct it, half of the problem is already solved. Most cliques form without those who are involved being aware of it. A concentratedted effort by the pastor not to be a part of a particular circle will help provide a good example. The planning of activities to include all the people and not just a few families will also go a long way in alleviating this difficulty.

A working church. If a church is a working church rather than a social church, it will be found that a great deal of the problem is solved. Actually, fellowship means "joint participation," and when this participation is doing the work of the Lord in winning souls, the cliques usually vanish.

The Fellowship Problem

One of the greatest problems facing evangelical Baptist churches is the one of where and with whom the church should fellowship. How involved should the church get with other circles, denominations and Christian enterprises?

Distinct areas of separation. An examination of Scripture makes it clear that neither the pastor nor the church should align itself with organizations that are liberal in doctrine. The Word of God says, "And have no fellowship with the unfruitful works of darkness, but rather reprove them" (Eph. 5:11). The best way to reprove them is to separate from them, making a clear-cut testimony in this respect. God's Word is definite on this. "Wherefore come out from among them, and be ye separate, saith the Lord" (2 Cor. 6:17). Separation is not simply a matter of moral reasons, but doctrinal as well. "Now I beseech you, brethren, mark them which cause divisions and offences contrary to the doctrine which ye have learned; and avoid them" (Rom. 16:17). This passage makes it clear that churches should be independent of all organizations that are contrary to the Word of God and that reflect unfavorably upon our Lord. The church that dares to take a stand and sever all relationships with apostate organizations will be blessed of God.

Vague areas of separation. It is to be admitted that there are some churches with whom we do not entirely agree, yet they hold to many of the basic doctrines of the faith. This is a rather nebulous area and has caused no little disturbance in evangelical circles. The best rule is simply not to get involved in organizations that could cause embarrassment to the pastor and the church, even though in some cases there may be no specific Scriptural basis for a clear-cut separation. For example, most cities have evangelical ministerial associations. Probably each of the churches represented would subscribe to the main fundamentals of the faith; however, cooperation with them in an evangelical enterprise could be both inconsistent and unfruitful. How, for example, could you cooperate in a prophetic conference with churches that may hold a different view of the Rapture or the Millennium? Your eschatological view of the Millennium has a great deal to do with your motive in missions. Are we "trying to bring in the kingdom" through social reform? While it is admitted that not all amillennialists and post-millennialists are modernists, it is certainly inconsistent to hold a missionary or prophetic conference with such groups.

Again, how would you hold an evangelistic conference with a Holiness or a Pentecostalist group? While agreeing with you on the basics of salvation, they insist on a second work of grace and an after-service involving tongues.

A great many ministers in the evangelical ministerial association are also members of the local Council of Churches, which includes liberals. These groups often promote mass evangelistic campaigns and other united projects within the community. The complications with such cooperation are numerous. It is the better part of wisdom, therefore, not to affiliate with local ministerial associations.

The following questions can serve as guidelines in determining the position a church should take:

1. Is such affiliation inconsistent with Scripture?
2. Will such cooperation conceal the issues and reflect upon a clear-cut stand?
3. Will such affiliation in any way be disadvantageous to the church in promoting the cause of Christ?
4. Will such association embarrass us as a church?

Wonderful areas of fellowship. First, the most obvious area of fellowship is your own association of churches. This does not intimate that your particular association is so exclusive as to think you are "the only ones" doing anything for God. However, to delight in one's family does not imply that other families are not happy also, and have their place. The finest blessings and fellowship should be with those who subscribe to the same doctrinal statement and have the same objectives and purposes. It is good for pastors to fellowship within their own national, state and local associations. Sometimes, because of competition or slight differences among men, there is a tendency to become bitter or indifferent to the work of their fellowship. The pastor and the people of a church should be prayerfully careful not to permit themselves to feel that they are the only ones, even in their fellowship, who are taking a stand.

Second, recognize that there are churches of like precious faith that are not in our particular associational family. A number of independent churches are doing a job for God. We need to encourage them and work with them as the Lord leads. I have had a number of wonderful opportunities in witnessing and preaching in independent Baptist churches without in any way compromising my position or reflecting upon my association.

Another possible area of church fellowship can be found among those in the American Council of Christian Churches, where God's people from different denominations are holding forth the Word of Life and taking a sound stand "outside the camp."

The Problem of Problems

While we have spent some time mentioning a few of the problems in church life and its administration, it is important that we do not give the problems more emphasis than they deserve. Some pastors and churches are "problem-oriented," and seem to delight in the fact that they are involved in some ecclesiastical altercation. Problems there are, but there is also a great job to be done for the Lord in building the church and in bringing honor to His name. Do not be so problem-oriented that the ministry becomes negative in its presentation. Be dedicated to preaching the positive message of salvation and in building up the saints for the ministry of witnessing.

CHAPTER TWENTY-TWO

Reaching Beyond the Pulpit

When people ask about my present work as president of a college, my first response is that it certainly isn't boring. There is so much variety and challenge that it's actually exciting. I also found the ministry to be that way; thus, my experience as a pastor was a happy one. The purpose of this chapter is to reflect on the variety of opportunities and challenges for the pastor as he reaches beyond the local church to a broader constituency. This does not mean there is a higher plateau above the work of the ministry in the local church. It does mean that it is possible to broaden one's ministry and, at the same time, make oneself more skilled and productive in the local church ministry. There is a reciprocal interaction here. Communication skills can be used outside the church while being honed for better use within the church. For example, writing out one's sermons could be the first step in developing writing skills and could even result in a book. At the same time, refining one's writing skills will help one speak more carefully and accurately. Reading, they say, makes a man full and writing makes him more accurate. So, let us look at this and other areas in which the pastor can reach beyond his pulpit to minister to others.

Radio Opportunities

One very natural way a pastor can multiply his ministry is in the area of radio. Early in my ministry, when I pastored the Bible Baptist Church of Trenton, New Jersey, we were involved in a weekly radio ministry called "Echoes of Heaven." As I recall, the program proved to be quite challenging, because the message was in manuscript form and it was a first venture in writing. This ministry developed further in Richland, Washington, where I broadcast a fifteen minute weekly program (also called "Echoes of Heaven"), six days a week, as well as the Sunday morning worship service. Then, while I pastored that same church, we added another daily fifteen minute program called "Bible Clinic," where we answered Bible questions submitted by the public. I can't begin to tell you how those opportunities sharpened my skills and helped me in those early days. Frankly, I think I overdid it, which is typical of youth "rushing in" with more zeal than knowledge. But that initiative of reaching out to do more was good discipline and probably helped me more than it did those on the listening end.

What is interesting is that those early days were foundational for other radio ministries in Everett and Tacoma, Washington. Today, in Grand Rapids, Michigan, we are involved in a radio ministry six days a week on our own college station. Plans are now underway to syndicate my five minute offering, "Let's Take a Break," for several more stations. One opportunity has led to another over the past years, and the Lord has seemed to use them to prepare me for this present addition to my presidential responsibilities. It all started back in Trenton, New Jersey, over thirty-five years ago. Also, this "beyond the pulpit" involvement has helped the churches I've pastored bring in new people, and it is helping the college and seminary today. Here are some suggestions you might think through:

1. Consider a fifteen-minute-a-week broadcast on Sunday morning. Write or type out your message and

tape it sometime during the week.

2. Expand to a daily five-minute program three days a week and then, if possible, to a daily program. Again, try to write or type out your messages.

The Ministry of Writing

Assuming you are studying regularly and that your sermons have substance and interest, there is no reason why material from those sermons cannot have a wider, broader use. It would be interesting to see a study of pastors in the last one hundred years who were also known for the power of their pen. Several come to mind.

One of the great pastors of all time was Charles Haddon Spurgeon (1834-1892). His writing ministry still reaches thousands. It should be remembered that many of his writings were messages delivered in the pulpit and later edited for publication. Besides his pastoral work and his many responsibilities at the Pastor's College, of which he was president, he wrote several books. He is probably the prime example of "reaching beyond the pulpit."

Spurgeon's monthly church magazine, *Sword and the Trowel,* was the means of publishing more than two thousand sermons. The forty-nine volume set of *The Metropolitan Pulpit* was a great work, to say nothing of *The Treasury of David,* a homiletic commentary on the Psalms in seven volumes. Add to this his various devotional books and special lectures to students and one should indeed be impressed.

Another good example of a pastor "reaching beyond" is G. Campbell Morgan (1863-1945). During his lifetime, he wrote sixty books and a dozen booklets. When one reads his commentaries one is impressed with a man who was able to articulate truth in a clear, unique fashion. He pastored the Westminster Congregational Chapel, Buckingham Gate, London, which was a dying church amid the "white elephant of Congregational-ism." Under his pastorate, the church grew and was greatly blessed of God. It is interesting that after many years he returned to the same church at age seventy-two and pastored there until his eightieth year. This great pastor was a student of the Holy Scriptures and his ministry reached out from his church to thousands the world over.

A. T. Pierson, another fine example, filled the Met-ropolitan Tabernacle pulpit when Spurgeon became ill in 1891. He pastored churches both in London and Amer-ica and was a leading Bible conference speaker. His books are too numerous to list here. (A chapter from one of his books is reprinted in this book: "The Genius of Indus-try.") F. B. Meyer and scores of other contemporaries could be added to the list of pastor-authors.

The pastor's study is a good beginning for messages that reach out to a world hungry for the truth. Think about it.

My own personal experience, in a more limited way, may be an encouragement to you. Some of my first writ-ings were from radio manuscripts. The material from which I preached was used in radio, and then extended to an even wider audience through the printed page. From there I have written hundreds of items for the Sunday School papers of Regular Baptist Press, many of which were first used in the radio work. I also have been privi-leged to write five quarters of adult Sunday School mate-rial and the four-year curriculum for high school age young people for Regular Baptist Press. Much of the ma-terial in those courses began in the studies of churches I pastored.

Another example of hard application of study and commitment is this book. The first edition (Regular Bap-tist Press, © 1976) was born out of a syllabus I used while teaching pastoral theology at the Los Angeles Baptist Seminary. It reflects the things I have learned over the years while in the ministry. Out of these experiences in the pastorate came a desire to help others, a sharing of the material at the seminary and a book used by other colleges and seminaries. As you work and exegete Scripture, prepare messages and illustrate them, this experience may lead you to share your messages in print. Let's talk about how this is done.

1. Begin by writing out your messages word for word. Edit them—or have a friend with editing abilities do so—with a view to publishing.

2. Edit a church paper. Desktop publishing makes it easier than ever to get involved in such a project. In my Tacoma church, I was the editor of *Temple Tidings,* a six-page weekly publication. Some of this material is still being used by the Regular Baptist Press Sunday School papers.

3. Write short articles and submit them to various publishers. They can be used as "fill-in" material of one hundred words or less. Next, attempt longer or more detailed articles of five hundred words. Don't get discouraged by rejection slips. That's part of the learning process.

Several months ago I received a phone call from a young pastor who spoke of a series of messages I had delivered to a group of ministers in his part of the country. He stated that I had encouraged the pastors to reach beyond their pulpits and get involved in writing. He decided to do just that and had written several hundred articles for Regular Baptist Press. I was then surprised to learn that the Press had hired him as editor of their Sunday School papers division. The same thing happened when I talked to one of the editors of Radio Bible Class. "I first started writing," he said, "after I met you in Hong Kong, where you encouraged me to get started if I felt I had any ability in this field. I was encouraged by this." He then thanked me for the part I had played in getting him started in this ministry. There are so many men who have something to say and share in writing but never take the first step in getting it done.

Many other areas could be considered here, including television and photography, where interests or hobbies could develop into paraministries and even, in some cases, full-time ministries.

Your Pulpit Ministry

While it is true that the church often takes a dim view of a pastor "working on the side," it generally feels complimented when he gets involved in areas that enhance the church's ministry as well as his own personal ministry. Thus, another way to reach beyond the pulpit is in the area of outside speaking. While this can be overdone and result in the neglect of the church, when kept in balance it is another means of extending one's ministry. Summer conference work, evening Bible school teaching and special messages for youth are examples of areas that can be developed with real spiritual and intellectual profit.

Reaching beyond your pulpit is not a matter of self-aggrandizement. Its purpose is not to create a "star status" in the religious world. God forbid that we would so prostitute our ministry. Reaching beyond your pulpit is designed to help you be all that you can be for the Lord in the quest of reaching a greater circle of people for His cause. With this desire to glorify God in mind, there are few limits.

APPENDIX

GIVE ME A MAN

"For the eyes of the LORD run to and fro throughout the whole earth, to shew himself strong in the behalf of them whose heart is perfect toward him."

2 Chronicles 16:9

"And I sought for a man among them, that should make up the hedge, and stand in the gap before me for the land, that I should not destroy it: but I found none."

Ezekiel 22:30

Our God is looking for a man;
   His eyes run to and fro
In patient searching for that one
   Through whom His strength to show.

"A man," He said, "give me a man
   Of faith, perfect in heart;
A man through whom I'll show My
     hand
And serving—strength impart."

Council and league were offered God,
   With power of place and plan;
Machinery large and iron strong,
   God said: "Give me a man!"

But Hell's aggressive power prevails,
   Relentlessly its hand
Strikes heavy, hard, against us all;
   God's answer is: "A man!"

His flashing eyes go to and fro
  Searching earth's breadth and
  length;
Our God still seeks a yielded man
  Through whom to show His strength.

C.U.W.

Many years ago I purchased a book in a second-hand bookstore entitled *Life-Power, or Character, Culture and Conduct,* by A. T. Pierson. It was published by Fleming H. Revell in 1895. I have never seen another copy in any bookstore or any pastor's library. (Incidentally, Dr. Pierson was ordained in 1860 in the Presbyterian Church. Thirty-six years later he became convinced that the views held by the Baptists were Biblical, and he was immersed and severed his relationship with the Philadelphia Presbytery.)

This book, dedicated to the memory of Charles Haddon Spurgeon, has meant more to me in shaping my life for the ministry than any other single book on the subject. It has six chapters:
  1. The Elements and Secrets of Power
  2. The Power of a Presiding Purpose
  3. The Use and Abuse of Books
  4. The Genius of Industry
  5. The Ethics of Amusement
  6. The Inspiration of Ideals
We are reprinting the fourth chapter in this volume. Digest it! Apply it! It could make a major difference in your ministry.

The Genius of Industry

It pertains to human nature to have some goal. Every true man aspires toward success. But the question arises, What is the path to this goal? Is there a royal road, or must we follow the old beaten track of humble plodding, as did William Carey?

No doubt there are on this subject opposing opinions. Some believe, whether they openly confess it or not, that the glory of the highest success is not within the reach of every honest toiler; that it is, like other legacies, the good fortune to which some are heirs, but which others are denied—the inheritance only of those whom nature has well endowed. These are the advocates of genius.

Others hold that genius has no monopoly in the race for success; that all true heights of worthy attainment and achievement are possible to those who have the average share of human endowments, the full complement of faculties, upon condition of the faithful culture of natural powers and the use of opportunities. These are the advocates of industry.

We would enter an earnest plea for mediocrity, and write a hopeful and hearty word in behalf of the "Genius of Industry."

It will certainly be encouraging to most readers if it can be shown that a high plane of action and achievement is open to those who claim no very uncommon endowments. Most men and women are ordinary, rather than extraordinary; and it were a pity to be compelled to conclude that, for such, fate has already ordained that even a high endeavor shall accomplish but little, reserving the golden crown of success for those who have the richest legacy of natural gifts. Must he who would be rich first consult the Sibyl of Fortune as to the traditions of his birth—whether or not he were born with a silver spoon in his mouth? Far more disappointing is it, if the higher wealth of learning and culture, influence and usefulness, can be gathered only by him whose childish prattle was in the dead languages, or who learned to read without a knowledge of the alphabet!

If a great mind—native, innate endowments of a

brilliant order—be essential to great power, large influence, efficient service, most people must give up in despair. The very fact that such gifts are rare, unusual, shuts such out from success, and shuts them up to a forlorn hope. For, as Emerson said, "If there be such a thing as genius, it is, like the passes on the railroads, marked 'special, not transferable, and good for this trip only.'"

The most formidable foe to human progress has been caste, the arbitrary elevation of an elect few above the many, and the erection of barriers, more or less inflexible, to prevent the average man from advancing beyond the common mass or rising above the common level. He is a philanthropist who in any department of life helps to break down caste barriers or encourage aspiration after excellence.

There are men who deny the existence of any such order of mind as is denominated genius. Some count it often nothing more than a studied eccentricity. If a man rush out of his house in mid-winter without a hat, like Lyman Beecher; wear one boot and one shoe, like Horace Greeley; walk up a church aisle with his wife's parasol high in the air, like a famous Connecticut divine; wear his hair in a cue, like the Chinese; put on his coat hindside before, waddle like a duck, gesture like a lobster, or do any other absurd or ridiculous thing, he is a genius. Someone wittily says: "Genius means idiosyncrasy, or, better still, idiosyncraziness." Certain it is that not a few seek to build up a reputation for being very uncommon by doing and saying very uncommon things.

It would seem best to concede that there is such a thing as inborn genius, in the sense of a naturally superior order of faculties. The very men who have denied it often disprove their own assertion. Now and then a child comes into life with a mind, like an already burnished jewel, shining with an imprisoned flame. If genius be defined as simply a peculiar natural aptitude for some particular study or employment, who can deny Napoleon's inborn fitness for a warrior and general, or James Watt's aptness for mechanics, or Isaac Watts aptitude for versification? What irresistible attraction toward the jingle of verse must that have been which led the young Isaac (the same story is told substantially of Alexander Pope), in the midst of a flogging from his impatient father for boring him with his doggerel, to dare a further application of the birch by entreating:

"O papa, spare me but this time,
And I no more will make a rhyme!"

If genius be defined as the creative faculty, who can doubt that men have been poets and painters, musicians and inventors, almost from the cradle?

One of the surest proofs of the existence of genius is to be found in the many undeniable instances of precocity or early cleverness. William Pitt was a marvel of such precocity, and in his early childhood seemed to have an instinctive perception of the natural affluence of his own gifts. When but seven years of age he surprised his tutor by a prophecy that he would succeed his father in the House of Commons. Lady Holland declared that at eight years he was the cleverest child she had ever seen; and when, at the age of fourteen, he went to Cambridge, he was in learning, as well as in mental maturity, a grown man. Young Pascal had such a genius for mathematics that, without ever having studied even the most elementary and rudimental work upon the "exact science," he actually invented a Euclid for himself, constructing his own definitions and axioms, and going step by step to the thirty-second proposition of the first book, unaided.

Julius Caesar, as a general, stands among the very first in history, having no equal except Napoleon; as a statesman the highest rank is conceded to him; as an ora-

tor he rivaled Cicero; and as a writer he excelled Xenophon and was excelled only by Tacitus. He was what the
Germans call a "many-sided man," touching life by every fiber, and great in everything he touched. Beside his
masterly Commentaries, the memoirs of his own life, he
wrote on grammar and on rhetoric, composed trage-
dies, satires, and lyrics, and reformed the calendar as
well as the state. Yet with all he was a man of indefatigable diligence.

Da Vinci was an example of universal genius—
musician, poet, sculptor, architect, engineer, astronomer, chemist, mathematician. Michelangelo, as poet,
painter, sculptor, or architect, shines conspicuous in a
firmament studded with constellations of glory. Ed-
mund Burke, in the amplitude and variety of his powers,
probably surpasses every other orator or statesman of either ancient or modern times. He was a perfect prodigy:
like Bacon, a philosopher; like Newton, an originator;
like Shakespeare, a myriad-minded man. He understood political economy like Adam Smith and could
judge art like Joshua Reynolds; a man of boundless gifts,
boundless knowledge, and boundless vocabulary.

While it may be conceded, therefore, that there is
such a thing as genius, it must be confessed that it is rarely found, and still more rarely found coupled with those
practical faculties popularly called "talents," which assure to the aptitude or creative faculty the actual success
it seems to forecast.

It is striking how seldom men of genius make and
leave upon the world a bold mark, a grand impress. Often
they die young; the mind, unnaturally mature, weigh-
ing down the puny body, that cannot get its natural, normal growth and strength. Sometimes, men, born acknowledged geniuses, precocious as children, grow in
years and stature, but early cease to grow in wisdom and

power, and die, scarce in life's prime, imbeciles, if not id-
iots. In other cases, utterly lacking in that practical faculty, known as common sense or worldly wisdom, they
forfeit all high attainment, splendid achievement, or noble success, spending life in wild vagaries or chimerical
dreams, the impracticable and visionary schemes so
strangely allied to genius, and which, because of their
unsubstantial character, have been vulgarly called
"moonshine."

We have a representative portrait of this unpracti-
cal type of genius that seems to unite a large brain to a very
small measure of common sense, in the comical story of
the philosopher who is described as standing in profound reverie before the barn door, through a hole in
which a calf had pushed out his tail. Being roused from
his meditation by the inquiry, "What are you thinking
about?" he answered, "Wondering how the calf squeezed
through that knothole!"

Early cleverness has so often been succeeded by premature imbecility or decay that one is sometimes tempted to think precocity a kind of deformity, or, at least, disease. Over against these examples of premature
development, how many cases may be cited of boys who,
beginning with a dullness verging upon imbecility,
have, like Daniel Webster, in the end far outrun those
who at first were like to have been winners in the race of
life! Sir Isaac Newton is said to have been a pronounced
dunce in his early school days; to have stood low in his
classes, and to have seemed lacking even in relish for
knowledge. The contemptuous kick given him by the
"smart boy" of the school was in the end a real uplift, for
the stinging insult roused Newton to determine that he
would rise above the lad that despised him.

To say no more, it is a fatal disadvantage attending
the most brilliant gifts, if their possessor is led to suppose

that anything can be accomplished without hard work. Yet how often consciousness of rare endowments leads to fitful application or absolute mental indolence, very much as heirs to wealth often prove heirs to laziness! Of many a highly gifted man it may be said, as Davy said of Coleridge, that "with the most exalted genius and enlightened mind, he was the victim of a want of order, precision, and regularity. With brilliant powers, but infirm of purpose; great intellectual endowments, but not the gift of industry and the sense of independence—his life was essentially a failure." Genius demands industry as its handmaid, and therefore requires concentration and observation. Montesquieu says: "First I arranged the principles of philosophy, and afterward arranged the facts on the shelves which I had thus prepared to receive and classify them." No true genius will despise order and method.

On the other hand, there is this to be said to the praise of the genius of industry. It is a kind of genius which is susceptible of culture, if not of out-and-out creation. It is not so rare as to be discouragingly exceptional; it is not a gift involving risk, like the fatal goodness depicted in some pious fiction, which is, to those who would attain a goodly old age, a forewarning of disappointment. Moreover, while genius often fails to leave a marked impress on history and humanity, industry has a record universally honorable and even brilliant. The men who have wrought the grandest achievements of culture and usefulness have not been as a class highly gifted, certainly not magnificently endowed; they have been at best only well balanced.

If we stop further to compare genius and industry, we shall see that there is no real good implied in the former which is not attainable by the latter.

I. The affluence of nature which often distinguishes

genius is quite indistinguishable from that affluence of culture which is the fruit of application.

Every thorough acquisition adds just so much permanent and substantial wealth to one's stock of attainment; and in this slow way all true riches of mind must be gathered. In the intellectual world there are no stock markets or brokers' boards whereby the indolent may rise to competence and affluence by happy speculations, without patient waiting and courageous industry. Here no man becomes suddenly rich by chance or change of fortune, turn of tide or accident of birth. Little by little he accumulates, if at all.

As he truly applies himself, he feels conscious that his nature is expanding; his powers, feeble perhaps by nature, get strong by culture. He finds that he is outgrowing himself; the self of years ago he scarce recognizes in the self of today. His thoughts strike deeper, have a broader sweep, a higher reach, a wider range, a mightier grasp; and so the whole man is enlarging: not his attainments only, but his power to attain; himself expanding continually.

Wealth comes to a few without their own exertion. But, as a matter of political economy, we find that there are laws of accumulation, and they are five:

1. Adaptation, natural or acquired, for one's chosen pursuit or calling
2. Adherence to it, or perseverance in work
3. Ambition or aspiration after excellence
4. Application of mind—the concentration of all faculties on the thing to be done
5. Economy, or the combination of frugality and judicious expenditure

So it is with mental wealth—accumulation of power. Paul writes to Timothy that the end and aim of Biblical indoctrination, reproof, correction, and instruction is to make the man of God "thoroughly furnished"—a most happy phrase to express the thought which we are laboring to enforce and illustrate. The expression is used by no chance or accident. When God would hold up the model of manhood he does not present the highly gifted, the richly endowed; that would discourage those who by nature have but the most ordinary powers. He presents what is within the reach of all—a thoroughly furnished manhood. This is something not inherited, but acquired; not born in us, but bred in us. The secret of all thorough furnishing lies in hard work.

Where there is found a patience that can wait slowly to gather, a perseverance that can hold fast an end yet unreached, a method that can store up results in an available form, an industry that does not shirk effort, there is all that is essential to a man thoroughly furnished for his work; give him time and health, and the wealth of success is his. One by one the links in his mental armour will be forged and joined, and by and by in full panoply he shall stand forth, like a warrior in his coat of mail. He who aspires to be a complete man, thoroughly furnished unto his life-work, will not depend upon any genius he may be thought to possess, but by industry make large general preparation for his vocation.

Affluence of mind and soul is therefore attainable; we are none of us doomed to feebleness and narrowness. God has made us and fitted us for growth.

The glory of humanity is largely its elasticity: it is capable of indefinite expansion. The lower animals seem endowed with a similar order of faculties with ourselves; they certainly perceive, reflect, reason, remember. But they reach a limit beyond which no education seems competent to carry them. The humblest man who is not radically deficient has a possible future whose dimensions suggest infinity. Everyone should therefore seek to grow into greatness of manhood.

They used to say of Lord Chatham that there was something in the man finer than in anything he ever said; and this is a delicate expression for that truest preparation for life's noblest work—the preparation found in the man himself.

II. Genius, again, seems marked by a *peculiar readiness;* it is never taken unawares. For example, some gifted public speakers, at times, when there is and can be no preparation with immediate reference to the occasion, seem to be *semper paratus.* We say of them that they have extempore gifts, and we summarily dispose of the matter by attributing to them a genius for oratory.

Here again we are largely mistaken. Power in the pulpit, on the platform, on the rostrum, proves generally the genius of industry. It means, again, hard work—the thoroughness of application which insures that large general preparation which never leaves one without resources from which to draw suddenly, unexpectedly. There is very little, if any, literally extempore effort or utterance which is worth anything, unless by extempore we mean "not what is the fruit of that moment of time, but of all time previous." A mind habitually studious, industrious, thoughtful, is constantly laying by in store against the time to come. Accumulation is perpetually going on, gathering materials which, at short notice, or under the white heat of intellectual fervor, assume a glow of beauty and even of brilliance, and are readily moulded and shaped for any desired end.

Great orations and sermons are not so much products of the sudden inspiration of genius as of long, laborious preparation. Like chemical solutions, which suddenly shoot into crystals when exposed to the air, great efforts of oratory may take their shape or form at the moment, but the crystallization is the final result of the skill with which thought has been distilled, held as in solution, and combined. Dr. John M. Mason was asked how long he had been preparing a certain one of his grand discourses. "Ten years," he answered. In reply to a similar question, Lyman Beecher said, "Twenty-five years"; and Dr. Nott, "Thirty years"; or as some say, "All my life."

In such thoughts as these we may perhaps find a key to those words of the Master Teacher of the ages: "Every scribe which is instructed unto the kingdom of heaven is like unto a man that is an householder, which bringeth forth out of his treasure things new and old" (Matt. 13:52). The faithful student is day by day gathering a "treasure"; and, when there comes some occasion for utterance by pen or tongue that by its suddenness forbids specific preparation, he falls back upon his treasure, and brings forth things new and old; old to him, embracing thoughts and facts long since accumulated; new to others in their form of presentation and method of application. Like weapons stored in an armory, they are in readiness for use when emergencies arise.

Dr. Bellamy was once asked by a young clergyman what he should do for matter for his discourses. "Fill up the cask," quaintly answered the doctor; "then if you tap it anywhere, you get a good stream; but if you put but little in it, it will dribble, dribble, and you must keep tapping, and get but little after all." Now, in all seriousness, what is it that fills up the cask? Is it genius? Could there be a happier phrase than that of Dr. Bellamy to describe the accumulations of a painstaking industry that stores up and lays by the results of study, until the very fullness of mind, like the height of a column of liquid, gives force to the stream in which thought finds vent through utterance, shooting up crystal jets or scattering its opaline spray?

Genius gives facility, undoubtedly; but so does industry develop facility. A few may inherit money, but most men must earn it. So it is of mental wealth. No achievement is at first easy. Talking and walking are arts acquired only at the price of many a stutter and stumble; repetition at last makes these triumphs so easy as to be no longer matters of conscious effort. So, when the orator, with the fluent utterance of a full stream, pours forth words of beauty and of power, who knows but that this fluency has been begotten of such laborious mastery of the powers of speech as is attributed to the prince of Athenian orators, who, if we believe Demetrius Phalerius, spake with pebbles in his mouth to cure his stammering; drilled his reluctant tongue to the roll of the letter "r"; removed the distortion of features which made his awkward speech repulsive, by watching in a mirror the faces he made; hung over his left shoulder a naked sword, that in his private practice he might prevent that shoulder hitching; ran up steep and rough walks to learn a loud, full emphatic enunciation; and acquired the power to breast the tumult of a popular assembly by first declaiming upon the democratic rostrum of a sandy beach, and with no audience but the clamorous waves of the Aegean Sea.

Henry Clay acquired the silvery flow of his persuasive speech by similar effort; from the age of twenty-seven, for years, daily speaking upon the contents of some historical or scientific book which he had read, and choosing for his very unsenatorial auditors a field of cornstalks or of cabbageheads, or the oxen and asses.

Curran, the Irishman, was known at school as "Stuttering Jack," and, having once failed utterly when attempting to speak in a debating club, he was insolently referred to as "Orator Mum"; but the taunt loosed the tied tongue, and from that day perseverance assured his success, though, like Demosthenes, he had to seek even the help of a mirror, to cure his awkwardness.

Of some men we are wont to say that they possess a native aptness for the platform, because we observe a certain readiness, fluency, and accuracy of diction, which are at once set down as marks of genius. But men have to learn to talk; as no one can spell without having learned his letters,or parse without having learned the principles of grammar, neither can one compose correctly and elegantly, or speak accurately and forcefully, without understanding the origin, the meaning, and the difference of words. Some may acquire more rapidly or even more easily than others; but, like runners in a race, whatever be the differences of speed—whether we run or walk, limp or hobble—it is step by step that we all get toward the goal. If there be such a thing as "intuitive" orthography, etymology, syntax, or prosody, that is to be preferred which comes not by intuition but by acquisition.

Accuracy of diction depends on a patient mastery of the etymology of words—the study of their derivation and of their exact meaning, even to the nicest shades of discrimination—or the science of synonyms. Forsyth tells us how Cicero attained that wonderful command, that mastery of language, which makes his orations to this day stand out in Latin literature as the Parthenon stands out in architecture. He quietly pursued his studies, attending the lectures of Molo, the Rhodian rhetorician—a consummate advocate and teacher—and diligently laboring to improve his style by translations from the works of Greek writers, especially the "Economics" of Xenophon.

The younger Pitt told the late Lord Stanhope that he owed greatly whatever readiness of speech he possessed to a practice which his father had impressed upon him. The Earl of Chatham, one of the most illustrious English orators, thus advised his still greater son, while yet pur-

suing his early studies: "Take up any book in some foreign language with which you are well acquainted, in
Latin, or Greek especially; read out of this work a passage, translating into English, stopping when you are
not sure of the exact English word to be used as the equivalent, and studying it until the right word comes to your
mind, and then proceed." And to this practice the accurate Pitt traced that aptness in finding the right word
which led a brilliant contemporary orator, Charles
James Fox, to say, "I never hesitate for *a* word; William
Pitt never hesitates for *the* word,"

Thus this man—already instanced as an example
of precocious and marvelous genius, who was, at twenty-one, one of the first men of Parliament, and, at twenty-
four, prime minister—great as were his natural endowments, did not rely on them, even in oratory. No gymnast
or agonist in the Isthmian games ever trained himself
more assiduously than he strove to bring out the muscles
and sinews of his mind into the perfection of symmetry
and strength, and make all his great powers the obedient
servants of his imperial will. At twenty-one he had read
almost every known Latin and Greek author, and was familiar with civil law, natural philosophy, and mathematics.

Most great orators have patiently studied the dead
languages because in such application they found a help
to the mastery of the living tongue which was their vernacular. When Dr. Arnold was asked, "Why need a boy
study Latin; what will he do with it?" he replied, "I wish
him to study it, not for what the boy will do with the Latin,
but for what the Latin will do with the boy." So the highest
benefit of the study of other tongues is not so much any direct use to be made of them as rather the discipline of
mind and power of utterance secured in one's own language. Every time a classical student stops to seek the ex-

act English equivalent for a Greek or Latin word or phrase he is enriching his own vocabulary. There is but one right word and best word, and to get that he must often study the whole class of words to which that belongs as a kinsfellow.

How closely allied are such words as efficient, effective, effectual, efficacious; culture, cultivation; circling, cycling, circular, circulating; part, portion, partition; pretense, pretension, pretentiousness; grace, gracefulness, graciousness; gratitude, gratefulness; devout, devoted, devotional; honored, honorary, honorable; aggregate, segregate, congregate; priceless, precious, inappreciable; proximate, approximate, approximating, approaching, approachable; stable, steady, steadfast, stationary; sentiment, sentimentalism, sentimentality; distinct, distinctive, distinguishing, distinguished; enough, sufficient; opposite, apposite, etc!

Nothing more assists in the direction of acquiring a true knowledge and mastery of one's native tongue than the patient following of a few simple rules:

1. Never to hear or read a word which is not understood, without noting it, with a view to consulting the dictionary.

2. Never, in writing, to proceed until the word that is wanted is found.

The writer remembers years ago, while yet a lad, to have stopped in the midst of a sentence because a certain verb which was needed refused to come to his aid. There was a vague impression that there was a word which expressed the changes of unsteady popular sentiment or public opinion, and which had about it the suggestion of the motion of the sea. It was not "waver," nor "oscillate," nor "vacillate"; "undulate" came near it, but it was only next of kin—Leah would not do for the mind which was looking for Rachel, her sister; and the dictionaries were searched, and Roget's "Thesaurus" and Crabb's "Synonymes" were ransacked, until at last the word was found—"fluctuate"—and the sentence was triumphantly completed: "Public opinion is subject to sudden and uncertain fluctuations." That seems a very small matter in itself; but two results followed: first, that word "fluctuate" was never wanted, even in extemporaneous speech, without being found at the tongue's end (it is to be hoped there is implied no genius for fluctuation!); and again, it was always easy after that to draw the exact shades of discrimination between those words whose acquaintance had been made on the way to the one desired.

The reader of "Ivanhoe"—that finest romance of Sir Walter Scott—pronounces its author a genius. The fact is, that book is a conspicuous illustration of the genius of industry—patient, persevering toil. For years Scott had made himself familiar with the era of chivalry, plodded over, in imagination, the weary march of the Crusaders, studied the characteristics and contradictions of the Jewish character, searched carefully into the records of the times in which the scenes of his story were laid, and even examined diligently into the strange process whereby the Norman French and Anglo-Saxon elements were wrought into a common tongue. He read and studied and pondered until he got thoroughly furnished for his work by getting thoroughly imbued and infused with his subject. Then, when he took up his pen to write, it was as when an artist sits down before his easel, full of his theme; every touch was a master-stroke. Those graphic outlines of character which, vividly as in profile, set before us the Jewish maiden and the Saxon lady, the king of the Lion Heart and the outlaw of Sherwood Forest, the swine-herd and the pilgrim, are not so much the product of inventive genius as of patient study. A careful and laborious search into authorities had thoroughly furnished the "Great Unknown" for his work. But mere genius could no more have brought those materials into their happy and harmonious combination than it could have filled the armory and museum at Abbotsford with all those curious and rare relics of the olden time.

That was a suggestive explanation, given both by Titian and Sir Joshua Reynolds, of the facility and rapidity with which the chisel, in one case, and the pencil, in the other, dashed off as by a few master touches or strokes a bust or portrait. On one occasion, being reproached for demanding what seemed an exorbitant price for the work of a few hours, "Sir," said the great artist, "did you say 'a few hours'? It took me thirty years to learn to do that in a few hours." Back of those few master strokes lay the practice, study, and toil of a lifetime. That rapidity and facility meant close application, patient industry, now matured into mastery of art. This is the real gauge by which often to determine the value of a product: how long it took not only to do a certain thing, but to get ready to do it.

Other apt illustrations of these principles may be borrowed from the science and art of music.

When such men as Thalberg or Gottschalk, sitting at the piano, discourse in the language of melody and harmony, one is struck dumb with amazement at the complete mastery obtained over the instrument. The piano seems to talk, speaking whatever language the mood of the master requires, whether of joy or sorrow, of mirth or mournfulness, of hope or despair; the dirge of burial, the song of bridal, the dance of the carnival. Surely this is genius for music! But what if those who hear the performance could go back and stand by the piano when the master was a pupil, taking the first lesson? How awkward his attempt to play those simple exercises! He can think of nothing but how he is sitting, holding his hands,

and managing his fingers. Practice and habit, the handmaids of genius, have helped him to lose sight of what is
merely mechanical in what is spiritual, till in the inspiration of musical enthusiasm he forgets the instrument, and becomes no longer a mere practicer of scales
or an imitator of others, but a composer, a creator of musical harmonies. Carissimi, the Venetian composer, and
director of the pontifical chapel at Rome, when complimented upon the ease and grace of his melodies, replied,
"Ah, how little you know of the difficulty with which this
ease has been acquired!"

There is a curious law of the body by which certain
muscles come to operate involuntarily; their action becomes self-regulating—autonomic; self-operating—
automatic; so that as in breathing or even walking, we exercise them without effort or even thought. The mind has
its autonomic and automatic action—a result of careful
discipline and trained habit.

The notion that any grand attainments or achievements of any kind come without hard work was quaintly
rebuked by Rufus Choate when someone remarked to
him, "It is really very wonderful how many great successes have come of accident." "Nonsense! you might as
well let drop the Greek alphabet and expect to pick up the
'Iliad.'"

The seven sages of Greece have each left some characteristic saying, and three of these axioms are very pertinent to our theme and thought. While Solon's motto
was, "Know thyself," and that of Pittacus, "Know thine
opportunity," that of Periander was, "Nothing is impossible to industry." Those who know the inside history of
literary productions know what incredible pains Plato
bestowed on his "Republic," Addison on the "Spectator,"
Tennyson on his simplest sonnets, writing "Come into
the Garden, Maud," fifty times, etc. Marked as are the re-

sults of judicious reading and communion with inspiring minds, nothing perfects the man and his work like practice that brings facility and at last mastery. Pains and patience work wonders.

III. Genius is supposed to imply *versatility*. But here, we are persuaded, there is another great mistake. Are we to understand that there are a few gifted men who can do equally well in any or all pursuits? A famous Latin sentence tells us, indeed, of one whose faculty was so flexible in all directions that one would have said he was destined especially by nature for everything he took in hand;* and that there are a few cases of such general aptitude may be admitted.

*Shakespeare makes reference to such versatility:
"Hear him but reason in divinity,
And, all admiring, with an inward wish,
You would desire the king were made a prelate;
Hear him debate of commonwealth affairs,
You would say it hath been, all in all, his study;
List his discourse on war, and you shall hear
A fearful battle rendered you in music!
Turn him to any cause of policy,
The Gordian knot of it he will unloose,
Familiar as his garter." (Henry V, 1., 1.)

A man taught for thirty years in Canada who came near to being practically a universal master. Whether in the chair of natural science or history, of belles-lettres or philosophy, of art or theology; whether at work dissecting an animal or classifying fossils, explaining the mysteries of ethics or of botany, drawing up a legal document or writing a treatise on Egyptology, he would have been found equally at home in any one department. Yet, even this amazing versatility manifested only a general aptness for intellectual pursuits. It does not follow that even he could have solved a difficult problem in mathematics, excelled in mechanical invention, rivaled great painters and sculptors, or made a successful general. At the most, the rarity of such universal genius makes such an example no criterion of judgment for the rest of mankind. We are neither led to hope nor left to despair because of exceptional success. The man just referred to, with all his versatility, was a most indefatigable worker. If his universal aptitude came by birth and genius, his universal information came by hard study and habitual industry.

But generally speaking, genius cannot bear grafted fruit. If the native scion be incorporated with a foreign stock the product will have one form and another flavor. Spurgeon had a genius for preaching: does it follow that he could have built fortresses and planned defenses like Vauban, or organized and wielded an army like Wellington or Washington? Michelangelo was a poet, painter, sculptor, and architect; yet all these are kindred arts: does it follow that he could have made an astronomer like Galileo, an emperor like Charlemagne, or a navigator like Columbus? We bow before the genius of such men as Chrysostom, Abelard, Peter the Great, Kepler, Milton, Shakespeare, Jonathan Edwards, Stephenson; but the versatility, often supposed to qualify genius, is very rare even among great men. These very masters might not have attained eminence in other spheres. Their success partly hinged upon the possession of large faculties, and partly, also, upon their sagacious employment and investment of them in a suitable direction.

Even those who think themselves endowed with genius would best trust only to industry, and industry in one great pursuit; miscellaneous scattered exertions are like random shots that strike no mark. The best kind of genius is a genius for application. It is scarce worthwhile to undertake to be everything at once, like Artemus Ward's "Versatile Statoo," and general intelligence sometimes implies particular ignorance; hence the wisdom of Lord Brougham's motto, "Know something of everything and everything of something." Sydney Smith cautioned students to beware of the foppery of universality—following all sciences, excelling in all arts, chemistry, mathematics, history, reading, riding, fencing, Low Dutch and High Dutch, and natural philosophy. He says the modern precept of education is, " 'Take the Admirable Crichton for your model; be ignorant of nothing.' On the contrary, I would have you possess the courage to be ignorant of a great number of things, that you may avoid the calamity of being ignorant of everything."

It is, moreover, a very encouraging and stimulating fact that men who have deserved the highest niches in the Westminster of history, for attainments in science, art, and letters, have not belonged exclusively to any rank or class. From the lowly beginnings have some of the grandest men of history arisen to their loft eminence! Shakespeare was the son of a wool-trader, and Akenside of a butcher; John Foster, Mr. Fox, and Dr. Livingstone, of weavers; John Hunter, Opie the painter, and Gibson the sculptor, of carpenters; Ben Jonson and Hugh Miller, of bricklayers; Turner, Arkwright, and Bishop Taylor, of barbers; Haydn, of a wheelwright; Bunyan, of a tinker; Luther, of a miner; Burns, of a day-laborer; Canova, of a stone-cutter; Thorwaldsen, of a wood-carver; Richard Cobden, of a farmer; Virgil, of a potter; Columbus, of a carpet-weaver; Demosthenes, of a blacksmith; Whitefield, of a tavern-keeper; and Lincoln, of a rail-splitter. The list might be indefinitely extended; and such are the depths of poverty and obscurity out of which great men have often come, that it almost seems, sometimes, as though, in society as in the sea, the great fish swim nearest to the bottom.

The indebtedness of genius to industry will further appear by the *late hour of life* in which the fruit often ripens. Sir Henry Spelman did not begin his scientific study till past fifty; nor did Franklin till then fully enter upon his investigations in natural philosophy. Handel was forty-eight before he published any of his great works. Scott and Dryden were unknown as authors until each had reached forty; and there are many like examples.

The struggle through which the successes even of great men have come sometimes tempt us to say that difficulty makes men. John Foster is a prince among essayists, and his miscellanies have been compared to nuggets of solid gold. They ought rather to be called beaten gold; for revision and correction cost him, by his own confession, as much labor as the whole previous composition, which was arduous, slow and painstaking.

Fortune has long since been said to favor the brave; and there is no bravery like the courage of that persevering industry which will not be daunted, dismayed, or driven back by difficulties. Not more surely do "winds and waves prove on the side of skillful navigators," says Smiles, "than does fortune prove on the side of the industrious." George Stephenson, who won his grand triumph at Rainhill only at the price of fifteen years of labor to improve his locomotive, was wont to say to young men, "Do as I have done—persevere," even as William Carey, disowning all genius, said, "I can plod."

The brilliancy of a fine work, like the beauty of a mosaic at St. Mark's or at St. Sophia's is due to small fragments, laboriously collected, and put together with minute art. Those who imagine genius is like a volcano in a state of eruption forget that volcanoes have never produced anything but lava and scoriae.

In view of all this, it is not surprising that, as was remarked at the outset, some—and among them those

who were unquestionably geniuses themselves—have
doubted whether there be any genius but the genius of industry.

Some have boldly defined genius as only "common
sense intensified"; but this seems to be a begging of the
question, for common sense is not so called because it is so
exceedingly common—in fact, it is very rare; and, if genius imply uncommon gifts, then, paradoxical as it may
seem, common sense may be among them. But if common sense be taken as simply the characteristic quality
of a well poised character, it is more frequently found in
the average man than in those marked by the most brilliant qualities.

There is another sort of common sense, or average
faculty of the common man, of which, with proper training, great results may be predicated. Beccaria held that
any one might become a poet or orator. Locke, Helveticus,
and Diderot believed that all men have an equal aptitude
for genius, and the chemist Dalton and the elder Disraeli
held essentially the same view. Dr. Young, the philosopher, boldly affirmed that what any man has done any
other can do. Buffon did not believe in any other genius
than that which is the result of profound attention directed to a subject. Ary Scheffer said, "With a strong soul and
a noble aim one can do what one wills, morally speaking." Sir Fowell Buxton said, "The longer I live the more I
am certain that the great difference between men—
between the feeble and the powerful, the great and the insignificant—is energy, invincible determination, a
purpose once fixed, and then death or victory." Dr. Arnold said, "The difference between one boy and another
lies not so much in talent as in energy." Dr. Ross said of
men who would yet be recognized as men of genius, that
they were "all plodders, hard workers, intent men." Vol-
taire, while he admitted genius to exist, believed that only

a very slight line separates the man of genius from him of ordinary mould, and that line was not an impassable barrier. Hogarth said, "Genius is nothing but labor and diligence." "Industry and perseverance" was the motto of Banks, the sculptor; and Guizot affirmed that "good ability, with industry and system, accomplish all things."

Alexander Hamilton once said to an intimate friend: "Men give me credit for genius. All the genius I have lies just in this: when I have a subject in hand I study it profoundly. Day and night it is before me. I explore it in all its bearings. My mind becomes pervaded with it. Then the effort which I make the people are pleased to call the fruit of genius: it is the fruit of labor and thought." Dickens declared that this was the secret of whatever success he attained—the quality of attention. Hugh Miller modestly states in his autobiography: "The only merit to which I lay claim is that of patient research—a merit in which whosoever wills may rival or surpass me; and this humble faculty of patience, when rightly developed, may lead to more extraordinary developments of idea than even genius itself."

In the lexicon of all true workers, as Richelieu and Napoleon said, there is no such word as "fail." Mirabeau called "impossible" a blockhead of a word. Lord Chatham, when told by a colleague that a certain thing could not be done, calmly replied, but with all the weight of his giant will, "I trample upon impossibilities." And so he did. He moved forward with the confidence of one beneath whose iron tread mountain barriers turned to dust.

Chatterton, genius as he was, said that God had given his creatures long enough arms to reach anything if they chose to be at the trouble. As Dr. Chapin said, not only must we strike while the iron is hot, but strike till it is made hot. There are some who wait for opportunity, as the blockhead waited for the stream to flow by, that he might cross; and there are other men who know how, on the anvil of resolve, to forge a key that unlocks all closed doors.

A distinguished teacher, a college president, spoke of genius as "the power of making efforts," and John Foster declared it to be the faculty of "lighting one's own fire." Perhaps Comte de Buffon was a prejudiced witness when he said, "Genius is patience and patience is genius, the result of a profound attention directed to a particular subject." He knew that with him success was the reward of peculiar patience. In youth he showed no uncommon powers; his mind was slow, if not sluggish, and he was constitutionally lazy. Born to affluence, a soft bed in a warm room proved very attractive. Too polite to get up before the sun, he waited until the monarch of the day had left his Oriental pavilion far behind, before he ventured modestly to emerge from behind his bed-curtains. But somehow a day so tardily begun reached its close too soon for Buffon to work out any marked results in natural history, though he might have written the autobiography of a sleepyhead, or a work on the pleasures of slumber, or the natural history of dreams. After struggling hard for some time to wake early, he found to wake was not always to rise. He desperately called to his aid, his manservant. "Joseph," said he, "I'll give you a crown every time you get me up before six; and never you mind what I say or do—get me up and you shall have your crown." The faithful valet knocked at the door persistently; but the count had, every morning, some new indisposition: he was ill, had not slept, would rise soon, etc. Sometimes he was angry at the persistence of his servant, who loved his master, or his money, too well to slight orders; and when he did rise, was angry because he had been allowed to lie abed, contrary to his injunction. But Joseph, having tried in vain to force his master to leave the bed, one morning determined to earn his crown. He dashed under the bedclothes a basin of ice-cold water. The effect was electric: that was not the sort of bath or pack the naturalist liked, and he did not long give the hydropathic remedy a chance to test its virtues. It was by the persistent use of such means that Buffon at last broke the chains of his indolent habits; and he used to say that to Joseph he owed three or four volumes of his "Natural History."

While thus convinced of the absolute need of thorough work, we concede the existence of genius, or a higher order of native endowment, as admitting of no serious question. It is vain to expect to make out of the raw material of manhood, by any process, a Homer, Shakespeare, Dante, Milton; a Beethoven, Mozart, Handel, Haydn; an Aristotle, Newton, Bacon, Humboldt; a Salvator Rosa, Raphael, Titian, Michelangelo. When Bush, the commentator, was asked how he could account for the meteoric shower of 1834 he said he could not tell, unless "Dr. Cox's brain had burst." And the Arabs have a quaint way of expressing their confidence in an inborn fitness which cannot be diverted from its true native direction: "You may bathe a dog's tail in oil and wrap it in splints, but you cannot get the crook out."

If aptitude for a pursuit can be made to order, where is the stupidity of the simple soul who asked, after the death of Canova the princely sculptor of Possagno, whether "his brother was intending to carry on his business"? It is one of the rewards which surely crowns honest, earnest self-culture, that one rises in the scale of being to a height to which every other man must also climb if he would get there. No man can go to bed a dunce and wake up a Solomon or Socrates, though some happy, lazy speculator may go to bed a pauper and wake a millionaire. As

Emerson said, "You reap what you have sown. Those who sow dunce-seed, vice-seed, laziness-seed, usually get a crop. Men can no longer fly at a dash into eminent position."

Probably in this, as in most other things, the truth lies between extreme statements: neither are we to attribute all successes to innate genius, nor is it true that there is no such thing as genius. To state the matter moderately, genius is natural aptitude in a certain direction, fitting one in some uncommon degree for some particular class of employments. All else that we associate with genius—facility, rapidity, certainty of achievement—belongs to industry. If, on the one hand, it be true that without the inborn genius no amount of mere industry, however well applied, will make the poet, painter, orator, or musician, it is not less true that without diligent application no man, however gifted, achieves the highest distinction and success. Even where aptitudes exist, they do not make industry unnecessary.

No one doubts the genius of Kepler. Yet the great philosopher and astronomer, referring to his own successful investigation, quotes Virgil's line:
    "Fama mobilitate viget, vires acquirit eundo,"
and adds, "So it was with me: diligent thought on these things begat still further thinking, until at last I brooded upon the subject with the whole energy of my mind." Newton, endowed with the first order of mind, yet acknowledged that he wrought out the grand results embodied in the "Principia" only by application, diligence, and perseverance. Said he to Dr. Bentley, "If I have done the public any service it is due to nothing but industry and patient thought."

John Hunter the surgeon said his own mind was like a beehive, so incessant was his industry. Plato wrote over and over the beginning of his "Republic." Lamb expended a week's work upon a single one of his humorous letters; their sparkle is like the radiance of a diamond elaborately polished into brilliance. Dickens shut himself up like a hermit for weeks while he wrote a Christmas carol, and, like Balzac, when he came out of his long seclusion and intense labor he looked like a mere ghost. The poet Moore thought ten lines of "Lalla Rookh" enough for a day. Kinglake and Wordsworth reviewed and corrected manuscripts day by day for weeks and months. Buffon spent half a century over his "Studies of Nature," and copied it eighteen times before it went to press. Each final cast of thought went through at least five moulds before it took its final form; and even after this he would recompense a sentence twenty times, and once spent fourteen hours in searching for the proper word to round off a period.

Michelangelo said of Raphael, whom we have been wont to regard as scarcely second to the great Florentine himself, that he owed his place in the front rank among the artists of his day simply to diligent, persevering endeavor; that "he did not get so far by his genius, but by his industry." "Industry can here mean nothing else than the success that an artist seeks in the unwearied improvement of his work. Industry is not persevering activity or diligence in general which allows itself no rest, but absorption in the one thing to be accomplished—a creative longing to work out into visible form the idea or ideal before the mind."

How genius summoned industry to its aid is seen in Vaucanson, the wonderful maker of automata, and machinist; in Jacquard, the loom-maker, to whom Lyons owes so much of its splendor; in Heilman, who brought machine-combing to such perfection that his apparatus seemed gifted with the delicate accuracy of human fingers and the delicate intelligence of the human mind.

The Latin motto is: "Opportunity has hair in front; behind she is bald: if you seize her by the forelock you may catch and hold her; but if suffered to escape not Jove himself can catch her again."

The innumerable examples of the noble achievements of industry show us how much it is worth to watch and catch opportunity. Handel and Haydn, Bach and Beethoven, Arnold and Murray, Cobden and Peel, Lytton and Brougham, Hunter, Harvey, Herschel, Titian and Palissy, Hugh Miller and Charles Bell, Watt and Wilkie, Scott the novelist and Scott the commentator, Albert Barnes, Morse and Edison the electricians, Palmer the sculptor, and the lamented Garfield, are examples of eminence due to obedience to this law of improving opportunity.

The study of the lives of great men, or men of great achievement, will satisfy us that all grand results in discovery and invention, science and art, thought and mechanism, are traceable to indefatigable industry and assiduous application. Moses Stuart said: "Original sin is aversion to work." John Randolph declared he had discovered the philosopher's stone: "Pay as you go." Samuel Smiles thinks that in all departments of life the philosopher's stone which turns everything, even time itself, to gold is, "Do with your might." Even Hercules must have his labors. If there be any one thing that helps to make men, it is the very difficulties that dismay all but the brave. They bring out grit; they develop backbone; they make men tenacious and pertinacious. Pertinacity is a good thing, though it is often perverted. On the wrong side, it becomes a fearful proof of total depravity; but enlisted in a high and noble cause it becomes the persistence of heroism, the perseverance of saints, a condition and guaranty of success.

If, then, the talisman of life be not the genius of industry, it certainly is the industry of genius. The men who sway the world, move and mould mankind, and shape history, are simply men of strong will, mighty purpose, and untiring application. If genius gives aptitude for success in certain spheres, it cannot do any more. *Success itself comes of order, method, concentration, accuracy, promptness, diligence, and perseverance—the seven handmaids of industry.*

On a broken helmet in Battle Abbey you may yet read, "L'espoir est ma force," which, in the fine fashion of heraldic sentiments, bespeaks the omnipotence of a high expectant purpose. The Horatian phrase, "Nil desperandum," has been the inspiration of many a successful life. If necessity is the mother of invention, diligence is the mother of success. It is worth a great deal to be able to say, with Richter, "I have made as much out of myself as could be made of the stuff; and no man should require more."

If we use genius of the inventive and talent of the administrative faculty, then talent is, in the long run, the surer winner of the race. In any department of activity no one needs to forfeit success. Let him honestly and earnestly resolve to make the most of his endowments and opportunities, whatever they may be; let him determine upon thoroughness—in other words, to avoid the snare of superficiality, putting his whole ability, however little, into whatever he attempts, and attempting nothing which is not worthy to enlist the whole man—and success is sure.

In the classic arena it is not the highly gifted only who bear off the palm of victory. That honor is reserved often for those of only very moderate abilities. With no remarkable powers, conspicuous only for honest, patient application, conscientious fidelity, they gradually pass by every competitor and take the front rank. So plain is this fact that the best minds have long since come to admit that a high grade of scholarship, and even intellectual greatness, depend, ultimately, mainly on habits of thoroughness; and that where these are found, or can be created, there is no such thing as hopeless stupidity or mental imbecility.

While lecturing on balloons, Mr. Glaisher, of the Observatory, Greenwich, gave some very sound advice on this point. He said: "Many depend too much upon natural abilities for success, and others have too little confidence in their own powers. All should know that the power of a man's mind is not solely dependent upon his ability, but that his real momentum is the product of his talents multiplied into his industry. Great talents without industry must yield to moderate talents combined with industry. If you wish to be able to overcome difficulties as they meet you in life (and we must experience great pleasure in overcoming them), you must train yourselves to conquer them while young."

Reynolds, whose motto was "Work! Work! Work!," and who was wont to rebuke the mere talker or idler by saying, "Let us be doing something," has finely summed up the substance of this argument: "If you have genius, industry will supply its place." Graham, master of the Scottish Academy, used to quote that wise saying to his pupils. David Wilkie, among others, heard it, and it fixed itself in his mind. "I was determined, therefore, to be very industrious, for I knew I had no genius." In the highest successes of his artistic career he affirmed, "The single element in all the progressive movements of my pencil was persevering industry."

Let us set the highest value upon the "divine faculty of work." The old crest is suggestive that bore a pickaxe with the motto, "Either I will find a way or make one." And a sagacious Frenchman rightly discovered the lack of energy peculiar to the inhabitants of a particular district by this very simple sign: he observed that pupils who from that quarter came to the Veterinary School at Paris did not strike hard upon the anvil, and he correctly inferred that there was little force among the people of those parts.

Work wields the weapons of power, wins the palm of success, and wears the crown of victory. No worthy end is gained without it. We need not be discouraged by feeble mental powers, but educate and strengthen them by study, as we expand a narrow chest by deep inspirations, or as we bring out the knotted, corded muscle with athletic exercises. No heroic soul is daunted by difficulties; the very determination, patience, perseverance which they develop make the man great. "Father, my sword is too short," said a young Spartan to his brave old sire. "Add a step to it!" was the laconic answer.

BIBLIOGRAPHY

Adams, Arthur Merrihew. *Pastoral Administration*. Philadelphia: Westminster Press, 1964.

Adams, Jay E. *The Christian Counselor's Manual*. Grand Rapids: Baker Book House, 1973.

_____. *Competent to Counsel*. Nutley, NJ: Presbyterian and Reformed Publishing Co., 1974.

Baker's Dictionary of Practical Theology. Grand Rapids: Baker Book House, 1967.

Baxter, J. Sidlow. *Rethinking Our Priorities*. Grand Rapids: Zondervan Publishing House, 1974.

Bays, Bertie Cole. *Some Preachers Do*. 3d ed. Valley Forge, PA: Judson Press, 1953.

Benson, Clarence H. *The Sunday School in Action*. Chicago: Moody Press, 1944.

Blackwood, Andrew Watterson. *The Funeral*. Philadelphia: Westminster Press, 1942.

_____. *The Growing Minister*. Nashville: Abingdon Press, 1960.

_____. *Pastoral Leadership*. Nashville: Abingdon Press, 1949.

Bliss, Edwin C. *Getting Things Done*. New York: Bantam Books, 1980.

Collins, Gary R., assistant ed. *Minister's Research Service*. Wheaton, IL: Tyndale House Publishers, 1970.

Colton, C. E. *The Minister's Mission*. Grand Rapids: Zondervan Publishing House, 1951.

Conant, J. E. *Every Member Evangelism*. New York: Harper and Brothers, 1922.

Cooper, Kenneth H. *The Aerobics Program for Total Well-Being*. New York: Bantam Books, 1982.

Cuyler, Theodore. *The Young Preacher*. Old Tappan,

NJ: Fleming H. Revell Co., 1893.

Dobbins, G. S. *Building Better Churches.* Nashville: Broadman Press, n.d.

Dolloff, Eugene Dinsmore. *The Romance of Doorbells.* Valley Forge, PA: Judson Press, 1951.

Engstrom, Ted W., and R. Alec MacKenzie, *Managing Your Time.* Grand Rapids: Zondervan Publishing House, n.d.

Flynn, Leslie B. *How to Save Time in the Ministry.* Grand Rapids: Baker Book House, 1975.

Gaebelein, Arno Clemons. *Half a Century: The Autobiography of a Servant.* "Our Hope" Publications, 1930.

Hogue, Wilson. *Homiletics and Pastoral Theology.* Winona Lake, IN: Free Methodist Publishing House, 1946.

Jackson, Paul R. *The Doctrine and Administration of the Church.* Des Plaines, IL: Regular Baptist Press, 1968.

Jowett, J. H. *The Preacher: His Life and Work.* New York: George H. Doran Co., 1951. Reprinted by Baker Book House, Grand Rapids, 1968.

Kent, Homer, Jr. *The Pastoral Epistles.* Chicago: Moody Press, 1958.

Kerr, William, senior ed. *Minister's Research Service.* Wheaton, IL: Tyndale House Publishers, 1970.

Knight, Walter B. *Knight's Treasury of Illustrations.* Grand Rapids: Wm. B. Eerdmans Publishing Co., 1963.

Laird, Donald A. and Eleanor C. *The Techniques of Getting Things Done.* New York: McGraw-Hill Book Co., 1957.

Leach, William H. *Handbook of Church Management.* Englewood Cliffs, NJ: Prentice-Hall, 1958.

LeBoeuf, Michael. *Working Smart.* New York: Warner Books, n.d.

Linamen, J. H. *Business Handbook for Churches.* Anderson, IN: Warner Press, 1958.

Lloyd-Jones, David Martyn. *Preachers and Preaching.* Grand Rapids: Zondervan Publishing House, 1972.

Matthews, Reginald L. *Missionary Administration in the Local Church.* Des Plaines, IL: Regular Baptist Press, 1972.

Meyer, F. B. *Jottings and Hints for Lay Preachers.* London: Andrew Melrose Co., 1906.

Molloy, John T. *Dress for Success.* New York: Warner Books, n.d.

Moyer, Elgin S. *The Pastor and His Library.* Chicago: Moody Press, 1953.

Narramore, Clyde M. *The Psychology of Counseling.* Grand Rapids: Zondervan Publishing House, 1960.

Osborne, Cecil G. *The Art of Understanding Your Mate.* Grand Rapids: Zondervan Publishing House, 1970.

Pierson, A. T. *Life-Power or Character, Culture and Conduct.* Old Tappan, NJ: Fleming H. Revell Co., 1895.

Riley, W. B. *Pastoral Problems.* Old Tappan, NJ: Fleming H. Revell Co., 1936.

Rossin, Donald F., and Palmer Ruschke. *Practical Study Methods for Students and Pastors.* Minneapolis: Rossin and Co., 1956.

Scripture Portions for the Afflicted. Presbyterian Board of Publications, 1840.

Spurgeon, Charles H. *Autobiography.* Edited and condensed from 4 original volumes by David Otis Fuller. Grand Rapids: Zondervan Publishing House, 1946.

_____. *Commenting on the Commentaries.* Lecture 1. Grand Rapids: Kregel Publications, n.d.

_____. *Spurgeon's Lectures to His Students.* Condensed and abridged by David Otis Fuller. Grand Rapids: Zondervan Publishing House, 1945.

_____. *Second Series of Lectures to My Students*. London: Passmore and Alabaster, 1897.

_____. *The Soul Winner*. Abridged by David Otis Fuller. Grand Rapids: Zondervan Publishing House, 1948.

Stott, John R. W. *The Preacher's Portrait*. Grand Rapids: Wm. B. Eerdmans Publishing Co., 1961.

Tead, Ordway. *The Art of Leadership*. New York: McGraw-Hill Book Co., 1935.

Thourlby, William. *You Are What You Wear*. New York: New American Library, 1978.

Turnbull, Ralph G. *A Minister's Obstacles*. Old Tappan, NJ: Fleming H. Revell Co., 1965.

Whyte, Alexander. *Bible Characters (The Old Testament)*. Vol. 1. Grand Rapids: Zondervan Publishing House, n.d.

SUBJECT INDEX